# *HOMELAND DEFENSE:*
# CIVIL UNREST AND
# FEDERAL INTERVENTION WITHIN
# THE UNITED STATES OF AMERICA

Major General Barrye L. Price, Ph.D.
U.S. Army, Retired

ISBN: 978-1-7353348-4-4

Library of Congress Control Number: 2020945283

Printed in the USA

ARC Communications, LLC.
P.O. Box O
College Station,Texas 77841

Email: arccommunications@arc-culturalart.com.

# *Dedication*

Writing this book has been one of the more difficult experiences of my life, as this opportunity finds me critical of people, institutions, and positions that I revere, respect, value, and admire—like the President of the United States and police officers. I often speak to the television each time there's another senseless death of a person who didn't move quickly enough; or who was victimized for being non compliant, when they may have been simply responding to blatant disrespect shown to them by authorities.

We must find ways to deescalate the encounter—where cooler heads might prevail. To that end, I dedicate this book to my brother, dear friend, and former San Jose Police Chief, Christopher Moore, who is the quintessence of what a police officer should be—an ambassador, a public servant, and a voice of reason during the "white noise" that we are hearing at present. I had the distinct honor of promoting Chris to Captain, Major, Deputy Chief, and Assistant Chief of Police, and even had the opportunity to speak at his retirement from duties as the Chief. Likewise, I owe significant praise to my bride of seventeen years—Tracy--who is a calming and loving presence in my life. I also thank my son William, who's life I pray will be absent of many of the racial trials that I have endured. I also thank Alissa Wendelken for her assistance in mining the data from the Mapping Police Violence website—she's truly an Excel/Access spreadsheet genius. I also thank my Sister in Christ, friend, Agent, and publicist Dr. Florita Bell Griffin for pushing me to speak up and out; and her husband Dr. Richard Griffin for his friendship and sage counsel. Finally, I thank my friend and Brother-in-Arms, Lieutenant General H. R. McMaster for always being present for me.

# Table of Contents

# FOREWORD

There is a growing realization among Americans that our society has become more divided in recent years. Our common identity as a nation is under duress from a powerful combination of forces that includes identity politics, vitriolic partisan rhetoric, bigotry, and racism. Ignorance catalyzes this combination; those who know least about issues and who are strangers to their fellow Americans seek affirmation of their biases rather than information about important issues or understanding of their neighbors. Foreign adversaries such as Russia endeavor to undermine our free and open society by exploiting America's divisions, polarizing communities further, pitting them against each other, and weakening Americans' confidence in the democratic institutions, processes, and values that bind us. As Barrye Price points out, these divisions and civil unrest associated with them are not new. But learning from the past to address the problems of the present, requires a clear understanding of history. As bias and vitriol contaminates the information environment today, the manipulation of history remains an important tool for those who want to sow division and conflict rather than foster unity and goodwill. We are in Dr. Price's debt for helping set an important part of the historical record straight as an important step in arresting our drift away from one another.

If misinformation and misunderstanding is a principal cause of the disease that is weakening confidence in our common identity as Americans, *Homeland Defense* is part of the cure. As author of the Declaration of Independence and third President of the United States Thomas Jefferson observed, "Whenever the people are well informed, they can be trusted with their own government; that whenever things get so far wrong as to attract their notice, they may be relied on to set them to rights." Reading this book purposefully and think about how, armed with a better understanding of the past, Americans might reverse the trends of recent years and come together with renewed confidence in our future. We might ask ourselves:

i

1.  How might we improve civic education to instill pride in the vision of our founders and the uniqueness of our democracy while recognizing, as our founders did, that the American experiment requires constant nurturing and improvement?

2.  How might we inspire more Americans to serve in organizations that bring people together from all racial, ethnic, religious, and economic backgrounds such that, as happens routinely in our military, prejudice gives way to common understanding, mutual trust, and pride in serving the nation and one another?

3.  How might we encourage our fellow Americans to at least give equal time to what unifies us when we discuss what divides us?

4.  How might we urge our representatives in the Legislative Branch of government to set an example for bipartisanship and address fundamental causes of polarization in America such as the gerrymandering of Congressional districts?

5.  How might we rekindle hope among rural and urban communities that have lost sight of the American dream by improving education, abolishing the soft bigotry of low expectations, strengthening families, and fostering new economic opportunity that reduces the growing chasm between wealthy and poor Americans?

6.  How might we build trust in American institutions at the national and local levels with an emphasis on police-community relations and the rule of law?

While we might prioritize actions necessary to prevent civil unrest, Price also emphasizes that how military and law enforcement respond to maintain public order can either help foster reconciliation or exacerbate division. *Homeland Defense* contains important lessons that would be painful to relearn through experience. An emphasis on professionalism and training is necessary to foster confidence among policemen and soldiers because confidence is essential to preventing breakdowns in discipline. And civilian, police, and military leaders must establish a climate in their organizations that fosters restraint and encourages risk-taking to prevent escalation or the indiscriminate use of force against innocents. Price also makes clear that federal, state, and local leaders must understand not only how to apply their authorities under the Posse Comitatus Act, but also how to do so in a way that moves toward reconciliation.

Although Americans should be concerned about the polarization of our society, we should remain confident -- confident in our institutions, our values, and who we are as a people. Confidence, however, should not encourage complacency. There is work to do. As the civil rights activist and patriot Rosa Parks observed, "To bring about change, you must not be afraid to take the first step. We will fail when we fail to try." After reading *Homeland Defense*, readers might resolve to take their own first step, reach out to their fellow Americans, engage in respectful debate, reject demagoguery rooted in bigotry and racism, and strengthen our democracy.

H.R. McMaster Author, *Dereliction of Duty: Lyndon Johnson, Robert McNamara, The Joint Chiefs of Staff, and the Lies that Led to Vietnam;* and *Battlegrounds: The Fight to Defend the Free World.*

# *PREFACE*

"My Life's Direction"

The words by which I live shall be the words by which I'll die; Although an entertaining thought I often wonder why?

Will my life ever be complete; Will I overcome life's famed deceit?

The truth is unknown and often misconstrued; It is spoken by soothsayers whose demeanors often rude.

Shall I fight with life's hypocrisy, Shall I combat man's futile greed; Or should I be just as cynical and fulfill my every need?

For this is the best of all possible worlds as written in Voltaire's "Candide"; He felt that times were bound to change and felt there was a need.

Though spoken clearly and written the same; He did not know that times would change.

Some men remain in bondage, while others have been freed; Yet some still fight the struggle to overcome man's futile greed.

Well, I will plant the seeds with hopes of growth; I will meet and beat life's challenges--for success I must do both.

For now is the time to take a stand; To come forth and be counted for I'm a strong man.

And should my fate be compromised or I fall victim to another's hand; At least I will have died for what I believed, which was my initial plan.

These themes of commitment, sacrifice, resilience, and courage have governed my person ever since I penned these lines on September 10, 1985--four months into my 31 year US Army career. Within the poem, you read about the promise of tomorrow. You hear my belief that the truth has sometimes been a moving target. You witness my desire to combat hypocrisy, and, finally, you encounter martyrdom -- my solemn commitment that I would willingly give up my life for that which I believe.

Since breathing life into the poem, it has been my credo, my mission statement that's guided me. It's kept me grounded, and focused. It's given me strength for the fight -- regardless of the circumstance. Intended as an unequivocal statement of who I was and how I would live my life, it has always ensured that my audio was in sync with my video. You see, since age 12—when I lost my earthly father, I have lived my life as though the world was watching me. By the time I received my commission at age 22—I had had a ten-year head-start on my peers towards living a transparent life where my private and public personas were one and the same.

*Homeland Defense's* roots are unequivocally rooted in my poem. First, it's a book about the vital and evolving domestic role for the US military, which depends on commitment, sacrifice and courage. It unveils truths that were codified during times immemorial when the Government always sided with management during labor disputes; when racial segregation was not only local practice, but Jim Crow practices were the laws of the land. Likewise, this book unmasks the hypocrisy of military leaders who questioned the loyalty of African- American Soldiers involved domestically in riot duty in 1992, as they had during the Detroit Riot of 1967.

Although I spent the first four years of active duty within the 5th Infantry Division at Fort Polk, Louisiana, my true journey towards understanding defense of the homeland and the value of American citizenship did not occur until my second assignment within the 11th Armored Cavalry Regiment located in Fulda, Germany. I arrived in the famed Blackhorse Regiment on October 13, 1989 as an ambitious and idealistic twenty-seven year old from Gary, Indiana, driven by a creed focused on impact which was uniquely my own. I understood what it meant to be a person from Gary, Indiana; had a pretty good understanding of what it meant to be a Hoosier; and I was tremendously comfortable in my own skin, but I would learn rather quickly in a foreign and divided country about the unique privileges of American citizenship—privileges that were lost on me during the first 27 years of my life. A myriad of circumstances and people would play seminal roles in my conversion. First and foremost, I was in a country ideologically divided, located at the most likely fissure of the most probable invasion route that would turn the Cold War in to full-scale, high-intensity kinetic warfare between the US and the former Soviet Union. At that time, I served within an Armored Cavalry Regiment patrolling more than one thousand kilometers of Interzonal Border separating East and West Germany. Finally, I was immersed in an environment of phenomenally talented and upwardly mobile men who were tremendous examples of who I endeavored to become as a Christian, man, husband, father, Soldier and American—chief amongst them was Colonel A.J. Bacevich, Ph.D., my Regimental Commander.

I was on that border on November 9, 1989 when freedom prevailed and the Iron Curtain collapsed. I quickly realized my role as an ambassador for America and our value-stream through the lens of my German Army counterpart—Lt. Col. Dietmar Philip. My participation in the first Gulf War strengthened my resolve and made my commitment to our nation, its shared values, our flag and our way of life irreversible. During the next two and one-half years in Germany, I witnessed two vastly conflicted economies merge, and watched as the "haves" from West Germany absorbed the "have nots" from East Germany. These lessons were seminal in my growth and maturation as an officer within the United States Army.

I departed Germany for graduate school on April 29, 1992. As I landed at Houston's Intercontinental Airport, I was greeted with the news that Los Angeles was on fire. Nearly three decades later, I still vividly recall the flood of emotions that consumed me, watching and listening with horror as American strip malls immolated across millions of American TV screens… questioning with each fresh explosion and

2

firestorm of successive public and police reactions (and overreactions), and considering all the while how what I was witnessing comported with my liberating experience of the previous three years.

Likewise, this "welcome back to America" informed my next five years of study as I pursued a Ph.D. in History from Texas A&M University, as I was in Kuwait when the video of the beating of Rodney King made national news. Yes, I was in a war-torn land, imparting the virtues of our way of life, an ambassador on freedom's frontier whose life and personal story spoke of the promise of our nation, its virtues, and its capacity to truly become that shining city on a hill. The Rodney King video told quite a different story, and the world watched with baited-breath to witness how America would deal with what appeared to be a severe abuse of power by police.

Five years later, I traveled to Los Angeles for a series of interviews with the "who's who" of the Los Angeles Riots—Mayor Tom Bradley, Former Los Angeles Chief of Police Darryl Gates, Los Angeles County Sheriff Sherman Block, LA Police Department Chief Willie Williams, Assistant Police Chief Bernard Parks, President of the Police Commission Jesse Brewer, and former Rodney King attorney, Milton Grimes. During my June 1, 1995 meeting with Milton Grimes I received what Paul Harvey coined: "the rest of the story." It was during this meeting that I was able to view the full video of the Rodney King beating. Unlike the 13-second clip that I had viewed while deployed for combat operations in Saudi Arabia and Kuwait, this version was much longer and it had an audio track, so I could hear—along with the sounds of a hovering helicopter whose lights illuminated the scene--both the commands and dialogue from the officers involved.

Unlike what I had witnessed during the 13-second soundless clip, I was horrified as I watched 82 seconds of nothing short of a brazen assault on Rodney King by supposed enforcers of the law. What was even more surprising were two things: first, there were two other passengers within the car with Rodney King—Bryant Allen and Freddie Helms; second, I counted at least 16 officers on the scene. As four officers (later acquitted) brutalized Rodney King, the remaining 12 broke up into smaller groups. A group of six appeared to establish a perimeter to contain Rodney King within the immediate area of the beating; while others appeared unaffected by what was transpiring—they even began socializing with one another. No one intervened! No one exclaimed: "That's enough!" No one seemed to care about the image of the events, or the irreparable damage that this event might have on the Los Angeles Police Department for decades to come. The officers simply could not fathom the possibility that someone was videotaping this savage beating by supposed enforcers of law and order. As the exhausted officers completed their assault on Mr. King, they "hog tied" him, and dragged him to the side of the road with less decency than one would provide to an animal injured on the road.

We now live in an era--twenty-six years after the Los Angeles Riots--when this type of behavior appears more common place. Every week a new video of heavy-handed policing is exposed to the nation via our 24-hour news cycle. This violence, often in counter-response to police responses when encountering very often nonviolent and allegedly non compliant suspects. The mood of a crowd which may result in a riot oftentimes starts when individual and collective police response isn't measured, when it lacks discipline and restraint by the officer. These responses are viewed most often as uneven by minorities because they lack democracy and they demonstrate a lack of accountability by law enforcement officials. Clearly, the commission of a misdemeanor should never result in the death of the alleged assailant.

This volume will reveal tremendous growth of the nation's ability to defend the homeland, while also exposing vulnerabilities and areas which can be improved. My research over three decades has revealed that we have solid doctrine, phenomenal training and first-rate nonlethal equipment. Our active-duty military defending the homeland have done yeomen's work in quelling civil unrest. They have been praised as both heroes and calming influences domestically in our nation's most volatile and racially charged riots. Our greater challenge remains the challenge of solving the problem before it arises—armed with the reality that the greatest purveyor of discontent is not the "tinder box" notion that's aligned with socio and economic disparities, nor the morbidity statistics normally associated with the inner city. Quite to the contrary, the most significant catalyst for civil unrest remains in the present day, what the Kerner Report revealed in 1968: the greatest precipitant, accelerant, and catalyst for civil unrest continues to be our supposed first-line of defense: the police. Perhaps most tragic is the reality that the burden of proof continues to be on the victim, who is often triple-victimized by their personal legal history, their environment, and by their race—immaterial of what the evidence appears to reveal.

My greatest fear is being realized as I edit my page proofs: that America could itself face the uncertainty and volatility as witnessed during the Arab Spring of 2010. One could certainly argue that we're seeing this phenom as a result of the murder of George Floyd in Minneapolis, Minnesota in May of 2020. A closer look at the Arab Spring reveals the simple goals of democracy, employment, economic freedom, human rights, and regime change. Are these not the same demands of the unheard voices that take to the streets to riot? Every time people assemble in protest, there is the possibility of a riot. People are assembling now across America more than ever and they are assembling for a host of emotionally charged issues—from separating children from their parents at US Borders—which ushers in memories of slave trades where families were indelibly broken; to the disruption led by the Black Lives Matter apparatus -- which is forcing the nation to look at itself and the uneven practices levied by police towards Black and Brown American citizens. There is also the political vitriol unleashed by this "Era of Trump" -- which inflames and illuminates passions based on confusion, racial divisions, and a significant level of mistrust in our democratic institutions. This mistrust provides the perfect fissure for a radicalized and charismatic leader — not a figure head, but a person with great leadership skills — who could leverage social media to cast a wide net. Like the Arab Spring, America would face a synchronized cybersecurity threat which would mobilize the disenchanted, the voiceless, the marginalized, and those who believe that our formal government has lost its way. And let us not forget that these crowds are easily infiltrated by ne'er-do-wells whose sole purpose is destruction, looting, police-focused violent acts, and racial division and discord.

Finally, I would remind the reader to always remember that the crowd remains the unknown variable whenever it assembles. Since the

Whiskey Rebellion of 1794, the dynamic and volatility of the crowd has remained constant. It gathers after a catalyzing event like the video-taped murder of George Floyd, or the slain body of 18-year-old Michael Brown lying prostrate in the middle of the street for four and one-half hours. In the case of Michael Brown that same crowd responds to the police, who follow the standard protocol of preserving the sanctity of an alleged "crime scene." This crowd is emboldened as it gathers to view Michael's cloaked body--which served as the outward symbol of a history of tumultuous relations between local African-American citizens and Ferguson police. The forensics of what happened between Michael and a local Asian store owner earlier that day; and the confrontation between police officer Darren Wilson and Michael Brown were secondary to the convergence of public opinion that was taking root as the crowd amassed.

Likewise, we witnessed in Ferguson the dynamic of the crowd change over the hours that Michael's body lay covered in the middle of Canfield Drive. As articulated in Army doctrine from the 1960s, the crowd was initially a "casual" crowd, unorganized and without common purpose. As Michael Brown's mother arrived on the scene, and wasn't allowed access to his remains, that crowd became "cohesive"—that is, held together by common interest. When Michael's stepfather arrived on the scene, the crowd became "expressive," with well-defined leadership. One can readily recall televised images of inflammatory language from police in riot gear, and antagonistic and provocative tactics by police on an armored vehicle. These lapses of restraint, coupled with the changing dynamics of the crowd, set the conditions for the increasingly "aggressive" crowd, with Michael Brown's stepfather emerging as the strong leader with significant influence on the emotions of the crowd. Moreover, we can never forget the profound and most alarming phenomena within the crowd—what Collective Behaviorists call "anonymity,"-- the damage wrought by the notion that you as an individual are not responsible for what you do as a member of a crowd. Certainly, Frederick Douglass best understood the eternal significance of our American values of sacrifice and dissent when he stated:

*If there is no struggle there is no progress. Those who profess to favor freedom, and yet depreciate agitation, are men who want crops without plowing up the ground... This struggle may be a moral one; or it may be a physical one; or it may be both moral and physical; but it must be a struggle.... Power concedes nothing without a demand. It never did and it never will.*[1]

# *INTRODUCTION*

Defense of the US homeland is as complex as any military operation, as employment of a federalized force—despite President Donald Trump's argument of his authorities and powers under the Insurrection Act--occurs with significant constraints. Not only are there constitutional implications that govern employment of a military force domestically, but there are also statutes, doctrinal and training implications, and an actual requirement of an application of support from the State Governor to the President of the United States, who assures that all State assets and resources have been exhausted. This volume examines the evolution of riot control doctrine in federal troop actions to quell racial violence throughout U.S. history, but especially following the 1968 assassination of Dr. Martin Luther King and the verdict of the Rodney King beating trial in 1992. It also considers how the role of federal troops and their preparedness have changed since the Los Angeles Riots of 1992. This book will evaluate the legal basis for military intervention, examines causal factors for civil unrest, and offers conclusions which may help determine the future of this very important domestic military role.

Although each disturbance evaluated within this volume is unique, sustained investigation of urban unrest in America reveals that similar adverse conditions persisting over extended periods may best describe the underlying causes of the contagion which leads to riots. The 1968 *Kerner Report* provided the United States of America with significant insights into the psychology of the riots that consumed many urban centers during the 1960's. During that decade, the nation was tremendously frustrated -- by poverty, by the war in Vietnam, by heavy-handed tactics and widespread abuse by police, and by the persistence of segregationist practices and theories. Many observers of continuing racial violence in present-day America contend that we are experiencing a resurgence of several major issues of the 1960's. This study will conduct an autopsy of that contention.

In examining civil disturbances within the United States, several intertwined questions are paramount: "What role should federal forces play in quelling civil unrest if there is a resurgence of urban violence?"

"Will these forces be prepared to respond immediately to this  eventuality?" "How has the Army's civil disturbance training and doctrine evolved?" "What is the 1878 Posse Comitatus Act and how has it affected the role of federal troops in conducting riot duty?" "What is the continued relevance of this 1878 statute in the modern era?" There is significant debate surrounding the constraints of the law which limits the military's ability to search, seize, and detain American citizens. "What conditions have prompted state and local authorities to require federal intervention; and how have federal troops performed during those civil disturbances, especially in Washington and Los Angeles?" "Will the inflammatory, inciteful, and volatile penchant of President Donald J. Trump during this modern era enjoin scores of Americans to return to a time immemorial and thus cause a setback in racial relations?" "Who is responsible for policing the police?" History—both past and present--is replete with evidence that would-be protectors and defenders of law and order are both the cause and catalyst of civil unrest within American cities.

"How have deployments in major disturbances influenced Army doctrine, training and planning?" Finally, "should our nation consider the riots in Ferguson, Missouri (2014), Charlotte, North Carolina (2016), Minneapolis, Minnesota (2017), St. Louis, Missouri (2017), Berkeley, California (2017), Charlottesville, Virginia (2017), Louisville, Kentucky, Minneapolis, Minnesota, Washington, DC, Atlanta, Georgia, Philadelphia, Pennsylvania, Seattle, Washington, Portland, Oregon, Los Angeles, California, and Kenosha, Wisconsin (2020) as a signal of what's to come and thus solicit a revisit and revamping of doctrine on civil unrest and federal intervention?"

The only published single-volume work on the 1968 Washington, D.C.,  riots is journalist Ben Gilbert's *Ten Blocks from the White House*. A review of more than fifty works on the 1960's revealed either no mention or very little discussion of that riot. A review of thirteen undergraduate history textbooks, used across the country in college survey history courses, uncovered very little discussion of the event. Indeed, extracts from the thirteen textbooks would not provide enough material to form a solid paragraph on the rioting that transpired in the nation's capital.

One of the more alarming quotes on the riot is found in a 1993 textbook entitled *Enduring Vision*. After claiming that "In Washington, D.C. more than 700 fires illuminated the night sky," the work stated that, "Rampaging blacks there forced Army units in combat gear to set up machine-gun emplacements outside the Capitol."[1] The passage created the illusion of blacks storming, the Capitol, which did not occur. With respect to the set up and placement of machine-guns, an Associated Press photo on the front page of the *New York Times* clearly depicts a small machine-gun emplacement on the steps of the Capitol building, with no ammunition belt protruding from the side of the gun, indicating that it was not loaded.[2] The presence of the machine-gun on the Capitol steps, however, is not surprising. The Army's riot control doctrine, *Field Manual 19-15· Civil Disturbances and Natural Disasters*, called for the display of machine-guns, no larger than .30 caliber, concluding that "the psychological effect produced by the sight of machine-guns serves as a strong deterrent against rioters challenging the application of force by the disturbance control troops."[3]

Eugene Methvin offered a chapter on the Washington riot in *The Riot Makers* (1970). Several of Methvin's contentions are unsubstantiated and factually incorrect. In one instance, he quoted a paratrooper who supposedly stated: "When we went to help [the casualties] snipers started shooting, bullets bounced around my feet. I was in Vietnam a year and never came as close to getting hit as I did today."[4] However, the Department of the Army After Action Report stated that there were "no verified reports of sniper incidents occurring in Washington, D.C."[5] Methvin also alleged that the Army's riot techniques were based on nineteenth-century manuals. Again, Methvin's assertion is factually incorrect. The Army's civil disturbance manual had been revised five times since its introduction in 1945, with one modification distributed just one month before the D.C. riot.

The only scholarly writings that deal specifically with the post-King assassination riots are dissertations by James R. Gardner and Richard Guy Sedlack.[6] Gardner's study focused on the aftermath of the unrest from the Department of the Army's perspective. His treatment of the Washington riot constituted only two pages of his 343-page dissertation.

Sedlack's study is an exploratory effort into disaster relief literature which relies on official statistics of arrest records and fire data associated with the D.C. riot. He offers only a cursory overview of the employment of federal troops in the nation's capital.

Conversely, there exists an abundance of published historical, sociological, and psychological studies on the 1992 Los Angeles riot. *The City in Crisis*, more commonly known as the *Webster Report*, provided an excellent account of the events in Los Angeles and blamed the city's police department for the volatile situation which turned into the perfect storm. The staff of the *Los Angeles Times* furnished an excellent day-by-day synopsis of the riot in *Understanding the Riots: Los Angeles Before and After the Rodney King Case.* Likewise, The Institute of Alternative Journalism produced an insightful and informative collection of essays and articles by more than sixty independent writers and journalist in its volume, *Inside the L.A. Riots: What Really Happened—and Why It Will Happen Again.*

An examination of more than 100 volumes and articles associated with the Los Angeles riot, coupled with interviews of the principals charged with returning the city to normal (mayor, chief of police, sheriff, president of the police commission), revealed an emphasis on assessing blame for the 1992 riot. Less clear was the collective and coordinated effort by the aforementioned to control the riot and return order to the city. Past writers have not had access to classified military after action reports, planning documents, and situation reports. As a result, in both Washington and Los Angeles, conclusions were based largely on media accounts. In many instances, these conclusions are limited and suspect.

This volume is organized chronologically and divided into seven chapters and an Epilogue. Chapter 1 surveys the history of federal intervention, the legal basis for federal action, and the evolution of civil disturbance doctrine from 1794 to 1967. It recounts several examples of the Army's deployment in civil unrest, and highlights several instances when soldiers initiated civil violence (Brownsville and Houston, Texas). Chapter 1 also recounts how the Military Intelligence Division—an entity which informed our nation's policies and its perceptions of national threats -- viewed Negroes in the very same light as the United States viewed Bolshevism during the "Red Scare" of the early 1900s. This chapter also examines the so-called "Negro Problem" within the Army during World War II, and assesses various recommendations and actions taken by the Army to remedy the "problem."

Chapter 2 examines the Detroit riot of 1967. The after-action reports from units deployed to Detroit served as the guide for reforming the Army's civil disturbance policies and standing operating procedures. Although active forces performed admirably during the riot, the Michigan National Guard did not fare so well. Recommendations for intensive training for all Guard units on the use of force, better command and control procedures, and more training for officers and soldiers on riot control formations followed the Detroit experience.[7] Chapter 2 recounts how the rioting in Detroit led the nation's leadership to search for the underlying causes of mounting urban unrest. Detroit was the catalyst that prompted President Lyndon Baines Johnson to create a National Advisory Commission on Civil Disorders, chaired by Otto Kerner, commonly known as the Kerner Commission. Its report in March 1968 concluded "that the single overriding cause of rioting-in U.S. cities was not any one thing commonly adduced- unemployment, lack of education, poverty, exploitation-but that it was all those things and more."[8]

Chapter 3 argues that "lessons learned" during the Detroit experience were not "lessons lost" as federal troops quelled the 1968 Washington riot. The "restrained and effective" use of military forces after the assassination of Martin Luther King, Jr., in Washington, D.C., proved that the Army's civil disturbance doctrine and policies were sound. The chapter also argues that the outbreak of violence in D.C. after King's death substantiated many of the findings of the *Kerner Report,* released just one month earlier. Chapter 3 concludes with lessons learned and a post-mortem of the Army's performance in Washington.

Chapter 4, entitled "From King to King: 1969 to 1991," examines the systematic dismantling of the role of federal troops in civil disturbances during those years. It evaluates the woeful performance of the Ohio National Guard at Kent State University in May of 1970; the Regular Army's violations of the Posse Comitatus Act at Wounded Knee, South

Dakota, in 1973; and the Florida National Guard's efforts in Miami in 1980--a riot which in many ways mirrored the 1992 Los Angeles riot.

Chapter 5, entitled "Discerning the Divide," examines the background and origins of the 1992 riot in Los Angeles. The chapter contends that numerous well-publicized instances of police brutality over an extended period created the "tinder box" which would ignite in May of 1992. It argues that a peculiar brand of justice existed for Los Angeles's minority communities, that federal troops played only a minimal role in quelling the 1992 Los Angeles riot, and that the advantages gained by the Guard, Regular Army, and state and local police from 1968 to 1974 were lost by the time Mayor Tom Bradley requested federal assistance in 1992.

Chapter 6 offers conclusions, reflections, a comparative look at past riots with the Los Angeles riot of 1992. It considers whether the Posse Comitatus Act is a statute, a statue, or a shield which should be rescinded or further revised. Chapter 6 also considers what future role the Army might play in civil disturbances.

Chapter 7 considers the *Kerner Report* fifty years later and addresses potential remedies within local police departments to counter causal trends which finds heavy-handed policing at the epicenter of the cause versus catalyst debate. This chapter also considers whether the "Age of Trump" represents a rollback to a time immemorial, and assesses the continued relevance of the major contentions of the *Kerner Report*. Finally, the Epilogue considers the murder of George Floyd, the fanning of flames by President Donald Trump, and provides a reflective desire to live up to our best selves as American Citizens. The Epilogue will examine the May 2020 response to the murder of George Floyd, the lessons-lost by current civil leaders, and the "over-response" by President Trump and the way ahead.

This study is first to employ the declassified primary source data File 103, "Civil Disturbance Operations," U.S. Army Staff, of Record Group 319 (RG 319), located at National Archives in College Park, Maryland. It also draws upon other archival material including the Records of U.S. Army Commands (RG 338), the Records of the Provost Marshal (RG 389), and the Records of the Adjutant General's Office (RG 407). This work is the first to incorporate other declassified military after-action reports, situation reports, and year end summaries from the United States Army Continental Command, Forces Command, and the National Guard Bureau. Other official correspondence, government documents, U.S. census data, congressional reports, and Army contingency plans were also consulted. A variety of contemporary journalistic reports and personal interviews with several civil and military figures involved in the 1992 Los Angeles Riot round out the sources for this study.

## CHAPTER 1

## *FEDERAL INTERVENTION IN CIVIL DISTURBANCES, 1794-1967: A SEARCH FOR DEFINITION*

*From 1807 on, presidents . . . nearly always chose to use Regulars. There was a variety of circumstances dictating this choice, but these can be summed up as reflecting a lack of reliability of militia to overcome local prejudices and act with unity under national authority.*[1]

Federal intervention within a U.S. State or Territory is tremendously complex. This chapter surveys the first 150 years of the role of Federal Troops within the Continental United States; establishes the legal basis—both constitutional and by established statute; examines the evolution of civil disturbance doctrine and training; recounts actual deployments of Federal assets in the role; and introduces the so-called Negro problem that spans the life of this vital domestic military role.

Throughout the history of the United States the American military has assisted the Federal government with maintaining domestic order. From 1794 through the eve of the 1967 Detroit riot, the armed forces evolved from a focus on defending the frontiers and keeping foreign adversaries out, to arguably the most powerful and technologically advanced military force in history. Although the American military has enjoyed widespread recognition as the world's premier military power, within the confines of the continental United States the Army's role has lacked clarity, continuity, and consistency. From the Revolution to the long hot summer of 1967 the Army, militia, and National Guard had quashed civil unrest throughout the nation. In unusual circumstances, however, the Army's soldiers had also rebelled against the local community at such places as Brownsville and Houston, Texas.[2]

The U.S. Constitution clearly stipulates that the President holds the power to deploy the military in cases of civil unrest in order to preserve public order. Article II, Section 2 places the President as commander-in-chief of the Army, Navy, and militia called into the service of the United States. Article II, Section 3 charges the President with the faithful execution of laws. Article IV, Section 4 guarantees every state in the Union a republican form of government, and requires the Federal Government to protect states against invasion.[3] As a result of these provisions the President has possessed considerable authority to order troops on varied and diverse missions to preserve order.

As we will see in the events described here, presidential intervention has played a decisive role—often, though not always, a positive one—in defusing the country's often explosive domestic crises. Not surprisingly, in a country born in revolution and replete with conflicting allegiances, early American citizens were nervous about a continued role for the military on American soil. The Army's role in quelling civil unrest during the first eighty-nine years of the Republic was correspondingly sporadic, restrained largely by public opposition to a standing Army. Many citizens feared that the government would utilize the Army to tyrannize its people, and as historian Robert Coakley observed, American citizens believed that a standing Army "could be the instrument only of a monarchy, not a democratic state."[4]

Despite this concern, the U.S. Army did not usurp power nor was it used by presidents to harass their opponents or suppress dissidents, although Federalized military forces were first used as early as 1794 by President George Washington to control civil unrest during the Whiskey Rebellion. At that time, prompted by violent resistance in western Pennsylvania to a federal tax on the production of whiskey, President Washington federalized 15,000 militiamen from Pennsylvania, Maryland, New Jersey, and Virginia and placed them under the command of Virginia Governor General Harry Lee.[5]

The precedent established by Washington was reinforced during Fries' Rebellion in 1799, the Tariff Nullification controversy in 1832-33, and the Dorr Rebellion in 1842.[6] Due to the demand for federal troops to enforce fugitive slave laws along the Kansas border in 1854, U.S. Attorney General Caleb Cushing wrote an opinion, commonly known as the "Cushing Doctrine," stating that, "A marshal of the United States . . . has authority to summon the entire able-bodied force [all males over 15 years of age] of his precinct, as a *posse comitatus*. The authority comprehends not only bystanders and other citizens generally, but any and all organized armed forces, whether militia of the state, or officers, soldiers, sailors, and marines of the United States."[7]

Regular Army forces deployed throughout Kansas from 1854-58, quelled the Mormon troubles in Utah in 1857-58, and recaptured the federal arsenal from John Brown at Harper's Ferry, Virginia in 1859. During the American Civil War the U.S. Army not only fought conventional battles against the Confederate States of America, but also suppressed draft riots, operated railroads, took over necessary industries, and played a major part in developing the role for former slaves within the larger society after the war.[8] Beginning with the passage of legislation on 29 July 1861, Congress vastly strengthened Abraham Lincoln's authority to use both militia and the Regular Army to suppress insurrections and to execute the laws of the Union. Under the President's war powers, military commanders supplanted civil authority and exercised both police and judicial functions. In an effort to control dissent and disloyalty Lincoln suspended the writ of *habeas corpus* in specified areas in 1861. Concurrent with this action the President issued a proclamation suspending the writ for the duration of the war for all "rebels, insurgents, and persons, wherever found, who discouraged enlistment, resisted the draft, or were guilty of disloyalty."[9] President Andrew Johnson declared insurrections ended on 20 August 1866, thus revoking Lincoln's proclamation of 1861.

As well as restoring order, however, the military sometimes engaged in more questionable activities. During the elections of 1862 and 1864, for example, military personnel policed the polls and, in many instances, required loyalty oaths from citizens before allowing them to vote. Conservative congressmen and Democrats publicly charged that these repressive measures were used to maintain the Republican party in power. Beginning in 1863, Abraham Lincoln appointed military governors with civil and military powers within Louisiana and Arkansas, as a part of his presidential reconstruction efforts. Lincoln hoped that these military appointees would mobilize loyal electorates while other Army officers initiated educational programs for ex-slaves. In 1865, as a result of public dissatisfaction, Congress enacted the first laws restricting the use of federal armed forces in executing the laws.[10]

During the same year Congress, supporting the Army's work with blacks, created the Bureau of Freedmen, Refugees, and Abandoned Lands in the War Department.[11] Following the conclusion of the Civil War, the Army was used extensively as if it were a federal police force. Governors, sheriffs, U.S. marshals, revenue agents, and other local figures requested and received detachments of troops. To historian Joan Jensen, "the role of the military in Southern reconstruction was always an ambiguous one. . . resulting in hostility, law suits, and confusion on the part of officers over the extent of their powers."[12]

Southerners responded to Reconstruction by organizing such white supremacist groups as the Ku Klux Klan. Klansmen not only beat, whipped, and murdered blacks and white Republicans, but they also terrorized and killed militiamen charged with protecting blacks during Reconstruction.[13] Congress responded to the Klan's coercive tactics with the passage of the Ku Klux Klan Act in 1871. This statute gave President Ulysses S. Grant the authority to intervene militarily in reconstructed states without the formal request of the state legislatures and governors.

Public criticism followed the deployment of federal troops in southern communities during the 1876 elections. This use of military forces, coupled with frequent military deployments between 1865 and 1876, for purposes normally reserved for civil authority, provoked a congressional reaction. In December 1876, the U.S. House of Representatives passed a resolution requesting that President Grant submit all documents pertaining to the use of troops in the states of Virginia, Louisiana, Florida, and South Carolina from 1 August to December of that year. President Grant defended the legality of his use of troops based on the provisions of the Constitution, varied precedents, and the Enforcement Acts which, according to Robert Coakley, "acted against the Klan. . . at election time."[14] Coakley noted that the President viewed the Klan as the true oppressor of the democratic process. Congress sought measures to control the employment of troops domestically and reached a compromise in May of 1878. In an amendment to the Army Appropriations bill, Kentucky Democratic Representative J. Proctor Knott offered what became known as the Posse Comitatus Act. This bi-partisan act received overwhelming support in both houses of Congress, and it repealed the

Cushing doctrine. Among the provisions of the statute was the restriction that "whoever, except in cases and under circumstances expressly authorized by the Constitution or Act of Congress, willfully uses any part of the Army as a *posse comitatus* or otherwise to execute the [civilian] laws shall be fined not more than $10,000 or imprisoned not more than two years, or both."[15] The Act prohibited the use of the Army in any law enforcement role. In its original form, the Act did not impose any restrictions on the Navy, Marine Corps, or the Coast Guard because the Act was proposed as a result of the alleged misuse of the Regular Army.[16]

At the time of the statute's introduction, the generally accepted reason for its implementation was the excessive use of troops by Republican governors and presidents. Congressmen opposing the Act charged that it would strip the president of the power to use troops to suppress internal disorder except on request of a state governor or legislature. In actuality, all the Act really did was repeal the Cushing Doctrine. Robert Coakley argued that the Act simply meant "Army troops could not be used on any lesser authority than that of the President."[17] Army lawyer H.W.C. Furman noted that President Rutherford B. Hayes "considered the Act to be little more than a restraint on the power of U.S. Marshals and not applicable to the Chief Executive."[18]

Controversies associated with the timing of the Act included the disputed Hayes/Tilden presidential election of 1876; the return of "Home Rule" to the states of Mississippi, Louisiana, South Carolina, and Florida; and the effective redeployment of federal troops in Louisiana and South Carolina. These varied themes tended to overshadow the events orchestrated by Hayes before signing the Act into law in June of 1878. For example, Hayes called a special Congressional session to have funds appropriated to pay soldiers who had gone without pay since June of 1876. Hayes' signing of the Act essentially gave the President, as Commander-in-Chief, absolute civil authority with regard to deploying troops. Perhaps Paul Jackson Rice best summarized the significance of the Act. He stated: "While the act was never a vision of clarity, its reputation for obscurity was probably due to the fact that, in broad terms, it had accomplished its mission. After the passage of the Act, it was understood that federal troops were not available to supplement civilian law enforcement officials."[19]

What does the Posse Comitatus Act mean with respect to the Army involved in state and local operations? Whether the military is involved in an urban riot, labor dispute, disaster relief or modern counter-drug operation, the legal authority to participate in domestic territory is normally limited to the support of civilian law enforcement agencies.

As with most laws, Posse Comitatus has several exceptions which grant the President increased authority and flexibility in the employment of troops.[20] In order to avoid breaking the statute, any use of the Army to enforce civilian laws must be grounded upon a recognized and valid exception. Three categories of exceptions to the Posse Comitatus Act exist. First, there are statutory exceptions based on specific laws enacted by Congress. These laws date back to the early days of the Republic. They were first enacted by Congress in 1792 and remain unchanged since that time. The procedures prescribed by these laws were first used by President Washington to suppress the Whiskey Rebellion.

The second category consists of two non-statutory exceptions to the Act. Both are based on "the inherent right of the sovereign to respond when emergency, preemptive action is required to preserve public order, and to use necessary force to protect its own property and functions."[21] This exemption is outlined in paragraph six of Army Regulation 500-50: Emergency Employment of Army Resources--Civil Disturbances, which authorizes the local military commander on the scene to respond to emergency situations during a public crisis.[22] General Frederick Funston's actions taken to prevent looting, provide medical aid, and restore order following the San Francisco earthquake of 1906 provide an excellent example of the use of this exception. Additionally, the state governors' authority to mobilize the National Guard to assist in quelling a civil disturbance illustrates their right to preserve public order.

Another exception to the Posse Comitatus Act is based on a joint resolution of Congress passed shortly after the assassination of Senator Robert Kennedy in June of 1968. The resolution directed all departments of the government to assist the U.S. Secret Service in protecting government officials and candidates for high public office.[23] Military resources were used to assist the Secret Service in this way during the Republican and Democratic party conventions of 1968.

An important extension of the domestic armed-services powers came in the early 1980s when Congress passed a series of statutes under Title 10 of the U.S. Code (Sections 371-381). These provided authority for the armed services to support law enforcement activities in areas such as intelligence, transportation, equipment loans, and training. The military began to support counter-drug operations during this period. Parallel congressional action also increased the government's authority to employ federal troops to assist in domestic disaster relief. The foundation of the 1878 Posse Comitatus Act, however, remained intact--military personnel could not participate in arrests, searches, and seizures.[24]

Following Reconstruction, the Army quelled violent labor disputes and enforced court injunctions against striking union workers. The Army's intervention in the national railroad strikes of 1877, the labor dispute at the Coeur d'Alene mines in Idaho in 1892, and Chicago's Pullman strike of 1894 created turbulence within the officer corps. Historian Jerry Cooper contended that "officers wished they could have avoided involvement in riot duty because of the lack of defined policy and law."[25] Policy decisions, normally made by the President or Secretary of War, were vague or unspecific, leaving local or state authorities in charge. Invariably, Republican and Democratic state officials supported management's position and pitted soldiers against strikers, making the Army a nonpartisan instrument in the sense that it was not helping one political party at the expense of the other. During the eleven-year period between 1885 and 1895, military forces were mobilized over 300 times for riot duty; 120 involved labor conflicts.[26]

During the eighteenth and nineteenth centuries, the Regular Army had no doctrine for civil disturbance duty. The first comprehensive plan for action against a domestic threat was not created until World War I, when War Plan White became the Army's plan for action against a domestic threat. The Regular Army's domestic plan focused on the "suppression of violence . . . without bloodshed," while the National Guard had a more aggressive focus.[27] National Guard Officer Henry Bellows' statement that "the attack is the basis of all successful tactics in riot duty as elsewhere. Defensive action can never of itself produce victory," was indicative of the National Guard's penchant for violent and decisive resolution of domestic crises.[28]

The doctrine that governed the Active Duty soldiers during the control of civil disturbances was the product of years of trial and error by the War Department's War Plans Division and the Military Police Corps. Several early attempts at formulating civil disturbance doctrine focused specifically on select National Guard units. Early chroniclers and writers of civil disturbance operations advocated meeting mass violence and dissent with overwhelming firepower.[29] One of the first attempts at developing civil disturbance doctrine was an 1891 drill regulation by Brigadier General Albert Ordway of the Washington, D.C. Militia. Ordway focused on the static defense of an armory by a battalion of four companies. He argued that "fire discipline" was synonymous with "control of fires," asserting that, "when it does become necessary to fire on a mob, it is merciful to make the fire short, relentless, and effective."[30] With respect to the soldier performing riot duty, the general asserted that, "they may kill, burn, or destroy with absolute impunity if their superiors lawfully order them to do so."[31] The militia's focus ran counter to the Regular Army's desire to avoid being regarded as an invading alien force.

During the twentieth century, the Regular Army's role in quelling civil disturbances was both infrequent and more diverse. The Army suppressed labor unrest at Nevada gold mines in 1907 and at Colorado coal mines in 1913 and 1914. It also quashed a race riot in Winston-Salem, North Carolina, in 1918. During the same year Brigadier General Louis Babcock, of the New York Guard, examined the law for the call-up and employment of his State's Guard. His volume resembled a standard operating procedure or continuity file for officers. Like Ordway, Babcock was a hard-liner with no patience for half measures in meeting dissent with force. He argued that, "nothing so emboldens a crowd as passive resistance and it should never be allowed." Babcock further asserted that, "any man in a crowd, on a roof, or at a window, plainly seen to fire a shot, throw a stone or assault a soldier, should be shot."[32]

Following the same basic logic as Babcock was Captain Edward S. Farrow, a tactics instructor at the U. S. Military Academy. Farrow's 1919 volume, although absent of notes, professed conclusions identical Babcock's.[33] Consistent amongst these early attempts at doctrine was the focus on using violent and overwhelming force to quell local violence. Farrow's views, however, were not those of the Army. The Regular Army did not have a sound and usable plan until the Military Intelligence Division prepared War Plan White in 1916.

War Plan White, a series of plans for controlling domestic upheaval, required significant involvement from the Army. According to historian Joan Jensen, the White Plan focused on "American civilians who might cause civil disturbances and possibly overthrow the [U.S.] government."[34] On the Military Intelligence Division's (MID) list of domestic adversaries were communists, Industrial Workers of the World, socialists, anarchists, pacifists, and radical political reformers. After federal troops quelled widespread racial violence in Chicago, Illinois, Omaha, Nebraska, and Washington, D.C., in 1919, the MID's adversaries list included African-Americans.[35]

The War Department replaced War Plan White in October of 1921 with Emergency Plan White. It called for the complete military occupation and control of the nine corps areas in the United States. At the foundation of the Emergency White Plan was the premise "that a well-organized movement for the overthrow of the [U.S.] Government was being orchestrated by a force of 600,000 to 1,500,000 civilians."[36] The MID postulated a situation in which these domestic insurgents would seize major industrial centers; cut off air, land, and water transportation lines and hubs; capture public utilities; and seize food stocks, which would eventually drive the starving civilian population to mob violence and anarchy. In response the military would intervene, recapture the food depots, and distribute provisions to the starving citizens. In this scenario, the military would possess the support of the local populace as it enforced martial law.[37] As far-fetched as the White Plan may appear in retrospect, to the War Department similar occurrences in Russia, Hungary, Poland, and Siberia demonstrated the plausibility of the plan's contentions.

Emergency Plan White was one of the most comprehensive military plans of its time. It included specific laws governing military actions, drafts of legislation under consideration, and corps area intelligence functions. The plan also included maps depicting area power lines, railroads, road networks, and signal communications in the designated area. Moreover, the plan provided an outline for developing corps area plans and a checklist to test the completeness of the plan.[38] It also detailed the employment of forces and the character of the military actions to be contemplated. The White Plan even gauged the probable media response to the employment of chemical agents by military forces against civilians. No stone was left unturned in these comprehensive contingency plans. Corps area commands divided the country into regions of responsibility. Table 1 depicts the ten service command headquarters, which provided command and control for the nine Army corps located across the nation.

Emergency Plan White also presented a preventative strategy to forestall opportunities for civic violence. Under the plan the corps area commander maintained vigilance within his area of responsibility by "carefully observing incidents and events which might develop into strikes, riots, or other disorders which could ultimately require the intervention of federal troops."[39] The character of the military action contemplated closely resembled the actions of local police. Under the provisions of Emergency Plan White, martial law would be in effect, thus, the military would temporarily govern the civilian population until the local government could be restored. During martial rule, military forces are subordinate only to the President of the United States and the War Department.[40] The use of Regular Army soldiers, under the direction of Army Chief of Staff Douglas MacArthur, to thwart the protest of veterans during the Bonus March in Washington in 1932 marked one of the first tests of Emergency Plan White.

During the early part of the twentieth century, a disturbing trend developed: Regular Army troops not only quelled domestic violence, but they also initiated it, and a primary reason for this violence was racism. On occasion, from 1906 through the end of World War II, African-American soldiers were the focus of domestic violence. According to historian Bernard Nalty, "besides fighting the wartime enemy, black Americans faced a second and far more dangerous foe--racism, which sharply restricted their opportunities within the armed services and in civil society as well. The accomplishments of blacks in combat all but disappeared when examined through the distorting prism of white supremacy."[41] When African-American soldiers from the frontier began moving into southern garrisons, white backlash occasionally resulted in altercations between citizens and soldiers.

| TABLE 1: Service Command Headquarters in the United States | |
|---|---|
| Service Command | Headquarters Location |
| First | Boston, Massachusetts |
| Second | Governor's Island, New York |
| Third | Baltimore, Maryland |
| Fourth | Atlanta, Georgia |
| Fifth | Columbus, Ohio |
| Sixth | Chicago, Illinois |
| Seventh | Omaha, Nebraska |
| Eighth | Dallas, Texas |
| Ninth | Fort Douglas, Utah |
| Military District of Washington | Washington, D.C. |

Source: Data extracted from the Army Service Forces Office of the Commanding General, Subject: Domestic Racial Estimate, dated 10 July 1945. Located in File 291.2, RG 389, NA.

One of the earliest disputes between African-American troops and white citizens during the twentieth century occurred in Brownsville, Texas. On the evening of 13 August 1906, ten to twenty African-American soldiers allegedly terrorized the community of Brownsville, firing randomly into buildings, killing one citizen and wounding another.[42] "Alleged" is the operative word in this event as it was confirmed immediately after the shooting spree that none of the ammunition of the 25th Infantry Regiment was missing. Testimony further revealed that the first five or six shots fired were from a pistol or revolver -- which the battalion had only recently received, but had not issued to troops. Testimony by the local mayor revealed that Texas Rangers and at least four local civilians owned the identical weapons that the Army had issued to its soldiers -- Springfields and Krag Jorgensens. The expended ammunition shell casings for these weapons was the only evidence used against the soldiers in Brownsville.

These members of the 25th Infantry Regiment had conducted a violent reprisal in response to the Jim Crow policies of the local community. City parks and local businesses were reserved for whites only, while unfounded stories of black soldiers attempting to rape white women circulated. Episodes of white physical violence were not uncommon, as "individual whites punched or threatened black troops who had done nothing to provoke this kind of treatment."[43] Race relations totally deteriorated between soldiers of the 25th Infantry Regiment and the local white populace within two weeks after the African-American soldiers' arrival in Brownsville.[44] As a result of the Brownsville incident, President Theodore Roosevelt commanded the dishonorable discharge of three African-American companies without initiating the customary trial by court-martial.[45] All told, 167 black soldiers, six of whom were Congressional Medal of Honor recipients, were forced from active service without benefits, pensions, back pay, allowances, or the opportunity to gain future federal employment of any kind.

Eleven years after violence erupted in Brownsville, a similar confrontation occurred in Houston, Texas, between African-American troops and local white police. On 23 August 1917, approximately 100 soldiers from the all-African-American Third Battalion of the 24th Infantry Regiment marched on Houston to avenge the beating of a noncommissioned officer by a local white policeman. Within three hours, sixteen whites--including five policemen--were dead, and twelve civilians were seriously injured.

Much like the situation in Brownsville, troops were in Houston only a short time-- twenty-six days--when violence occurred. Author Robert Haynes faults the *Houston Post* for the city's negative response to African-American troops. He argued that the *Post* attempted to sway the local prohibition vote on 20 August 1917 by headlining that day's edition: "3000 Negro Troops in Houston within the Month: Remember Brownsville. Make Harris County Dry."[46] This prophetic media admonishment fueled discontent between the local populace and African-American soldiers.

These two similar events involving African-American Regular Army troops in Texas raise the question of why African-American troops resorted to violence against the local white populace? William Tuttle believes the reason was based on the troops' experiences in World War I. In *Race Riot: Chicago in the Red Summer of 1919*, Tuttle describes a "new Negro whose self- respect and aspirations had been kindled by the [First World] war and who was determined to defend himself militantly against aggression."[47]

Although Tuttle's "New Negro" thesis was linked to African-American participation in World War I, the "New Negro" was already present considerably earlier within the all-Negro 24th and 25th Infantry Regiments. Both units had "earned their spurs" fighting on the Western frontier of the United States, in the Philippines, and in Cuba. The 24th Infantry had even served with General John "Black Jack" Pershing in Mexico. The experiences of the units in combat created great expectations of respect and full citizenship among the soldiers, but they were denied them by white military police, civilian police, and the local populace upon their arrival in Brownsville and Houston. To historian Ulysses Lee the military "was one of the few national endeavors in which Negroes had had a relatively secure position and which, at least in time of war, could lead to national recognition of their worth as citizens."[48]

Increasing racial tensions during World War II brought new theories and new proposed solutions, with geography playing a major role in the latter. The Army General Staff placed increased emphasis on what Major General George V. Strong (Assistant Chief of Staff, G2) called the "Negro Problem in the Army." With respect to the so-called

"Negro Problem," actions by the Army are replete with examples of acts of violence against black soldiers by white soldiers, white military and civil police, and the white local populace in cities and towns outside of the military installations. For example, a 12 August 1942 inquiry from Judge William Hastie suggesting that Negro troops be utilized in elite, amphibious, paratrooper, and commando units. Brigadier General I.H. Edwards, the Assistant Chief of Staff for the Army, responded "Negroes should be used to the greatest extent in shore and service elements."

In a letter from concerned citizen, A.J. Burke to President Franklin D. Roosevelt, Burke described a brutal beating of a black soldier at a Fort Worth, Texas, restaurant by two white military policemen. Documents also recounted the shooting of Private Rubin P. Pleasant by a Montgomery, Alabama, bus driver on 27 March 1943. Likewise, declassified records include weekly intelligence summaries from the various Army service commands--each highlighting the racial situation throughout its region in the Racial Appendix. There was a pervasive tendency within these reports to depict the Negro as the perceived enemy.

This view gives credence to Walter White's 1942 contention with respect to the Negro soldiers' perspective on fighting a foreign war. White stated, "The Army Jim-Crows us. The Navy lets us serve only as messmen. The Red Cross refuses our blood. Employers and labor unions shut us out. Lynchings continue. We are disfranchised, Jim Crow'ed, spat upon. What more could Hitler do than that?" [49]

In a memorandum to the Army operations officer, Strong identified numerous disturbances between black and white soldiers and civilians in southern states. In Alexandria, Louisiana, on 17 January 1942 for example, a riot was "alleged to have started when a white military policeman clubbed a colored soldier in front of a theater located in the heart of the Negro district of Alexandria."[50] General Strong attributed this racial conflict to differences between northern and southern blacks and whites. He argued that northern Negroes often rebelled against southern Jim Crow practices, while southern Negroes understood and accepted the status quo. Strong recommended that the "movement and stationing of Negro troops in areas where racial relations differ from their prior home environment should be reduced to a minimum."[51]

In May 1942, the Chief of the Military Intelligence Service also suggested a geographical solution to the growing problem of domestic racial tension. In a memorandum to the Army operations officer, Colonel Hayes A. Kroner recommended that "Northern colored troops should not be stationed south of the Mason Dixon Line" and that those already "in the south . . . be removed."[52] Similarly, a military police lieutenant colonel, writing to the Provost Marshal General, recommended that training and reception centers for Negro troops be confined to the states of "Arizona, New Mexico, Utah, and Nevada, which are very small in population and devoid of traditional race prejudice."[53]

In June 1943 federal troops deployed to quell a race riot in Detroit, Michigan. The unrest at that time was, in part, the result of the great northern migration of both blacks and whites to fill the abundance of jobs supporting the war effort. Historian Harvard Sitkoff viewed the racial violence in Detroit in 1943 as inevitable. He argued that "no city expected racial trouble more than Detroit, and none did less to prevent it. . . . Detroit, the 'Arsenal of Democracy,' seethed with racism and hatred. Racial clashes in schools, playgrounds, and factories, fights on buses and trolleys, and cross burnings throughout the city became accepted everyday occurrences. The city was described as 'a keg of powder with a short fuse.'"[54]

Although the riot was attributed to a racial incident that occurred on the bridge leading to Belle Isle, sociologists Alfred Lee and Norman Humphrey pointed to five precipitating events. First, media coverage of the controversial segregation of Negro blood by the Red Cross fueled racial discontent within Detroit's black community. Second, in-migration and employment had created an influx of over 500,000 southern whites with traditional southern attitudes towards Negroes, further exacerbating an already volatile situation. Third, overcrowding in dwellings, recreation and transportation facilities served as a source of great racial tension. Fourth, delinquency and crime within "the imprisoning walls of the slums bred frustration . . . demands outlets that take the form of juvenile delinquency and crime as well as diseases and other symptoms of moral and social disintegration."[55] Finally, Lee and Humphrey posited that prejudiced attitudes and acts of hate by "subversive groups [such] as the Christian Front, the Black Legion, the Ku Klux Klan, and many others that proselytize the psychologically conditioned with wonderfully satisfying 'panaceas.'"[56]

The 1943 riot lasted only twenty-four hours. According to *Time* magazine, "Detroit was quieted down, counted the toll of the worst riot in modern U.S. history: at least 23 dead, over 700 injured, over 600 jailed. Of the dead Negroes, police had shot at least eight."[57]

*Newsweek* gave a clearer picture of the devastation: "when the shooting, the stoning, the knifing and the bludgeoning, the arson and looting had ended after 24 hours, 35 were dead, some 700 injured, 1,300 under arrest, and a million dollars' worth of property damage."[58] Attorney Thurgood Marshall writing in 1943, claimed that, "the trouble reached riot proportions because the police once again enforced the law with an unequal hand. They used 'persuasion' rather than firm action with white rioters, while against Negroes they used the ultimate in force: night sticks, revolvers, riot guns, sub machine-guns, and deer guns. As a result, twenty-five of the thirty-four persons killed were Negroes. Of the latter, seventeen were killed by police."[59]

President Franklin D. Roosevelt acted decisively and effectively by sending 3,800 federal troops to help quell the violence in Detroit. A U.S. War Department memorandum from the Provost Marshal General to the Director, Operations and Training Division stated that "three military police battalions, a provisional battalion from Selfridge Field . . . and the Ninth Infantry [regiment]" were utilized in Detroit. The memorandum noted: "with the appearance of these troops, the situation was quickly brought under control. Motorized patrols were organized, liaison established, intelligence facilities coordinated, and necessary restrictions imposed. The troops remained on the scene until the disorders had subsided, after which they were withdrawn."

The Provost Marshal General was careful to point out that the troops' "primary missions were to disperse mobs and restrain violence, not to make arrests."[60] Unfortunately, this critical lesson of restraint had been lost by the time of the 1967 Detroit riot.[61]

On 10 July 1945, the Deputy Director of Army Intelligence distributed a memorandum outlining the racial situation across the United

States. In an assessment of 102 cities and thirty states, leaders in over eighty cities and twenty states believed that racial unrest was possible in varying degrees ranging from slightly possible to highly explosive. Surprisingly, government and military officials from Georgia, Alabama, Mississippi, and Tennessee contended that they did not anticipate any racial unrest in 1945.[62]

In a well-researched and excellent book, historian Ulysses Lee focused predominately on the role of Negro troops abroad during World War II. With regard to the Negroes' military service domestically, Lee noted racial disturbances on nineteen Army installations and in sixteen cities and towns that bordered military installations. According to Lee, "cases of physical racial friction, ranging from minor brawls to serious disturbances, ran into the hundreds."[63] Lee was careful to highlight that few disturbances involved mass violence between white and black soldiers, and that street brawls and weekend parties took on increased significance if the participants were in uniform. Lee argued that to Negro troops during the period of World War II, "the threat of disorder that might involve them was omnipresent; at times it was thought of as just one more of the inevitables of military service."[64]

Concurrent with the July 1945 release of the domestic intelligence estimate, the Army published *Field Manual 19-15: Civil Disturbances (FM 19-15)*. The manual was a relatively simplistic cut and paste synthesis of social control theories. *FM 19-15*, and its three revisions through 1967, stressed that the successful accomplishment of civil disturbance control required an understanding of group behavior, which included: the typical crowd actions and motives, basic patterns of group behavior, and individual characteristics which underlie behavior.[65] *FM 19-15* categorized crowds as "casual, cohesive, expressive, and aggressive." A casual crowd was considered to be an unorganized group of people without a common purpose or a designated leader. On the other hand, a cohesive crowd was held together by a common interest and was assembled for a particular purpose. According to the manual, an expressive crowd had well defined leadership and a specific purpose. Finally, an aggressive crowd had a strong leader with significant influence on the emotions of the crowd.

31

*Field Manual 19-15* accepted the view that social violence originated in a state of mind and the convergence of public opinion. According to the manual, rumors played a major role in crystallizing public opinion. A rumor could often be the spark that set off the explosion and changed a crowd into a mob. It was believed that rumors circulated rapidly and through distortion grew in their ugliness at each recitation. Finally, rumors were considered to be operative during actual rioting, helping to sustain the violence.

The Army's civil disturbance doctrine advocated a number of riot control formations and restrictive measures to control crowds. These measures included closing places where people could assemble (parks, stadiums and parking lots); imposing a curfew; and banning the sale of firearms, ammunition, liquor and gasoline in cans. Army doctrine, like Emergency Plan White, emphasized the importance of securing vital facilities, establishing a vigorous patrol system, designating a quick reaction force, and maintaining the psychological advantage over the rioters. Table 2 highlights the major changes to *FM 19-15* through the December 1964 edition.

| TABLE 2: Field Manual 19-15 Civil Disturbances | | | |
|---|---|---|---|
| **Edition** | **Changes to Manual** | **Weapons Utilized** | **Societal Events** |
| July 1945 | Initial Publication | • Artillery  • Chemical weapons<br>• Mortars  • Explosives<br>• Masks  • Rifles<br>• Grenades | • 242 Race riots 1943<br>• Domestic Intelligence Estimate July 1945 |
| April 1952 | • Added Section IX "Assistance or Intervention in Disasters" | • Tanks (Psychological Effect)<br>• Airplanes (Straffing and Reconnaissance)<br>• Grenades<br>• Mortars<br>• Masks<br>• Artillery<br>• Rifles<br>• Chemical Weapons | • Labor disputes<br>• Racial tensions |
| September 1958 | | • Rifles with bayonnet<br>• Machine guns<br>• Shotguns<br>• Sniper fifles<br>• Pistols<br>• Chemical weapons<br>• Sub-machine guns<br>• Mask | • Brown v. Board of Education<br>• Central High School desegregation<br>• PosseCommitatus Act revised to include Air-Force<br>• March on Washington (1957)<br>• Montgomery bus boycott |
| December 1964 | • Better illustations of riot control formations<br>• Appendix added for Field Expedient Riot Control Agents | • Rifles with bayonets<br>• Machine guns<br>• Grenade Launchers<br>• Mortars<br>• Chemical Weapons<br>• Shot guns<br>• Sniper rifles<br>• Automatic rifles<br>• Pistols<br>• Masks | • Civil Rights Movement<br>• Freedon rides<br>• Launch counter sit-ins<br>• March on Washington (1963)<br>• Desegregation:<br>  – Oxford, Alabama<br>  – Birmingham, Alabama<br>  – Tuscaloosa, Mississippi |

With the beginning of the Civil Rights Movement in the 1950s, the Regular Army's domestic disturbance mission focused almost exclusively on the role outlined in Article II, Section 3 of the Constitution--the faithful execution and enforcement of laws mandated by the U.S. Congress or Supreme Court. The Regular Army performed this mission in Little Rock, Arkansas, in 1957 and 1958 as it assisted the government with the desegregation of Central High School.[66] President Dwight D. Eisenhower established a precedent by intervening in Little Rock. One of the mandates of the Federal Government was to protect the civil rights of citizens within each state. To achieve this protection, no application or request from the state authorities was required.[67] Eisenhower became the first president to federalize an already mobilized state-controlled National Guard force being utilized in violation of a U.S. Supreme Court order.[68] One of the landmark cases of the use of federal forces in integration came in 1963, when James Meredith became the first black student to enroll in the University of Mississippi. As the U.S. Marshals protected Meredith by forming a perimeter around the university's administration building, violence quickly escalated beyond their control. The crowd fired scattered shots and threw bottles, acid, pieces of metal pipe and bricks at the marshals. What began on 30 September 1962 with 400 U.S. Marshals escalated within three days to a federal force of about 12,000 troops, of which about 9,300 were Regulars within three days.[69] Military forces remained in Oxford through Meredith's graduation in August of 1963. All told, Regular Army units from Fort Bragg, North Carolina, Fort Benning, Georgia, Fort Campbell, Kentucky, Fort Dix, New Jersey, Fort Hood, Texas, Fort Knox, Kentucky, Fort Lee, Virginia, Fort Leonard Wood, Missouri, Fort McPherson, Georgia, and Fort Rucker, Alabama deployed to Oxford.[70]

The State of Alabama was a desegregation powder keg from 1963 through 1965, requiring major federal support for integration efforts. Federal forces, headed by Major General Creighton W. Abrams, Jr., deployed throughout the state of Alabama in 1963 and 1964 to enforce desegregation legislation. As early as 1963 General Abrams described the Army's response to domestic violence. In a 19 May 1963, message to Army Chief of Staff, Earle G. Wheeler, Abrams argued that the Army had responded with an "ad hoc organization, hastily improvised."[71] Abrams recommended establishing an agency with its own staff to control the Army in support of the Civil Rights Movement and strongly emphasized the need for aggressive intelligence collection and dissemination. One can surmise that Abrams' recommendations fell on deaf ears as the Army would not establish an agency with centralized control for civil disturbances until 22 January 1968, after the significant employment of federal troops during the Detroit riot of 1967. [72]

On 11 June 1963, President John F. Kennedy federalized the Alabama Army and Air National Guard to assist deputy U.S. Attorney General Nicholas Katzenbach in gaining entry into the University of Alabama at Tuscaloosa and Huntsville. Kennedy performed the same function in September of 1963 when Alabama Governor George Wallace prevented Negro children from entering schools in Birmingham, Mobile, and Tuskegee.[73]

President Lyndon B. Johnson coupled Regular Army troops with federalized National Guardsmen in Army operation plan "Steep Hill Alabama" in March of 1965 to protect Martin Luther King, Jr., and the civil rights march from Selma to Montgomery.[74] On this occasion the Federal Government stepped in only after Governor Wallace refused to mobilize the Alabama Guard under state control. Wallace argued that the state of Alabama could not afford to call the Guard into service. Though Governor Wallace meant financially, he certainly believed that he would lose political capital if he complied with the President's directive.

Finally, in 2020 after the murder of George Floyd in Minneapolis, Minnesota, President Donald Trump insisted that the Insurrection Act of 1807 granted him authority to deploy federal forces at will--without limits and conditions. As discussed earlier within this chapter, Article II, Sections 2 and 3, and Article IV, Section 4 of our Constitution clearly delineates the President's role as Commander-in-Chief of the military, charges the office with the faithful execution of laws, and guarantees every State in the Union a republican form of government—while requiring the federal government to protect the States against invasion. The Insurrection Act of 1807 empowers the President to deploy military forces to suppress civil disorder, insurrection, and rebellion. Before invoking these powers, however, the President must first publish a proclamation ordering insurgents to disperse, but this isn't executed in a vacuum by the President alone. These powers are conditioned upon the following provisions: first, the State must submit and application after it has exhausted **all** of its resources. Second, the insurrection must make it impracticable for the State to enforce the law; and finally, the State must be incapable of Governing itself and its citizens. None of these factors where present in the George Floyd protests of 2020.

Of note, the National Defense Authorization Act of 2007, had a short-lived **amendment** to the Insurrection Act, which permitted military intervention without State consent based on the Governor of Louisiana's refusal to ask President George W. Bush to intervene in Hurricane Katrina. Most Americans believed that President George W. Bush was indecisive and slow to act after Hurricane Katrina—nothing is further from the truth. He was ready, but the Governor of Louisiana refused to ask for assistance. Of note, this provision was repealed in January of 2008 when all 50 State Governors issued a joint statement against it. [75] Hence, President Trump's committing federal agents to American cities was operating outside of his constitutional authority.

# CHAPTER 2

# DETROIT 1967: THE CATALYST FOR CHANGE

> *I remember being very much struck when I arrived [in Detroit] by the fact that the commander of the State National Guard indicated that he was waiting for us [Warren Christopher and General John Throckmorton] to tell them how they should deploy some 3,000 National Guard troops who had not yet been deployed into the effort to control the riots.* [1]

This chapter examines the Detroit Riot of 1967 and reveals how that riot ushered in tremendous reform of civil disturbance doctrine; of repurposing equipment to make it less lethal; of training required of military personnel—training that was offered to State and local police; and a recognition that the National Guard required intensive training on the use of force, better command and control procedures, and more training on the art and science of engaging people during riots. This chapter also reveals the seminal action which evolved from the Detroit Riot: President Johnson's creation of a National Advisory Commission on Civil Disorder—better know as the Kerner Commission, and a report that the President would later not even acknowledge, as the findings ran contrary to his hopes.

On 23 July 1967 Detroit police conducted an early morning raid on an illegal after-hours establishment known as "blind pig", in the black section of town.[2] Reports indicated that the club was selling alcoholic beverages after the city's 2:00 a.m. curfew. The raid drew a crowd of curious onlookers, which became enraged as police began carting off patrons. Widespread disorder erupted as the last police squad car drove off into the night; fires, looting, and violence followed until rioting overtook much of the city. At the outset, city officials were apprehensive about calling out the National Guard and opted to handle matters with local and state police. However, within fourteen hours the situation had escalated beyond the control of local and state law enforcement officials.

A *Newsweek* account graphically portrayed the scene: "the trouble burst on Detroit like a firestorm and turned the nation's fifth largest city into a theater of war. Whole streets lay ravaged by looters, whole blocks immolated in flames."[3]

As the unrest continued unabated, Governor George Romney mobilized the Michigan National Guard's 46th Infantry Division and instructed the commanding general of the division, Major General Cecil L. Simmons, to "use whatever force necessary" to restore order. As Guardsmen deployed throughout the riot area, they brought the full power of their arsenal to bear on rioting citizens, employing many of the same weapons that were being used by the Army in the jungles of Vietnam. The 46th Infantry Division fired rifles, machine guns mounted on armored vehicles, and blanketed the impacted area with chlorbenzylidene malononitrile—better known as CS. As General Simmons stated later, "this was in accordance with custom from time immemorial."[4]

The untested and fearful members of the Michigan National Guard had taken to the streets and literally executed the Governor's orders. Detroit had become a war zone in which the representatives of law and order--the Michigan National Guard--lost all semblance of weapons discipline. What transpired was a situation comparable to that in which the legendary vigilantes took charge of Dodge City in the 1860's--lawlessness, chaos, and a total disregard for restraint by the authorities responsible for social order. In one incident "Guardsmen fired fourteen shots into a car, wounding its four passengers. A search of the car revealed two empty wine bottles and a half-pint of whiskey, but no arms, no loot."[5] An unidentified Detroit citizen perhaps stated it best with his contention that, "with the amount of shooting going on around here, we're lucky 430 weren't killed."[6]

The continued escalation of violence forced a reluctant Governor Romney to request federal intervention after the first day of rioting, and President Lyndon Johnson issued an executive order for the employment of federal troops on 24 July 1967, almost forty-eight hours after violence began.[7] According to Assistant US Attorney General Warren Christopher, Romney's reluctance to request federal troops stemmed from local insurance companies aversion to the word "insurrection," which was the language in the request for intervention from States to the Federal Government. Romney did not want to void insurance policies by declaring that an insurrection was occurring in Detroit. Christopher reassured the governor that the U.S. Attorney General's office would intercede with the insurance companies if necessary. Upon this reassurance to the Governor, the Regular Army deployed brigades from the Army's elite airborne divisions, the 82d, located at Fort Bragg, North Carolina, and the 101st, located at Fort Campbell, Kentucky.[8] According to *Newsweek*, "this marked the first time that federal troops were deployed to assist in a racially motivated disturbance outside the South in a quarter century."[9] The earlier racially motivated disturbance referenced by *Newsweek* was the Detroit riot in June of 1943.

President Johnson's executive order brought the Michigan National Guard into federal service. Thus, control of all military personnel in Detroit fell to the designated commander for Task Force Detroit, Lieutenant General John Throckmorton, commanding general of the XVIII Airborne Corps. Upon arrival in the city Throckmorton had the daunting task of "bringing about a disciplined use of weapons by the federalized Michigan National Guard, who had been making frequent use of them."[10] Speaking of the military professional officer, as political scientist Samuel P. Huntington told his readers in 1957, "the peculiar skill of the officer is the management of violence not the act of violence itself,"[11] but the Michigan National Guard commander's statement that "The laws of the state will be obeyed. We will use whatever force is necessary," ran counter to Huntington's description.[12]

Due to reports of indiscriminate firing by the Guard, Throckmorton took steps to improve control over them. On 25 July he issued a directive to the Michigan National Guard commander, "to have all Guardsmen unload their weapons and put the ammunition in their pockets." Throckmorton also directed that Guardsmen were not to fire their weapons except when authorized by an officer. Finally, Throckmorton instructed the Guard "to stop shooting looters and to cease shooting out streetlights, which they had been doing because of their fear of snipers." Yet despite these orders, Throckmorton's deputy commander, Major General Charles P. Stone, "discovered that 90 percent of the approximately

500 guardsmen that he spoke with still had loaded weapons as late as the 27th and 28th of July--four days after General Throckmorton's order."[13]

Throckmorton, unlike the commander of the National Guard, possessed excellent credentials, as a thirty-two-year veteran with combat experience during World War II, Korea, and Vietnam. He was also the "commander of the 82d Airborne when it was sent to Oxford, Mississippi,... to enforce the admission of... James Meredith."[14] Upon his arrival in Detroit, the General assessed the situation before deciding on the best course of action for bringing about a truce between the rioters and civil authorities. After touring the riot area, he determined that fear saturated the city: "the National Guardsmen were afraid, the police were afraid, and numerous persons were being injured by gunshots of undetermined origin... From the time of our [Regular Army] arrival in the city, our major task was to reduce fear and restore an air of normalcy."[15] Throckmorton sent active duty units into the hardest-hit areas of the city to establish contact and rapport between the troops and city residents. Units assisted in cleaning streets, picking up garbage, and running checks for missing persons. These efforts resulted in improved cooperation between citizens and soldiers.

Ten days after the beginning of the riot, federal troops withdrew from Detroit and President Johnson released the Michigan National Guard from federal service. An additional fifteen days passed before local civil authorities regained full control of Detroit. When the violence subsided, forty-three people were dead, thirty-three of whom were African-Americans. Police officers were responsible for twenty-one fatalities, the National Guard claimed responsibility for nine, while active duty troops were credited with one death. Local store owners killed two looters, and four people died in riot-related accidents. State and local authorities determined that rioters bore responsibility for three of the deaths, and a private security guard mortally wounded one person.[16]

The post-riot military after action report served as the mandate for both reform and continuity of the Army's policies and standing operating procedures. Active duty forces performed admirably during the disturbance, but National Guardsmen did not fare so well. Former Deputy Assistant Secretary of Defense for International Security Affairs, Adam

Yarmolinsky, stated that "the experience in… Detroit in 1967 has disclosed a lack of training, indiscriminate firing, inadequate discipline, a low proportion of blacks, and frequent lack of equipment among National Guardsmen."[17] An examination of the post-riot statistics bears out Yarmolinsky's claim. During their seven days on duty in Detroit the 4,000 men of the Michigan National Guard expended 156,391 rounds of ammunition.[18] Although the Michigan National Guard received the standard written special instructions from the Department of the Army ordering restraint and fire control, these orders were either poorly enforced or ignored. The after action report recommended that the Guard undergo intensive training in the control and employment of weapons during civil disturbance operations.[19]

The report further stated that both the Regular Army and the National Guard were deficient in riot training. It recommended that the Department of the Army take an active role towards ensuring that the Guard receive more hours of training in riot control during Annual Field Training.[20] The Detroit experience illustrated an urgent need to train Guardsmen in the apprehension and handling of rioters, looters, and arsonists.

## President Johnson's Response to Detroit

The Detroit riot spurred the Army and the nation to seek solutions to the mounting national problem of urban unrest. Within the first nine months of 1967, more than 164 communities reported disorders, the most destructive occurring in Detroit.[21] Figure 1 depicts the locations of riots during 1967. The civil disturbance in Detroit, however, was the catalyst which led the Army to reassess the effectiveness of the Guard in quelling civil unrest. Additionally, the disturbance led President Johnson to create the National Advisory Commission on Civil Disorders, commonly known as the Kerner Commission, named for its chairman, Otto Kerner, Governor of Illinois. The Kerner Commission was comprised of a cross section of America's business, political, and social leaders.[22]

The President asked the commission to investigate the summer riots of 1967, determine why they occurred, and to suggest how they could be prevented in the future. Following nine months of work, the commission published its lengthy report in March 1968, concluding that:

> Our nation is moving toward two societies, one black, one white--separate and unequal... The single overriding cause of rioting in the cities was not any one thing commonly adduced--unemployment, lack of education, poverty, exploitation--but that it was all of those things and more, expressed in the insidious and pervasive white sense of the inferiority of black men. Here is the essence of the charge: What white Americans have never fully understood--but what the Negro can never forget--is that white society is deeply implicated in the ghetto. White institutions created it, white institutions maintain it, and white society condones it.[23]

**Figure 1:** *The U.S. Epidemic of Negro Riots*

According to an oral history of the civil rights movement, reaction to the *Kerner Report* was mixed. The military, as servants of democracy, did not have a public response to the report, which praised the Regular Army for its support to the commission and for its professionalism.[24] Vice President Hubert Humphrey questioned the conclusion that America was becoming racially polarized. Presidential hopeful Richard M. Nixon argued that the report blamed everyone for the riots except the perpetrators. President Johnson said privately about the Negro's plight, "He's still nowhere. He knows it. And that's why he's out in the streets. Hell, I'd be there too."[25] Publicly, however, Johnson said nothing about the report.

Public response to the bi-partisan *Kerner Report* was mixed. African-Americans viewed the report as hopeful, while many whites had a negative reaction. Opinions on the commission's conclusions were as polarized as the society itself. Authors like Lillian Boehme criticized the report as simply a "response… not an answer," calling it "a multi-billion-dollar blackmail note to the productive nation." [26] She concluded that it was a "worthless, except as a typically noisome, bit of flotsam cast up by the sewer-tide of statism in which the U.S. is drowning."[27]

Even President Johnson, who had promised the full support of the Federal Government upon appointing the commission in 1967, retreated to the safety of silence upon the report's release in March of 1968. In his memoir, *The Vantage Point,* Johnson asserted that he "made the difficult decision not to respond directly to the [Kerner Commission's] call for major new programs, because it would have killed my tax bill and possibly brought on an uncontrollable monetary crisis of 1931 proportions and consequences."[28]

Although this was the President's contention in 1971, there was evidence to the contrary in 1968. For example, Joseph Califano, the President's special assistant, sought the President's permission in February of 1968 to "leak the report to diminish its overall impact," and to highlight "its enormous cost and the unrealistic nature of its recommendations."[29] Essentially, Califano was conducting damage control. Former presidential military aide Hugh Robinson noted that "President Johnson felt betrayed by the Kerner Commission."[30] Likewise, Harry McPherson, special counsel to the President, forwarded a memorandum to Califano on 1 March 1968 which assessed the ramifications of the President's cold reaction to the *Kerner Report.* In his memo McPherson cautioned the President against failing to respond to a report by a commission that he [the President] had appointed. McPherson recommended "analyzing every single commission recommendation that affects the Federal Government; . . . treating it seriously, in other words."[31] In the president's defense, however, the report was compatible with most of his Great Society programs. The major disagreements between the

President and the commission's recommendations were over cost and the speed of implementation.

With respect to the commission's conclusions regarding "institutional racism," the commission's co-chair, New York Mayor John Lindsay, viewed the violence that erupted after the assassination of Dr. Martin Luther King [mentioned earlier] --as proof that the country was divided along racial lines. Lindsay argued that this was evident by the fact that many people and organizations that flocked to support King's vision and cause after his death were not King's supporters during his life. Lindsay asserted, "we must look to what is accomplished, not what is promised. We must discern and judge the reality, not the rhetoric."[32]

The true significance of the *Kerner Report* was not so much in its major revelations, but in its demands for action. Famed Brown vs. Board of Education psychologist Dr. Kenneth B. Clark, testifying before the commission, argued that the same problems, recommendations and solutions had been identified after all of the major race riots of the twentieth century. Clark asserted, "it is kind of Alice in Wonderland--with the same moving picture reshown over and over again, the same analysis, the same recommendations, and the same inaction."[33] Like most people seeking an end to the urban unrest of the 1960's, the commission did not condone violence as a conduit for social change, but the report was both a wake-up call and admonishment to America at-large. According to writer Gary Marx, the underlying premise of the report was "the nation would not deserve freedom from violence unless it can demonstrate the wisdom and will to undertake decisive action against the root causes of racial disorder."[34] British essayist and critic, William Hazlitt wrote in "Characteristics" that, "Vulgar prejudices are those which arise out of accident, ignorance, or authority. Natural prejudices are those which arise out of the constitution of the human mind itself."[35] Opposite *Kerner's* claims about "institutional racism," was the contention that institutions are not racist, only individuals are. Therefore, institutional racism exists because societal leaders either foster, condone, or promote racist values and views.

An examination of unemployment statistics bears out the *Kerner Report's* assertion of two societies, separate and unequal. According to

Herbert Hill, NAACP labor secretary, of the "185,000 unemployed in Detroit, 112,000 were Negroes."[36] *Kerner's* conclusion that white society was deeply implicated in the ghetto was also evident in Detroit's urban renewal program. Authors Henry Hampton and Steve Fayer contended that federal funds targeted for Detroit's urban renewal brought in new interstate roadways that "divided and destroyed black neighborhoods, displaced residents, and created a mechanism whereby more prosperous whites could ride over or around the city's black poverty on the way to shop or play or work downtown." Furthermore, by 1967, Detroit's African-Americans had accumulated a long list of grievances about their abusive treatment at the hands of the city's predominantly white police force. The police department ("called an army of occupation... by black residents,"[37]) was 95 percent white in a city whose black population exceeded 35 percent.[38]

The members of the Kerner Commission later identified underlying circumstances for unrest, stating: "We have cited deep hostility between police and ghetto communities as a primary cause of the disorders surveyed by the commission. In Newark, in Detroit, in Watts, in Harlem-- in practically every city that has experienced racial disruption since the summer of 1964, abrasive relationships between police and Negroes and other minority groups have been a major source of grievance, tension, and ultimately disorder."[39]

Table 3 supports *Kerner's* conclusions on causal factors, indicating that a lack of equity in opportunities for upward mobility for Negroes over a thirty-year period played a major role in fueling discontent. During the period in question Detroit fit nicely into sociologist Ted Gurr's model of relative deprivation, a perceived discrepancy between a person's value expectations and his or her value capabilities, as well as a gap between what people think they are entitled to receive and what they believe they are capable of attaining under the status quo.[40] Under Gurr's model something as routine as a police raid on an African-American night spot, illegally selling alcohol after curfew, becomes magnified and takes on increased significance. Given that such an incident led to mass upheaval and chaos in a major part of the city, Gurr's model does much to explain the causation of the 1967 Detroit riots.

| TABLE 3: Social -Economic Status of Black and White Males in Detroit | | |
|---|---|---|
| Category | Black | White |
| Median Income | 4,366 | 6,766 (plus 55%) |
| Median Education | 9th Grade | 10th Grade |
| Poverty | 34% | 13% |
| Unemployment | 8.6% | 2.7% |
| Rent | Blacks paid 58% more for rent than Whites | |

Source: Memorandum, 5 October 1967, Subject: Socio-economic profile of Detroit Michigan located in Record Group 282, National Advisory Commission on Civil Disorders, Series (9) Statistical Data: Socio-economic profile on selected cities located in the Lyndon B. Johnson Presidential Library.

## The Army's Post-Mortem of Detroit

Riot duty became a national priority for the Department of the Army as a direct result of the Detroit experience, although author Mark Perry may overstate the case that President Johnson, in his role as com- mander-in-chief of the military, decided that the war being waged on America's streets was of greater import than that being fought abroad in Vietnam. Perry contended that General William Westmoreland was adamant about receiving the 82d Airborne Division in Vietnam, but the Chairman of the Joint Chiefs of Staff stated that "the 82d couldn't be deployed, . . . because it was already engaged in combat operations in downtown Detroit, in barricaded ghetto buildings in the midst of one of America's worst race riots." Perry noted that "in late September [President] Johnson was forced to make the same choice."[41]

After the Detroit riot, the Department of the Army focused on a pro- gram that would prepare the Army for future urban disturbances. Jean Moenk, a command historian for the United States Army Continental Army Command, detailed how the Army developed its future riot pro- gram by developing a comprehensive training program for both the

46

Army and the National Guard; by coordinating planning between civil police, the Army, and the National Guard; and by establishing a task group to study every aspect of the Army's role in civil disturbances. [42]

The Army task group needed to redefine the Army's standing policy on the use of regular military personnel, equipment, and facilities in connection with civil disorders and disturbances. Prior to the Detroit riots, the Army deputy chief of staff said that "soldiers--other than National Guardsmen under state control--could not be used in connection with civil disturbances or related activities without the direct personal approval of the Secretary of Defense, his deputy, or the Chairman of the Joint Chiefs of Staff."[43] All requests for authority to use military personnel in connection with civil disturbances required forwarding through military channels with appropriate justification and recommendations. Likewise, any requests from local officials for the loan of military equipment went through a similar bureaucratic maze. To minimize red tape, the Department of Defense appointed the Army as its sole executive agent for planning and military support to civil authorities during civil disturbances.[44]

## Army Plans for Future Civil Disturbances

Following the major disturbance in Detroit, the task study group investigated preparedness for civil disturbances with the stated objective of solving problems as they were encountered. According to an Army Chief of Staff memorandum dated 4 August 1967, "this task group was not only to develop recommendations for appropriate changes in existing Army policies and procedures, but was also to serve as a committee to assure the adequacy and consistency of the Department of the Army's response to all immediate requirements regarding inquiries concerning involvement in the suppression of civil disorders."[45]

By the time the study group completed its investigation, the Army had begun implementing several of its proposals. Sixty-six recommendations for improvements evolved from the group, all of which were acted upon by the Army Chief of Staff by 18 December 1967. On 22 January 1968, the newly formed Department of the Army Civil Disturbance

Committee became responsible for supervising the completion of actions begun by the task group. The Civil Disturbance Committee also doubled as the Army's planning group when civil disturbances seemed imminent.[46]

As the task group pursued its study, it developed a set of plans codenamed Garden Plot. One set of plans concentrated on the Continental Army Command, while the second focused on the Department of the Army Civil Disturbance Plan. Garden Plot provided detailed plans for deploying 10,000 federal forces to twenty-five major cities simultaneously throughout the United States.[47] Execution of these contingencies required the use of Military Airlift Command (MAC) and Tactical Air Command (TAC) aircraft, as well as direct coordination between military forces planned for certain selected cities and municipal, county, and state officials.

The Department of the Army's plan for Task Force Washington—which covered the nation's capital--designated the execution of the civil disturbance mission in three phases: *preparation and deployment; employment;* and *redeployment*. Phase one would begin when the President directed federal intervention in a civil disturbance. Concurrent with the President's directive, the Army chief of staff would initiate civil disturbance control operations and direct the Commander-in-Chief, United States Strike Command (CINCSTRIKE), to deploy appropriate forces to the objective area within a specified period of time. During phase two, the Army Chief of Staff would use the deployed military forces under his control to restore law and order in the objective area. In phase three he would direct CINCSTRIKE to redeploy forces to their home stations. The Department of the Navy had responsibility to coordinate for the use of Sailors and Marines stationed in close proximity to a riot area.[48]

Washington, D.C., a high-priority city, required a separate plan for its protection.[49] The contingency for the nation's capital was written by the staff XVIII Airborne Corps, located at Fort Bragg, North Carolina. Their plan called for Task Force Washington to exercise command and control over federal forces when committed to assist the civil authorities in Washington, D.C. The plan also required the mobilization of Task Force Inside--selected tactical units at installations within a one hundred-mile radius of Washington--under the operational control of the Commanding General, Military District of Washington. Other major task forces earmarked for the nation's capital included Task Force 82, from the 82d Airborne Division stationed at Fort Bragg, and Task Force 5, from the 5th Infantry Division (Mechanized) at Fort Carson, Colorado.[50]

Although the Garden Plot contingency for the nation's capital was sound, the rapid escalation of violence on Friday, 5 April 1968 in Washington, D.C., led the Army Chief of Staff to activate a Task Force Washington staff from his personal staff.[51] The ad hoc twenty-nine-member staff was austere compared to the robust 150-man staff called for in the plan.[52] The augmented staff, however, functioned quite smoothly throughout the disturbance.

In the aftermath of the Detroit riot, the Army also revamped its training, doctrine, and planning for civil disturbances. In January of 1968 the Army opened the Senior Army Civil Defense Orientation Course (SEADOC) at Fort Gordon, Georgia. The course was designed to train senior Army officers (lieutenant colonels and above), National Guard officers and noncommissioned officers, and state and local police throughout the nation on riot control tactics, formations, and weapons. The course provided attendees with an understanding of crowd behavior.

The Army also created military police mobile training teams which traveled throughout the nation, giving riot control demonstrations to National Guardsmen and local and state police forces. The Washington, D.C. National Guard, underwent "a 24-hour FTX [field training exercise] in a realistic riot environment" at Fort Meade, Maryland.[53] A part of the requisite military training for all National Guard outfits after the Detroit riots was "32 hours of specific instruction in operational techniques to be employed against guerrilla-type actions, hit and run tactics, sniping, arson, and protection of firefighters, 16 hours of command and staff training, and an eight hour command post exercise."[54] As the *Kerner Report* stated, "By the end of October 1967, all state National Guard forces had completed the required training."[55] The Department of the Army also mandated that National Guard units undergo sixteen hours of refresher training annually after meeting the aforementioned minimum standard.

During the nine-month period following the Detroit disturbances, both civilian and military authorities procured new weapons for use in civil disturbance operations. According to *U.S. & World Report*, the Army developed a number of nonlethal weapons for use during riot control duty, including reels of barbed steel tape which could create anti-personnel obstacles; foam and foam sprayers capable of laying down a "five-foot layer of foam the width of a 200-foot street," a gas-powered paint shooting pistol which could mark agitators for apprehension on sight, dart and injector weapons to fire tranquilizers, and cattle prods to move crowds.[56]

The aftermath of Detroit demonstrated that the Army--with its Task Study Group and intensified planning and training--and the Federal Government, with the Kerner Commission, could be responsive. More importantly, the military authorities realized that their obsolescent policies and practices required revamping. The Army made remarkable changes and improvements in its approach to civil disorder from 2 August 1967 to 4 April 1968, as it faced the reality of a nation angered by increased racial tensions and protest against the Vietnam War. The riots in Detroit--a city that Rev. Martin Luther King called "a model city" in 1963, one that had been considered among the nation's very best in improving racial harmony-- caused the Army and nation to actively seek solutions to urban strife. In the aftermath of Detroit, when civil disturbance operations became a top national priority, the Army's implementation of focused training and contingency plans greatly enhanced the Federal Government's preparedness and response to the riots that ensued following the assassination of Dr. Martin Luther King on 4 April 1968.

Considerable controversy arose in the aftermath of the Detroit riot. Historians questioned who was best suited to undertake the civil disturbance mission, the National Guard or the Regular Army. Robin Higham, Paul Scheips, and Martin Blumenson argued that the Regular Army was better suited to the mission because of its discipline, cohesion, and responsiveness to orders. They also contended that the Regular Army maintained an impersonal outlook with respect to local prejudices and manifested superior training. A review of literature published in the latter half of the 1960's and 1970's revealed that in the eyes of many the Regular Army had demonstrated greater tolerance, possessed better unit cohesion, and was more responsive to orders than the National Guard. Alfred Lee contended that "[Regular Army] federal troops--on the rare occasions that they have been used--have brought the most exemplary degree of objectivity to riot control."[57]

Prior to the beginning of the civil rights movement in the mid-1950s, little debate existed as to who was best suited for the civil disturbance role. Dating back to 1794 the National Guard (or state militia) had held primary responsibility for riot control duty. Occasionally the escalation of violence and destruction by rioters in a specific locale required the deployment of both the National Guard and the Regular Army. With the beginning of the civil rights movement a different challenge emerged for National Guardsmen, that of protecting African-Americans and enforcing civil rights legislation. From this challenge, the historical debate evolved. After the Guard's poor showing in Newark, New Jersey, and Detroit, Michigan, during the summer of 1967, numerous questions arose about the Guard's competence and professionalism. Critics claimed that Guard units were poorly trained and often shared the prejudices of the local populace. Sociologist Alfred Lee argued that, "the part-time soldiers of the National Guard units… have shown themselves to be poorly disciplined and even more prejudiced than local and state police in identifying themselves with white control interests, as they understand them."[58] Thus Guardsmen were perceived as an extension of the segregated society, with vast arsenals and the authorities' permission to impose as much force as deemed necessary to restore and maintain order.

Robin Higham argued that, "the Regular Army had a better record in restoring order than the National Guard, because its outlook was more impersonal and its personnel were not as well read in local newspapers and as filled with local prejudices."[59] He concluded that the Michigan National Guard had not been trained adequately for riot duty. Higham's assessment was correct. Only after the Guard's abysmal performance in

51

Detroit and Newark, did the Department of the Army take corrective action to improve the preparedness of all Guard units.

Martin Blumenson noted that "the National Guards' activities were marked by slow response, tangled lines of authority, uncertain deployment, insufficient training, disruption of the military units, and isolation of individuals."[60] He also viewed the "Michigan National Guard['s] . . . 98.7 percent Caucasian [population] as a contributing factor in Detroit."[61] Blumenson argued that regular troops were better trained, capably led, more experienced and rarely lost their composure, no matter how difficult the situation became: "U.S. [Regular Army] troops are battle-trained, hardened, and tested; they are far better prepared to bring law and order to a troubled city than a National Guard unit sprinkled with raw recruits fresh from summer encampment."[62] Although probing and insightful, his study did not assess the legacy of the Army's Detroit experience. For example, Blumenson did not mention that a special board was convened in August of 1967 to explore why Negroes were not participating in the National Guard. The board found that the exclusion of Negroes within the Guard was a nation-wide phenomenon, with Guard units averaging only 1.3 percent Negro enlistment across the country.[63]

Paul Scheips, who examined the Army's performance in Oxford, Mississippi, and Detroit concluded that "the restraint with which the active Army conducted itself… has become its hallmark in civil disturbances, as befits the Army of a democracy."[64] He contended that General Throckmorton's main priority upon arrival in Detroit, was to bring about "the disciplined use of weapons by federalized guardsmen."[65] Scheips, through his numerous studies, contributed immeasurably to the study of the Army during civil unrest.

Roger Beaumont, though critical of the National Guard's performance in 1967, examined causal factors, environmental factors, and reactions by participants. Beaumont noted that, "most obvious, as the dust settled, after Detroit, was the gap in existing military doctrine and training between riot control and all-out-street-fighting."[66] He further contended that the police and the National Guard were not prepared, or trained, for the type of violence that they faced in Detroit. Beaumont, a former military police officer, stopped short of revealing to the reader the significance and impact of the Detroit riots on the various agencies responsible for social control: the Federal Government, the military, state governments, and state and local police forces. Detroit was a watershed that brought riot control to the forefront within the Johnson Administration and the U.S. military.

Sociologists William C. Cockerham and Lawrence E. Cohen coauthored an intriguing study on Regular Army paratroopers' attitudes toward riot duty. Their approach was quantitative and concluded that the Regular Army was better suited for civil disturbance than the National Guard. They asserted that "the area of Detroit assigned to the brigade of paratroopers rapidly became the quietest part of the city, thus prompting their commander to state that the key to quelling civil disorder is to saturate an area with calm, determined, and hardened professional soldiers."[67] They contended that with the exception of the Pullman Strike of 1894, federal troops encountered little opposition when they have intervened in domestic civil disorders. Moreover, they pointed out that "unlike some police and National Guard units, federal troops have not been accused of engaging in indiscriminate violence against rioters and demonstrators."[68]

Cockerham and Cohen's excellent study did not offer an explanation of why federal troops have shown great restraint compared with Guardsmen. In Detroit Guardsmen under state control took Governor Romney's instructions to use whatever force necessary to restore order literally, while Regular Army soldiers were severely limited in their use of force by both rules of engagement and by the Posse Comitatus Act. The National Guard under the control of a state governor could be utilized as a "cop on the beat," with full policing powers and authorities. On the other hand, the Regular Army, due to the constraints of the Posse Comitatus Act, had no authority to detain or arrest, or exercise any of the other powers normally associated with a police officer.[69] No matter how difficult it was to fathom the lack of restraint demonstrated by the Michigan National Guard, the unit operated within the scope of its authority in Detroit.

Charles P. Stone, who was sent to Detroit to evaluate and assess the capabilities and operations of the Michigan National Guard, asserted that their doctrine was sound: "what was needed was different emphasis on training, imaginative employment of techniques, better leadership, and better command and control."[70] Military leaders at every level of command must continually circulate in the areas for which they are responsible. In Stone's view, "they [leaders] must have firsthand information about what is going on; they need to correct deficiencies on the spot, anticipate problems that are developing, and insure that their orders are understood and properly implemented." Stone spent an average of 15 to 22 hours each day with the leadership of the Guard. He concluded in his assessment that "we cannot expect a National Guard unit to be able to compare favorably with an Active unit during the early phase of a civil disturbance."[71] Stone's contribution to the argument was the role of leadership in commanding and controlling troops deployed for riot duty.

Army officer Lewis Zickel identified overreaction as yet another aspect of poor training in the National Guard. According to Zickel, General Throckmorton stated that "it appeared that the National Guard had not been warned regarding the danger of overreaction and the necessity of great restraint in using their weapons. The young troopers could not be expected to know that their lack of fire discipline made them a danger not only to the civilian population but to themselves."[72] Zickel concluded that the focus of a civil disturbance force must be restoration and not suppression. Zickel's assessment was correct, but it stopped short of noting the actions taken by the Army to correct this deficiency. The Army's implementation of the orientation course for senior officers, its creation of a mock riot city (Riotsville) at Fort Gordon, Georgia, and its mandate of the minimum riot training requirements for all units in August of 1967 assisted in minimizing overreaction during 1968.

The *Kerner Report* highlighted the essence of the problem with its contention that "Controlling a civil disturbance is not warfare. The fundamental objective of National Guard forces in a civil disturbance is to control the rioters, not to destroy them or any innocent bystanders who may be present."[73] Anthony Deane-Drummond reinforced *Kerner's* conclusion, writing, "the record of the National Guard has shown itself (as a matter of some interest) to be more lethal than the Regular U.S. Army or the police, not only at Kent State University, but also at Detroit, Newark, and Watts; to name but a few."[74]

The period following the 1967 Detroit riot also raised numerous other questions and concerns with respect to causation and explanations of the riots themselves. Interdisciplinary conferences in the 1960s produced numerous edited studies that helped to increase the nation's understanding of urban unrest. Three basic explanations of riots and proposals for change evolved. First, the radical view argued that riots were the start of a revolution and a call for black separatism. Second, the liberal view, deemed the riots a response to inequality and called for massive federal spending to aid inner-cities. Finally, the conservative view argued that the riots were the work of hoodlums and called for the return of law and order. "Law and order" sometimes appeared to be a euphemism for racism within this third group.

David Boesel and Peter Rossi edited a collection of twenty-five essays on the anatomy of ghetto riots in their 1971 volume, *Cities Under Siege.* The study argued that riots were uprisings against the racist institutions that controlled the lives of urban blacks. The book focused on the uprisings in Newark, Milwaukee, Watts, and Cambridge, Maryland, and viewed these disorders as political events. Rossi provided an important contention with his statement that "As city after city experienced civil disorders it became increasingly difficult to hold to an interpretation which saw them as race riots." He further stated, "there were no mass confrontations between blacks and whites: indeed, blacks showed little interest in moving out of their ghetto areas into other parts of the city."[75] The Detroit riot of 1943, as well as much of the violence that occurred during civil rights protest in the South, pitted whites against African-Americans. The Northern and Western urban riots witnessed violence utilized as a protest--an indirect conduit of sorts for direct social change. Writer Bayard Rustin supported Rossi's contention with his assertion that by the 1960s riots had become "unilluminating and achromatic."[76]

Joseph Boskin's edited volume, *Urban Racial Violence in the Twentieth Century*, focused exclusively on U.S. race riots from East St.

Louis in 1917 through Detroit in 1967. The study described three distinct phenomena, with respect to riots, within America during the twentieth century. First, it argued that race riots were "invariably begun by marauding whites who invaded the fringes of the minority group communities." Second, Boskin asserted that uprisings of ethnic groups within their communities began in the 1930s, but occurred essentially in the mid-1960's. The author viewed these riots as acts of "retaliation against racism."[77] Finally the author assessed contemporary forms of racial conflict and violence. He argued that in the 1960's, "the typical riot did not take place. The disorders of 1967 were unusual, irregular, complex, and unpredictable social processes. Like most human events, they did not unfold in an orderly sequence."[78] Boskin's argument regarding the irregularity and unpredictable nature of the riots dispelled the notion that urban riots were *premeditated* endeavors by "black power" advocates.

Robert Connery's edited book, *Urban Riots: Violence and Social Change*, much like Boskin, Boesel and Rossi, and the *Kerner Report*, viewed "white racism" as a major precipitant of domestic violence. Sociologist Robert J. McNamara, however, argued that, "in the last analysis, only when white America can bring itself to see rioting as a symbol of the horror that has been inflicted on black America will serious attempts be made to help the ghetto populations help themselves."[79] Thus, McNamara believed that urban African-American violence is a protest against the status quo. McNamara's argument is very paternalistic, in that his solutions to the ills of the ghetto rest solely in white America's empathy and compassion toward African-Americans.

Louis Masotti and Don Bowen, editors of *Riot and Rebellion*, argued that during riots "white-owned property is particularly singled out for attack... White policemen become particular targets." This description generates memories of African-American proprietors attempt to save their businesses by painting the words "black-owned" for would be arsonists. The problem with the proposal of Masotti and Bowen is that fire sees no color and hears no voices, and its master is the wind. Masotti and Bowen also asserted that the ethnicity of active duty soldiers played a major role in quelling the 1967 Detroit riot. They contended that, "in Detroit, units of the 82d Airborne . . . more than half of whose ranks are

Negro, were able to pacify an area of the city in a few hours, inflicting no casualties and suffering none themselves."[80] Whereas the presence of black troops may have had a calming effect on the streets of Detroit, the magnitude of Negro presence within the 82d Airborne Division is exaggerated. Save for the pre-Cold War all Colored 24th and 25th Infantry Regiments and the 91st and 92d Infantry Divisions, African-Americans have never comprised 50 percent of the personnel of any Division in the Army. Moreover, active duty troops, contrary to Masotti and Bowen's contention, were responsible for one fatality in Detroit.

Roger Lane and John Turner's edited volume, *Riot, Rout, and Tumult*, provided perhaps the most diverse historical perspectives on racial violence. Harvard Sitkoff examined race relations and interracial violence during World War II. He argued that unlike World War I, "the very dependency of the [U.S.] government on the cooperation of the Negro intensified his demand for civil rights." Sitkoff noted that in 1943, "the Social Science Institute at Fisk University reported 242 racial battles in forty-seven cities."[81] He recounted numerous instances of racial violence--rioting, brutality--directed against Negro troops by white military police, and lynchings. Sitkoff presents a compelling illustration of how "tensions and violence within the military mirrored the mushrooming conflict on the home front."[82]

Historian Robert Fogelson's chapter in Lane and Turner's edited volume, has the same title as his book, *Violence as a Protest*. Within his chapter, Fogelson addressed several questions. First, he examined how the race riots of the 1960's compared to past episodes of interracial violence. He determined that the riots of the 1960s were not an extension of riots in 1917, 1919, and 1943. He argued that in "contrast with black rioters, who looted and burned stores and only incidentally assaulted [white] passers-by, the white rioters vented their hostility for the most part against [black] people, not property."[83] Fogelson further stated that in the first half of the twentieth century government authorities--military and police--did not attempt to restore order with the firmness exhibited in the 1960s. Second, Fogelson questioned why riots did not occur as frequently when blacks were most hopeless, but occurred with great regularity after two decades of apparent progress. To the latter question

Fogelson focused on the dichotomy between North and South and the apparent paradox between a racist South and a segregated North. He argued that riots occurred disproportionately in the North because the South had far fewer overcrowded ghettos. Fogelson viewed the urban ghetto as the tinder box during the 1960s, and I agree with his contention.

# CHAPTER 3

# TASK FORCE WASHINGTON QUELLS THE RIOT

*Rioters are the personification of the nation's shame, of its deepest failure, of its greatest challenge. They will not go away. They can only be repressed or conceded their humanity, and the choice is not theirs to make. They can only force it upon the rest of us, and what this [Kerner] Report insists upon is that they are already doing it, and intend to keep on.[1]*

This chapter reveals that the watershed event known as the Detroit Riot immeasurably assisted Federal Troops during their deployment to Washington, D.C., following the assassination of Dr. Martin Luther King. Improvements in equipment, training, doctrine, and planning played seminal roles in the Army's ability to quell the D.C. Riots with minimal violence from Federalized Forces.

Martin Luther King, Jr., once referred to riots as the voices of the unheard. The message of these unheard voices in Washington, D.C., and the restrained federal response to violence after King's 4 April 1968 assassination, is the focus of this chapter. The events suggest that Dr. King's assassination was the precipitant, or catalyst, for the turbulence in the nation's capital. The Kerner Commission, which was established during the summer of 1967, concluded that "unemployment," "lack of education," "poverty," "exploitation," "a pervasive white sense of inferiority of black men," and "police prejudice and brutality of minorities" (especially African-Americans) had resulted in riots in numerous urban centers in 1967.[2] Although a riot did not occur in Washington before the March 1968 publication of the *Kerner Report*, the District did fit the profile of a city where one could occur. Training, with a focus on restraint, had been directed by the Department of the Army after Detroit. This training minimized the use of force by police, National Guardsmen, and the Regular Army in Washington.

## Profile of Washington, D.C.

The prevailing conditions within Washington's black community during the 1960s made the nation's capital a prime locale for civil unrest. Only one of every three black students graduated from high school and 75 percent read below the national average. Only the state of Mississippi exceeded the District's infant mortality rate. Rates for sexually transmitted diseases were among the country's highest, and 25 percent of D.C.'s black residents lived below the poverty line. Unemployment rates within the black community often tripled those of white communities. Moreover, many employed blacks were often underemployed, working in jobs below their potential and skills.[3]

Census data reveal that the nation's capital transformed from a majority white city in the 1940s and 1950s into a predominantly black city by the 1960s. The data further depicts a significant disparity between black and white males with respect to unemployment, median income, and poverty. For example, in 1950 black males comprised only 34.3 percent of the city's male working age population, but comprised almost half of the unemployed population. Although census data characterized the median incomes for blacks as improving from 40 percent less than whites in 1950 to 14 percent less than whites by 1970, the city had 9.9 black families impoverished for every one white family facing poverty.[4]

During the late 1960s segregation and institutional racism were repudiated on paper, but prevalent in practice in the nation's capital. With Washington, D.C., "poorer Negroes were largely confined to virtually all-black areas, where high rents, congestion, and substandard conditions prevailed."[5] African-Americans' inability to secure credit and loans only added to their plight in a world where credit was synonymous with opportunity. A lack of public transportation in the African-American community denied blacks access to employment opportunities, and created an even greater dependence on Federal assistance.

In November of 1962, the first of a series of near riotous confrontations between local blacks and the police occurred when violence followed the annual Thanksgiving Day football game between two prominent high school teams. In his volume, *Ten Blocks from the White House, Washington Post* editor Ben Gilbert detailed numerous disturbances during the 1960's that nearly ended in riots. Violence was narrowly averted in September of 1965, when two white officers detained four African-American youths for playing ball in an alley. During another instance in August of 1966, citizens hurled stones at a local police station in Southwest Washington to protest an arrest. In August of 1967 a riot almost occurred after rumors of expected disorder circulated within the community.[6]

Armed with the lessons of summer 1967, Washington's civil and military authorities began preparing for possible violence in the summer of 1968. Major General Charles L. Southward, commander of the D.C. National Guard, confirmed that "some of his key men were attending anti-riot training based on the lessons of Newark and Detroit, being given at the [U.S. Army] military police school at Fort Gordon, Georgia."[7] The *Washington Post* ran a column that implied black power advocates were planning to burn the city on 18 and 19 June.[8] A sermon by Reverend Julius Hobson of Saint Stephen and the Incarnation Episcopal Church before 400 people asserted, "we need a revolution to change what's wrong... While we might be forced to make a revolution, it would fall [sic] this summer, because the authorities are ready and eager to quell it."[9]

*Washington Post* staff writer William Raspberry, in a reflective article on the twentieth anniversary of the 1968 Washington, D.C. riot, captured the essence of the mounting tensions and worsening conditions within the ghetto of the nation's capital:

> Housing discrimination continued apace, turning the Capital Beltway into a white noose around an increasingly black central city. Police brutality at the hands of a predominantly white police force was commonplace. Job discrimination, actual and imagined, kept the Human Relations Commission and the National Association for the Advancement of Colored People busy investigating complaints. Militant black leaders were commanding new respect, and the nonviolent King was at pains to defend his left flank. The dream was dying.[10]

## Violence Erupts After King's Assassination

With Robert Kennedy's 4 April 1968 announcement during a political rally in Indianapolis, that Martin Luther King had been felled by an assassin's bullet, a shock reverberated throughout the United States as the news spread like wildfire. It was a landmark moment of disbelief, denial, and confusion. Moreover, it was a watershed event for both supporters and detractors of King's message, his tactics and his person. The death of the nation's greatest advocate for nonviolence sparked some of the most severe episodes of violence in American history.

The news of King's death resulted in the mobilization of National Guard troops across eighteen states and thirty-six cities. Federalized troops deployed to Baltimore (11,086), Chicago (11,978), and Washington (15,530). Moreover, violence, death, or arson after King's assassination occurred in thirty-six cities and eleven states where only local and state police responded, and in total twenty-nine states and seventy-two cities across the United States of America were involved. (see Figure 2)

News coverage of the riot in the nation's capital captured the attention of America. The epicenter of the riot was the intersection of 14th and U Streets, Northwest--a hub within the local black community in Washington. Centered around this intersection were the offices of the Southern Christian Leadership Conference (SCLC), the Student Nonviolent Coordinating Committee (SNCC), and the National Association for the Advancement of Colored People (NAACP), as well as a myriad of small black-owned businesses. According to the *George Washington Law Review*, the intersection was in the heart of the community and doubled not only as a business center, but also as "a focal point for gatherings, demonstrations, and trouble."[11] *Washington Post* editor Ben Gilbert also noted that "police considered this intersection (14th and U Streets) the most volatile in the city's crowded Negro section."[12]

Shortly after 8:00 p.m. on Thursday, 4 April, when the news of King's death arrived in Washington, people began to congregate near 14th and U Streets Northwest. The mood was ugly. NBC News reporter Betty Wolden described the situation as "ominous--like before a hurricane strikes."[13] A crowd of 300 persons, encouraged by black activist Stokely Carmichael, began moving along 14th Street. Its members urged local businesses to close their shops in honor of Dr. King's memory. Just south of 14th and U Streets, the swelling crowd encountered Walter Fauntroy, a SCLC official and newly appointed chairman of the City Council. Fauntroy told Carmichael, "let's not get anyone hurt, let's cool it."[14] Carmichael allegedly responded: "all we're asking store owners to do is close the stores."[15]

*Figure 2: National Violence After Martin Luther King's Assassinations*

*NUMBER OF NATIONAL GUARD TROOPS USED: 68, NUMBER OF STATES: 18; NUMBER OF CITIES: 36 (INCLUDES WASHINGTON, DC)*

> Source: Department of the Army, After Action Report, 4-17 April Civil Disturbances, 13 August 1968, p. 17. Located in Record Group 319, Records of the U.S. Army Staff, National Archives, College Park, Maryland.

Evaluations of Carmichael's role in the riots have been mixed. Reports in the *Washington Evening Star*, the *Washington Post*, and *The New York Times* alleged that Carmichael instigated the violence that erupted in Washington. Familiar scenes of Stokely Carmichael telling blacks to, "go get your guns," on NBC's "Meet the Press" further reinforced the belief that he played an instrumental role in the D.C. riot. But did he? Ben Gilbert depicted Carmichael as an advocate of peaceful protest during the evening of 4 April 1968, reporting that Carmichael publicly scolded a teenager for punching out a window at the Republic Theater.[16] As the crowd became increasingly more anxious and uncontrollable, Carmichael departed the area. Adding credence to Gilbert's view was the fact that police did not charge Carmichael with inciting a riot or with any other riot-related charge. This decision, however, may have been to limit further violence, as the activist was popular and well respected by local blacks.

Violence began at approximately 9:30 p.m., when a marcher smashed the window of a People's Drug Store located at 14th and U Streets. Prior to this incident the spontaneous memorial march was apparently one of peaceful citizens, shocked and saddened by King's death, marching as a testament of their love and allegiance to the memory of their martyred hero. There is no indication that the marchers intended to turn their memorial march into an orgy of looting and destruction. Once violence began, however, a chain reaction occurred, and normally law-abiding citizens began destroying their neighborhood. Lawlessness escalated as members of the crowd began breaking windows, setting fires, looting businesses, and pulling occupants from their vehicles and beating them.

Not expecting disorder, city officials had removed police from the area after King's death in an effort to avoid provocation. But once looting began, police dispatched units to the troubled area. Overwhelmed by the rioters throwing rocks, bottles, and Molotov cocktails, police officers retreated to await reinforcement. As a result of mounting violence and their numerical inferiority, the police department activated its Civil Disturbance Unit, which deployed along 14th Street by 11:30 p.m. By midnight, 500 police officers had cleared the lower end of 14th Street, but looting continued. The police had responded quickly, but their 500-man force proved no match for the angry mob. By 1:00 a.m., 2,500 of the District's 3,000-man Civil Disturbance Unit patrolled the riot area. By 3:00 a.m., the city's damage assessment included 200 broken store windows, 150 looted businesses, more than 150 adults and about 50 juveniles arrested, 30 people injured, and one riot-connected death.[17] City officials concluded that 14th Street suffered the most damage, with only scattered looting and broken windows in other parts of the city. (see Figure 3)

As the sun rose on 5 April, police lined 14th Street, burned out buildings continued to smolder, and persistent tear gas hung in the moist morning air. The looting and burning during the previous nine hours left the 14th Street corridor covered with broken glass and rubble. Police, anticipating no further rioting until Friday evening, dismissed the Civil Disturbance Unit at 5:30 a.m. Meanwhile, local officials pre-pared to activate the National Guard for riot duty Friday evening. On that morning, however, the situation worsened as many residents missed work or school and congregated in large groups along several streets. Shortly after noon, a fire broke out in the Safeway market, a half block south of the intersection of 14th and U Streets. Window smashing, loot-ing and more fires followed. Police had not anticipated this resurgence of violence. As journalist Elsie Carper wrote, "District police were caught by surprise when looting and arson broke out . . . yesterday. There was only one patrol car at 14th and Harvard Streets, one of the early trou-ble spots. One policeman radioed, 'We need gas masks, gas and more troops. We are getting bricks here.'"[18] Outnumbered by looters, police began removing unprotected merchandise from store windows and se-curing the items at police headquarters.

## Figure 3: Main Riot Corridors

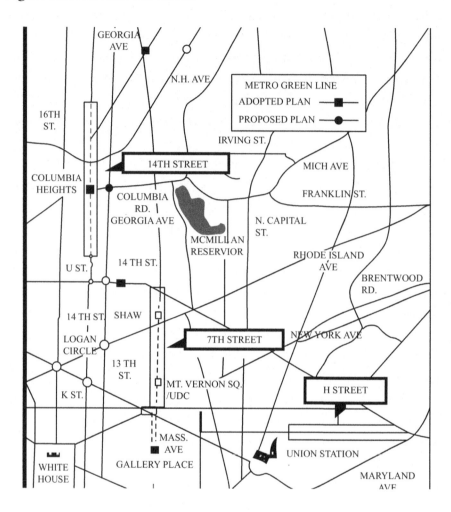

Source: "The Fires of April: 20 Years Later," *Washington Post*, 7 April 1988, sec. A, p. 14.

Local fire departments mobilized the majority of their personnel but lacked sufficient equipment to utilize all the additional firefighters. Nearby counties began sending fire-fighting equipment to assist the D.C. fire department. The contagion of rioting created a "carnival-like euphoria," with rioters looting and setting fires without fear of police reprisal.[19] Judge Alfred Burka concluded that "the April rioting resulted from an apparent breakdown, lack of respect or lack of fear of officers of the law.

It seems that the public has come to believe that what is done in a group is all right, although the same act committed by an individual would be punished."[20]

Within twenty-four hours of King's assassination, violence in the nation's capital prompted 1,272 arrests, resulted in eight fatalities, and caused 350 injuries. In response, Mayor Walter Washington imposed a daily curfew from 5:30 p.m. to 6:30 a.m.[21] City Officials declared a "Proclamation of Emergency," prohibiting the sale of alcoholic beverages, the dispensing of gasoline and other flammables, and the sale of firearms or ammunition.[22] To ensure compliance with the imposed curfew the mayor invoked a provision that allowed non-essential District government employees both a later start and early release from work without loss of leave or pay.[23]

### *Federal Intervention Requested by District Authorities*

On 5 April General Ralph Haines, Jr., the Army Vice Chief of Staff, Patrick Murphy, the District's Director of Public Safety, David McGiffert, Undersecretary of the Army, and Warren Christopher, the Deputy United States Attorney General, toured the areas hit by the riot. Haines described the overcrowded streets and rapidly spreading disturbance as evidence that the situation warranted troops.[24] Mayor Washington forwarded a memorandum requesting federal intervention and Haines directed that an operations center be set up in the Municipal Building. Haines concluded, "I am certain that on the basis of our recommendation, corroborated by reports from the area, the President issued his Executive Order at 4:03 p.m."[25] The Executive Order resulted in a seven-page letter of instruction (LOI) from the Army Chief of Staff authorizing General Haines to command troops in Washington. From this episode of violence and the President's Proclamation 3840 came the Continental Army Command's civil disturbance unit--Task Force Washington--commanded by the Army Vice Chief of Staff.

Proclamation 3840 represented the president's demand for law and order in the Washington metropolitan area. The legal procedures, unchanged since the Whiskey Rebellion, entailed a request for intervention by the mayor of Washington, D.C., and an order by President Lyndon B. Johnson to the rioters to cease, desist, and disperse, followed by an executive order to commit troops to Washington. The President also brought the District of Columbia's National Guard under federal control, which vastly limited its policing powers under Posse Comitatus.[26]

Questions may arise as to why the Army's Chief of Staff appointed his Vice Chief to command Task Force Washington. What qualifications and experience did Haines have that made him a good choice for the job? Perhaps first and foremost in the mind of the Chief of Staff was the rapidity of the escalation of violence in Washington and the subsequent necessity to act to contain the violence before it spread even further. The Chief of Staff realized that he could not afford to wait for the XVIII Airborne Corps command and control element to deploy from Fort Bragg, North Carolina. He thus turned to a veteran of proven quality and ability who was readily available and intimately familiar with the city, local commanders, and local and national politicians. Haines had been a driving force behind the significant changes that the Army had implemented after the Detroit riot. A cavalryman and four-star general, he had commanded troops at all but the four-star level of command, and had served in the Army's second highest post for more than a year.[27]

Upon assuming command General Haines established a headquarters at the District Metropolitan Police Station. He and his staff occupied a large conference room and two offices on the fifth-floor wing of the municipal building, near the offices of the chief of police and his assistants. Close proximity to police officials simplified liaison, the release of information, and the exchange of intelligence. It also provided quicker response to requests for assistance.[28]

General Haines' mission was to restore and maintain law and order in the Washington metropolitan area. Haines answered to the Chief of Staff and to requests from presidential representative Cyrus Vance. The Chief of Staff provided General Haines directives within a letter of instruction. This letter specified his mission, task organization, location for his command post, options for how troops would carry individual weapons (bayonets fixed or unfixed, sheathed or unsheathed, weapons in the ready position or at sling arms on the shoulder). It also provided examples of situations that necessitated the loading of a weapon, use of riot control agents, authorization for the use of force, and the methods for neutralizing and apprehending snipers.[29]

General Haines' instructions directed him to use minimum force whenever possible, and to restore law and order to the level permitting local and non-military law enforcement officials to resume control. The latter part of this mission was consistent with Article IV, Section 4 of the U.S. Constitution. The Chief of Staff's directive to use minimum force was the direct result of lessons learned by the Army during the 1967 Detroit riot. Troops used riot-control agents instead of standard rifle ammunition and employed deadly force only in life-threatening situations. Federal officials expected that these policies would prevent the loss of military and civilian lives. The Army focused on minimizing the use of force and maximizing restraint while quelling the Washington disturbance. The Chief of Staff stressed that firearms should not be used to stop looting, with individual weapons used as a last resort. Arrests and detention remained the responsibility of local law enforcement agents, federal marshals, and other Department of Justice personnel.[30]

Communications support for Task Force Washington consisted of telephone and radio facilities installed at the Metropolitan Police headquarters. Direct telephone lines connected Task Force Washington with the White House, Department of Justice, the Headquarters of the Military District of Washington (Task Force Inside), the Army Operations Center at the Pentagon, and the armory command post of the National Guard. Private telephone lines also ran to the command posts of subordinate units at Andrews Air Force Base in Maryland, Bolling Air Force Base, Fort McNair, and the Anacostia Naval Air Station in Washington and Fort Myer in Virginia. A preplanned network of portable radios connected established headquarters with mobile stations in leased automobiles.[31] This network afforded the operations center increased range over previous arrangements and permitted General Haines to contact his operations center from any location within the city.[32]

Logistics personnel had the arduous task of moving and housing military units performing riot duty in Washington. The Baltimore District of the Corps of Engineers real estate liaison representative coordinated the use of school facilities by deploying troops. Established plans allowed soldiers to occupy gymnasiums and adjoining locker rooms for sleeping and latrine accommodations, and use cafeterias for meals in some cases. These arrangements greatly increased the soldiers' comfort and allowed a degree of privacy not available in tent cities. Making use of such facilities allowed for well-coordinated logistical support of deployed units.

## Troops Arrive

Once the President authorized employment of both Regular Army and federalized National Guardsmen in the District of Columbia, the Department of the Army took immediate action to commit forces to riot control duty. The federal forces' primary mission was to contain looting, protect property, and prevent any further escalation and spread of riotous activities. The first unit ordered into the District, the 2d Squadron, 6th Armored Cavalry Regiment, traveled from Fort Meade, Maryland, to its assembly area at the United States Old Soldiers' Home in Washington at 3:19 p.m. on 5 April. After arriving at the Old Soldiers' Home, the 3d and 1st Squadrons began moving from Maryland. By 10:35 p.m., the 6th Armored Cavalry Regiment conducted riot control operations in the central city. Meanwhile, the 1st Battalion (Reinforced), 3d Infantry Regiment, entered the heart of Washington at 4:15 p.m. One company guarded the perimeter of the White House as a "show of force"; another protected the Capitol building; and two companies proceeded to H Street, N.E., between 1st and 15th Streets, where serious disturbances had erupted. Captain Leroy Rhode, commander of D Company, 3d Infantry Regiment, recalled the sight as he led his 150-man outfit from Fort Myer, Virginia, across the Memorial Bridge into the burning District of Columbia. "There I was," he said, "26 years old, and with a hell of a responsibility, especially since those were fellow Americans we might have to face out on the streets."[33] Simultaneously, the United States Marine Corps Student Battalion at Quantico, Virginia, reached its assembly area near the Naval Station Annex. By midnight on 5 April, 6,600 troops guarded Washington, D.C.

The 6 April edition of the *Washington Post* highlighted the deployment of area military units during the evening of 5 April 1968. Robert C. Maynard reported that the sector of 14th Street was sealed off by soldiers of the 6th Cavalry. He noted that the men were professional, firm, and courteous as they cleared the area of curfew violators. He further observed that six troopers were at every intersection. The troops' demeanor was orderly, well-controlled, disciplined, and unthreatening as they deployed throughout Washington, D.C. Maynard noted that "some of the troops carried clubs in lieu of rifles. Bayonets hung on the soldiers' belts." Soldiers located outside of the 13th Precinct Police Station, "in the 1600 block of V Street had bayonets fixed but sheathed on their . . . rifles. Magazines were not installed in the rifles." District National Guardsmen "were deployed among the city's eight fire battalions, fire alarm headquarters in the 900 block of R Street Northwest, and the headquarters of the Military District of Washington at Fort McNair" in accordance with their operations plan.[34] The 91st Engineer Battalion from Fort Belvoir, Virginia, arrived in East Potomac Park by 7:15 a.m. on the morning of 6 April. By that afternoon, three companies of the 91st deployed for riot control operations in the 1st, 2d, and 3d precincts, respectively.

A series of actions, according to contingency plans, occurred simultaneously for the Army's civil disturbance units earmarked for Washington. Units were in one of three categories: deployed throughout the District, deploying to the District, or alerted for possible deployment to the District. Both the 544th Supply and Services Battalion at Fort Lee, Virginia, and the 714th Transportation Battalion (Railway Operations) at Fort Eustis, Virginia, were on two-hour alert status at their home stations during the afternoon of 5 April and arrived in Washington later that same day. The 544th arrived outside of the District at 4:00 a.m. on 6 April. One company entered the 1st precinct at 6:40 a.m., with the remaining companies in reserve at Fort Myer. Upon its noon arrival at Anacostia Naval Station, the 714th Transportation Battalion remained in reserve. Rioting on Saturday, 6 April never reached the proportions of Friday afternoon, but fires were again a major problem as arsonists set 120 more blazes. Looting occurred in areas not protected by police and troops. A 4:00 p.m. curfew on Saturday helped authorities establish order before dark. Between 5:30 and 9:30 p.m. authorities arrested 600 people for curfew violations but only ten for looting.[35]

Critical to evaluating the effectiveness of the Army's intervention is assessing the role of military police. Staff at the Military Police School, located at Fort Gordon, Georgia, wrote the Army's civil disturbance manual. They also trained Army Reserve, National Guard and civil law enforcement personnel. An essential element in the Army force in Washington was the highly regarded 503d Military Police Battalion from Fort Bragg, North Carolina. Company C of the 503d was at Fort Gordon conducting a demonstration of riot control techniques when the battalion received alert instructions. At 2:15 a.m. on 5 April Company C received instructions from USCONARC to return to Fort Bragg after completing its demonstration. Despite the absence of Company C, the battalion received notification that its deployment to Washington might occur within two hours.

After Company C's 7:45 p.m. arrival at Pope Air Force Base, North Carolina, 1st Brigade, 82d Airborne received twenty-one aircraft for their immediate move to the Washington area. Later that evening, the Department of the Army (henceforth D.A.) decided to move the 503d Military Police Battalion forward in the deployment sequence ahead of the 2d Brigade. At 1:00 a.m. on 6 April, D.A. directed that the 503d depart after the 1st Brigade, 82d Airborne Division. The final aircraft carrying elements of the battalion did not leave North Carolina until 3:23 p.m.--twenty-three minutes after its 3:00 p.m. expected arrival in Washington.[36] This was the first of only a few missteps on the Air Force's part during the entire operation.

The 503d Military Police Battalion was critical to the Army's deployment because of its experience. The 503d deployed to Oxford, Mississippi, in 1962 to protect James Meredith's entrance to the University of Mississippi; protected demonstrators and marchers in Selma, Alabama, during racial unrest in 1965; participated in riot control operations in Washington during the Vietnam protest at the Pentagon in October of 1967; and the battalion's personnel trained civilian law enforcement and National Guard personnel on riot control techniques. Although the battalion had experienced normal personnel turnover since 1962, the 503d served continuously as the Army's premier riot control unit.[37]

After the commitment of Task Force Inside (local units within the local D.C. metropolitan area) to riot control operations, USCONARC began preparations to move the 82d Airborne Division and XVIII Airborne Corps headquarters element to the Washington area. Although Task Force Inside possessed sufficient forces to control the situation in Washington, the Army's post-Detroit riot plan called for the saturation of an area with troops, hence the deployment of the 82d Airborne. At 6:45 p.m., D.A. directed USCONARC to dispatch the 1st Brigade to Washington beginning at 9:00 p.m. with aircraft departing at five-minute intervals thereafter.[38] Due to misunderstandings at both Third Army and XVIII Airborne Corps headquarters, the first aircraft did not depart Pope Air Force Base until 11:45 p.m., three hours after the time initially established for takeoff.[39] While USCONARC estimated final arrival of the entire 1st Brigade by 9:05 p.m. on 5 April, the last aircraft did not arrive at Andrews Air Force Base, Maryland, until 8:35 a.m. on 6 April. The Department of the Army directed 1st Brigade to proceed immediately to an assembly area at Bolling Air Force Base, after which it entered the 11th and 14th Precincts for riot duty. By mid-afternoon on 6 April Washington was the only city east of the Mississippi River where federal troops conducted riot control operations.[40]

Since assuming command of Task Force Washington, General Haines spent most of his time directing troops on the streets and in coordinating with civil authorities. He realized at 9:00 a.m. on 6 April that the two large precincts east of the Anacostia River, though relatively calm at the time, might present a problem if invaded by determined looters. Two battalions patrolling precincts 11 and 14, the 1st and 2d of the 504th Infantry Battalion of 1st Brigade, 82d Airborne Division, were directly under Haines' command. Major General Charles S. O'Malley commanded Task Force Inside and had responsibility for the city west of the river. Haines observed that rioters made no attempts to damage federal buildings or foreign embassies and residences; and no calls for help had come from the police concerning government buildings. Haines also noted that troops utilized tear gas, instead of bullets, to force looters out of several stores and businesses. He closed his report with an estimate of damage. Precincts 2, 9, 10, and 13 were the hardest hit; little damage occurred in Precincts 1, 5, and 11; Precinct 14 showed marginal effects; and property destruction was negligible in Precincts 3, 4, 6, and 12.[41]

Shortly after 7:00 a.m. on 6 April, after looting increased in Precincts 9, 12, and 13, three infantry companies moved to Precinct 9, where crowds began to gather. Because the situation remained under control, however, Task Force Washington never committed its reserve. At 10:05 a.m., the 2d Brigade, 82d Airborne, began moving to Washington. The 2d Brigade's movement followed the 503d Military Police Battalion and members of the division headquarters to command and control both brigades.[42]

With its units deployed in all precincts, the Army had the riot under control. As more forces arrived from Fort Bragg, General Haines' was free to inspect units throughout the city. Following General Haines inspection, he joined Mayor Walter Washington and presidential representative Cyrus Vance for a forty-five-minute aerial tour of the city. They returned to police headquarters to pick up John W. Heshinger, chairman of the Washington City Council, and Police Chief John S. Hughes, for a tour of Precincts 1, 2, and 10.

General Haines departed from the civilian leaders to investigate a complaint from Senator Richard B. Russell (Democrat of Georgia) that federal troops had deployed to the Capitol without ammunition. Finding no shortage of ammunition, Haines discovered that each Marine received two full magazines before guarding the Capitol. Senator Russell's complaint was the only congressional criticism against Task Force Washington.[43] (see Figure 4)

At approximately 10:00 p.m. on 6 April, after 1st Brigade, 82d Airborne Division, arrived at Andrews Air Force Base, the airlift stopped. The airlift ceased because the Air Force was using the same planes and pilots to move the entire division from North Carolina to Washington, and "crew rest" and safety became major concerns for the Air Force.[44] By 10:55 a.m. the operations center reported to Haines that the Air Force was doing all that it could to provide the uninterrupted airlift of the 503d and the 2d Brigade to the city. The General could do nothing but wait.

Throughout the day on 6 April the increasing presence of military personnel in the city assisted in restoring law and order. As military strength grew, riot-related problems decreased, and when isolated looting and arson waned, the Army's major concern became traffic control. Thousands of automobiles poured into the District, and many soldiers became traffic police as sightseers flowed through parts of the fire-devastated sections of the city. With the 6:03 p.m., 6 April arrival of the 503d Military Police Battalion in its assembly area at Bolling Air Force Base, troop strength reached 12,000. Task Force Inside, in need of a mobile response force to assist local police, became the operational headquarters for the 503d Military Police Battalion. Arriving with the 503d was the headquarters for Task Force 82, and the arrival of the 82d Airborne Division's command element allowed General Haines to relinquish direct control of the 1st Brigade.

**Figure 4: Precinct Map**

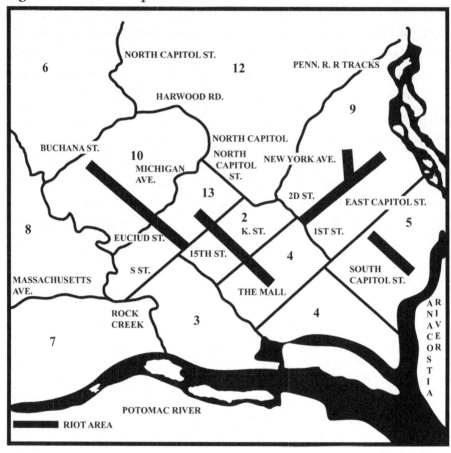

Source: Reprinted with the permission of Greenwood Publishing Group, Inc, Westport, Conn. Ben W. Gilbert, *Ten Blocks from the White House: Anatomy of the Washington Riots of 1968* (New York: Praeger, 1968).[44]

At 6:00 p.m., Haines issued his second fragmentary order since assuming command of the troops in the city. The order reflected the arrival of the 2d Brigade, 82d Airborne; it assigned a larger area of responsibility to Task Force 82 and shifted Task Force Inside units toward the western part of the city. Given responsibility for Precincts 4, 5, 9, and 12, Task Force 82 retained one battalion as a reserve for Task Force Washington. Task Force Inside was responsible for the remainder of the city. Haines also directed units in Precincts 1, 2, and 3 to shift positions to ensure tactical integrity of battalion-size units.

As darkness fell on 6 April the 2d Brigade began landing at Andrews Air Force Base. At 8:30 p.m., Major General Richard J. Seitz, commanding general of the 82d Airborne Division, assumed command of the 1st Brigade from Haines. Task Force Washington then possessed two subordinate operational headquarters--Task Force Inside and Task Force 82. By late evening on 6 April, 13,600 federal troops occupied the streets of D.C.[45] On Sunday, 7 April, the Army assisted civil authorities in cleaning up debris along main traffic arteries and helped sanitation, grocery store, and public utility employees restore essential services in fire devastated areas. The military watched closely as Washington held a Palm Sunday parade, planned long before the disturbance. Traffic direction again became a problem as visitors and curious suburbanites glutted District streets by driving into damaged sections of the city.[46]

At 4:45 p.m., General Haines, Mayor Washington, and other city officials conferred to plan for the partial restoration of normal city life.[47] Mayor Washington announced modified school hours, reestablished work hours for federal and District employees, reopened businesses, and extended the curfew from 5:30 to 6:00 p.m. Mayor Washington also agreed to minimize troop requirements in District schools. Immediately after this meeting, Haines began inspecting the city and his troops. In his 7 April report to the Army Chief of Staff, Haines commended the cooperative spirit between local police and federal military forces, but he voiced his displeasure with the military intelligence effort, commenting that over-reporting by a few intelligence units often caused over-reaction by the military. Haines also noted that he changed the mission of the federalized District National Guard from area responsibility to patrol duty.[48]

Throughout the night of Sunday, 7 April and the early morning of the next day, additional forces landed at Andrews Air Force Base. When the 1,882 men of the 197th Infantry Brigade from Fort Benning, Georgia, arrived at Andrews Air Force Base, General Haines directed them to move into Baltimore, Maryland. The 2d Brigade, 5th Infantry Division (Mechanized), from Fort Carson, Colorado, arrived at Andrews by 6:00

p.m. On the evening of 8 April Haines issued his fifth fragmentary order. This order directed Task Force 2/5, (2d Brigade/5th Infantry Division, Mechanized), to send one battalion to Task Force Inside and one battalion to Task Force 82. His order also directed Task Force 2/5 to prepare contingency plans for deployment to Fairfax County, Arlington, Alexandria, and Falls Church, between the District line and the Washington Beltway. Because General Haines wanted to avoid an obtrusive military presence in the suburbs, he restricted reconnaissance by members of Task Force 2/5 to the District.[49] Haines also lacked legal authority to commit federal forces into the state of Virginia, as the state's governor had not requested federal military intervention.

*New York Times* reporter Ben A. Franklin captured the military's change of mission in Washington, D.C., from quelling a riot to returning the city to routine activities. Franklin observed that "the 48-hour ordeal of Washington's Negro section appears to be ending tonight. Attention in the capital turned to a struggle to regain a semblance of normalcy. Authorities said schools, stores, and federal agencies would open as usual tomorrow."[50] Although widespread violence had subsided, tension in the District of Columbia remained until after Dr. King's burial in Atlanta, Georgia, on 9 April. No violence followed Dr. King's funeral, however, and the arrival of the 2d Brigade, 5th Infantry Division on 9 April at Andrews Air Force Base constituted the last large unit deployment to Washington. By the evening of 10 April federal officials considered phasing down military strength, which had risen to 15,530. City officials relaxed curfew hours daily until Friday 12 April, when they eliminated them altogether.

## Troops Depart

On Friday 12 April Mayor Walter Washington wrote to President Johnson asking for the orderly withdrawal of troops from the city. General Haines, Police Chief Layton, Mayor Washington and Public Safety Director Murphy then agreed on a plan to reduce the number of soldiers. This plan went into effect upon the President's concurrence and at 3:00 p.m. on Friday 12 April General Haines relinquished command of Task Force Washington to Lieutenant General A. S. Collins, Jr.[51]

Troops began leaving the city on 13 April. Calm continued during the next day, which caused the Army Chief of Staff to grant permission to release a limited number of units. By midnight, the 2d Brigade, 5th Infantry Division was en route back to Fort Carson, Colorado; the 544th Supply and Services Battalion had departed for Fort Lee; and two companies from the Marine Provisional Student Battalion returned to Quantico. As the 6th Cavalry departed from Washington and returned to Fort Meade, the roving patrols seen throughout the city were the only evidence of an active military presence. By 6:00 p.m. Sunday, 14 April, the Metropolitan Fire Department released its military guards.

On Monday, 15 April, the mayor issued a proclamation terminating the state of emergency. While officials discussed the total withdrawal of troops from the city on Monday, 15 April, the 2d Brigade, 82d Airborne moved into an assembly area at Bolling Air Force Base. General Collins, Mayor Washington, Police Chief Layton, and Public Safety Director Murphy signed the final agreement to phase out Task Force Washington on the morning of 16 April. The District of Columbia National Guard troops returned to their armories by noon and reverted back to District control by midnight. Headquarters, Task Force Washington, concluded its affairs at noon, and Headquarters, Task Force Inside, completed its functions at midnight. Federal military assistance in the capital ended at noon, 16 April, twelve days after it began.[52]

## *Evaluating the Army's Performance*

The aftermath of the Washington riot of 1968 revealed that the Army had learned numerous lessons from the 1967 Detroit experience. Chief among them was the importance of restraint by military forces. Examples of restraint included a low death toll, control of violence by the military and police, and the reduced application of deadly force. The low amount of ammunition expended is related to all of these factors. Table 4 indicates that the death toll in Detroit exceeded the combined totals of the three cities where federalized troops deployed in April of

1968. The civilian death toll in Washington was roughly one third of that in Detroit, and Table 4 indicates a significant improvement in the civil-military authorities' management of violence. The reduction of injuries from 2,250 in Detroit to 1,201 in Washington is further evidence of the responsiveness of the Army to the need to manage its application of force more effectively.

**TABLE 4: Comparative Statistical Data**

| Category | Washington 1968 | Baltimore 1968 | Chicago 1968 | Detroit 1967 |
|---|---|---|---|---|
| Fires | 1,243 | 1,208 | 213 | * |
| Arrests | 7,640 | 5,504 | 3,124 | 7,200 |
| Military Deaths | 0.00 | 0.00 | 0.00 | 2 |
| Civilian Deaths | 13 | 7 | 11 | 38 |
| Death of Police and Firemen | 0.00 | 0.00 | 0.00 | 3 |
| Total Deaths | 13 | 7 | 11 | 43 |
| Injuries | 1,201 | 1,096 | 922 | 2,250 |

Source: Chicago, Baltimore, and Washington data extracted from the Department of the Army After Action Report. Detroit data extracted from the National Advisory Commission on Civil Disturbances Report, 60-60, and 66.
*Data available in dollar amounts

Table 5 presents perhaps the greatest evidence of violence management by federal forces in D.C. This table depicts the results of months of intensified training by the Army in the wake of its fiasco in Detroit. The Army expended a total of twelve rounds of M-16 and two rounds of .45 caliber ammunition in Washington. In Detroit, the military expended 156,391 rounds of .50 and .60 caliber machine gun, M-1 rifle, and .45 caliber pistol ammunition. The expenditure in the District of Columbia equates to only <u>one</u> round fired for every 11,171 rounds fired in Detroit.

The aggregate number of rounds fired by the 38,594 federal troops deployed in Washington, Baltimore, and Chicago was 16.

| TABLE 5: Ammunition Expenditure by Federal Military Forces | | | | |
|---|---|---|---|---|
| Category | Washington 1968 | Baltimore 1968 | Chicago 1968 | Detroit 1967 |
| C.S. Grenades-teargas | 5,248 | 724 | 0** | * |
| Ball Ammo-bullets | 14 | 2 | 0** | 156,391 |
| Source: Data extracted from the Department of the Army After Action Report, 4-17 April Civil Disturbances, 13 August 1968, 12, 15, 1. *Not available **See note 56 | | | | |

The Army's response in Washington, D.C., placed greater emphasis on restraint, which obviously reduced the use of firearms and insignificantly reduced casualties. An 8 April 1968 article in the *Washington Post* asserted that "on balance, the first judgement has to be that they [soldiers] have served the city handsomely... Human life has been valued ahead of property."[53] Whereas the Army and Metropolitan Police Department valued restraint, several local proprietors viewed the lack of force by civil and military authorities as an invitation for continued looting and burning. Reporter Barry Kalb wrote that "many businessmen in the primary riot areas have complained that neither the city nor Federal Government provided adequate protection for private property during the height of the looting and burning."[54] Numerous complaints came from businessmen and members of Congress concerning what appeared to be a condoning of looting by civil and military authorities. Representatives William Jennings Bryan Dorn (Democrat of South Carolina), Thomas N. Abernathy (Democrat of Mississippi), Basil L. Whitener and Roy A. Taylor (both Democrats of North Carolina), and Senator Strom Thurmond (Democrat of South Carolina), led the attack from Capitol Hill.[55]

## *Army Doctrine Confirmed*

The Army's doctrine, outlined in *Field Manual 19-15: Civil Disturbances and Disasters*, was explicit on the conduct of operations, including planning, training, operational technique, and tactics. The manual was a working document, and units were intimately familiar with its contents and procedures upon publication of the March 1968 edition. The Army emphasized restraint, discipline, and psychological factors, including saturating an area with an overwhelming force. Historian Robin Higham wrote of a metamorphosis experienced by the Army after the Detroit riots. He further described the Army's "swing to sophisticated equipment and improved chemicals (mace), and then back again to the fundamental rules governing the handling of human situations… Emphasis was placed on the psychological effect of providing sufficient to even overwhelming, force to cow potential trouble makers before they got out of hand."[57]

Table 6 illustrates Higham's contention regarding the psychological effects of an overwhelming force. There was a 39 percent *increase* in troop strength in D.C., over the force deployed on the streets of Detroit. Washington resident William Cavanaugh noted the importance of psychological advantage in the tactical employment of soldiers in civil disturbance operations. He recounted:

> The police came marching up 14th Street to try to show force--to gain a psychological advantage, but their strategy was way off. They were all marching in a group in the same direction. One man could have wiped them all out. When the Army came in it was a different story. I wanted to get off the streets. I didn't want to deal with the Army. They sent a jeep down the street fast at first, and then three companies marching double-time. You knew they were there. That's psychological effect![58]

| TABLE 6: Number of Troops Deployed during Civil Disturbances |||||
|---|---|---|---|---|
| Category | Washington 1968 | Baltimore 1968 | Chicago 1968 | Detroit 1967 |
| Active Duty | 13,682 | 4,143 | 2,065 | 2,613* |
| National Guard | 1,848 | 6,943 | 9,913 | 7,000 |
| Total | 15,530 | 11,086 | 11,978 | 9,613 |

Source: Chicago, Baltimore, and Washington data extracted from the Department of the Army After Action Report, 4-17 April Civil Disturbances, 13 August 1968, 17 and 18. Detroit information was extracted from Paul Scheips, "The Army and Civil Disturbances: Oxford and Detroit," in Gary D. Ryan and Timothy K. Nenniger, eds., Soldiers and Civilians: The Army and the American People (Washington: National Archives and Records Adminsitration, 1987), 187.
*See Note 59

After studying the Detroit and Newark riots, the Army focused on minimizing the bloodletting by adopting very restrictive policies on the use of life-threatening weapons. The revised doctrine called for a shift in focus away from conventional Army weapons, such as machine guns and M-16 rifles, toward weapons that would diminish the loss of life, such as shotguns loaded with buckshot, and tear gas grenades and canisters. Brigadier General John Burk (the brigade commander of the National Guard forces deployed in Baltimore in April of 1968) later confirmed that absolute weapons' restraint was not only strongly encouraged, but demanded. Burk further stated that "Detroit was a perfect example of what not to do... if you fired ammunition after the extensive training undergone (physically, tactically, and psychologically) after Detroit, you failed!"[60]

The *George Washington Law Review* applauded the military commanders' ability to maintain tight discipline and control over their troops. Of the military's performance in D.C., a commentary in the *Review* stated:

> The planning and preparation of the National Guard
> and the active military units which participated

in quelling the April disturbances must be rated as near perfect. The military drew from its experiences in the riots of Detroit, Newark and elsewhere in recent years to formulate elaborate plans and provide specialized training in riot control. In addition, the military's special relation to the Nation's Capital and the previous experience of the military working with civilian officials of the District increased the ability of military units to efficiently restore order.[61]

The law review also commended the Pentagon's overall response, characterizing it as extraordinarily thorough. The Army also received high marks from another unlikely source--Capitol Hill. Senator Robert Byrd (Democrat of West Virginia), who had criticized the Army for not making arrests, requested that federal troops remain in the District indefinitely. He stated, "if Washington is to be subjected to a summer campaign of demonstrations, as has long been planned, the presence of federal troops will be reassuring." Senator Wayne Morse (Democrat of Oregon) noted that D.C. police, firefighters, and federal troops provided a shining example. Senate District Committee Chairman Alan Bible (Democrat of Nevada) commended city officials, civil leaders, and military authorities for their outstanding performance during a difficult time.[62] Task Force Washington also received praise from President Johnson and Secretary of Defense Clark Clifford. The President told the nation:

> During those days... military commanders and their superbly prepared men carried out their orders with calm professionalism... As the Commander-in-Chief I am particularly proud of the expeditious manner in which this mission was accomplished. The effectiveness of the wise and restrained use of force is attested by the fact that law and order was restored in each city without a single fatality caused by Federal and National Guard troops.[63]

District Fire Chief Henry Galotta paid a great compliment to the soldiers as well, stating that "before the troops arrived his men were apprehensive about going out, but with the troops here they did not mind." General Haines, later returned the compliment by saying, "we [the Army] have adopted the firemen and I believe they have adopted us."[64]

During the nine-month period following the Detroit disturbances, both civilian and military authorities had procured and developed new weapons for use in civil disturbance operations. According to *U.S. News & World Report*, the Army developed several weapons specifically for riot control duty, including reels of barbed steel tape for use as an anti-personnel obstacle; foam and foam sprayers which "could lay down a five-foot layer of foam the width of a 200-foot street;" a gas-powered paint shooting pistol which could potentially mark agitators for apprehension on sight; dart and injector weapons to fire tranquilizers; and cattle prods to control crowds.[65] There is no evidence, however, that of any of these items were employed during the D.C. riots.

## Lessons Learned

The riot control operation in Washington was a tremendous success for the Army and the Federal Government. The operation proved that the Army, with its Task Study Group and intensified planning and training, and the Federal Government, with the knowledge gained through the Kerner Commission, could be responsive. What was more important, the police and the Army realized that their policies and practices required revamping.

The actions of federal forces in quelling civil disobedience in Washington in April of 1968, though highly successful, were not without errors and problems. First among the problems encountered by Task Force Washington was the staffing of its headquarters. Contingency plans called for a 150-man command and control element from Fort Bragg, North Carolina's XVIII Airborne Corps, but the rapid escalation of violence on the streets of the nation's capital required hasty action, causing the Army Chief of Staff to draw personnel from the Department of the Army staff in the Pentagon. The failure by the Army rested in the area of augmentation. Task Force Washington Headquarters operated during the entire operation with only one-sixth of the manpower and resources mandated by contingency plans. Whereas this undermanned group performed admirably during its twelve days of operation, providing interim control to the ad hoc staff while the larger staff deployed to the area would have been a better course of action. Deploying the larger staff would have resulted in better command and control, better record keeping and more accurate reporting. It would also have provided depth in expertise, eight- to twelve-hour shifts for staff personnel, and most essential, execution of the plan by its authors, the staff of XVIII Airborne Corps.[66]

The Washington riots also revealed a potential problem area, operations in suburbs outside of the District. The District of Columbia metropolitan area includes portions of two neighboring states, Virginia and Maryland. Whereas the mayor of Washington and the governor of Maryland requested federal intervention, the governor of Virginia did not. Thus, no legal authority existed for a possible deployment into Virginia. The Army's after action report requested that the contingency plan for Washington consider provisions for coping with unrest in suburban Virginia in any future operation.

Another problem was USCONARC's deployment plan which envisioned operations in three distinct phases: preparation and deployment; employment; and redeployment. During the deployment phase "lines of authority and command relationships were not clear."[67] The Task Force Washington after action report stated that the problem began upon a unit's arrival at Andrews Air Force Base: "In some cases, units were attached less operational control, in other cases they were assigned but not to be employed without permission."[68] The report recommended greater clarity in the operations order as the optimal solution for delineating command, administrative support, and logistical support roles. The report also revealed a lack of standardized incident reports.

On a more positive note, the after action report stated that troops found chemical control agents an extremely effective tool for dispersing crowds, although soldiers discovered that the M7A3 (canister shaped) grenade often ignited, thus causing fires. The M25A2 (baseball shaped) grenade, though not a fire hazard, proved less useful to soldiers because it held a smaller concentration and volume of chemical agent than the M7A3. Troops also found CS (tear gas) crystals an effective deterrent for looters in unprotected damaged buildings.[69]

General Haines and the leadership of Task Force Washington stressed several factors as a result of the Army's experience in the District of Columbia. The first was the importance of prior planning, coordination, and liaison with local police, firefighters, and National Guardsmen. Task force leaders also emphasized the continued importance of establishing and enforcing a curfew, the use of helicopters for command and control, and the use of buses for transporting troops. Finally, leaders underscored the significance of a positive attitude, professional appearance, and strict discipline and control of the troops performing riot duty.

With the end of riot operations in Washington, the Army could breathe a major sigh of relief. Its monumental efforts in planning and training for active and National Guard forces and its insistence on restraint and the use of minimum force had paid dividends, not only in Washington, but also in Chicago and Baltimore during the same period. The Army forwarded the lessons learned in D.C. to units throughout the country so that they might benefit from the experiences of Task Force Washington.

## The Army's Post-Mortem of Washington D.C.

The prevalent view of historians of the era, such as Robin Higham, Martin Blumenson, Robert Coakley, and Paul Scheips, was that the Regular Army was better suited for the unpopular mission of riot control than the National Guard. They based their conclusion on such factors as training, discipline, cohesion, mission orientation, and, most importantly, the fact that an integrated Regular Army was not a reflection of a segregated society. However, an evaluation of the Washington riots divulged that the District of Columbia National Guard was very well trained and as prepared for the task as the active duty forces in April of 1968.

The evidence also revealed that 26 percent of the D.C. Guardsmen were African-Americans.[70] According to Martin Blumenson, the ethnicity of the Michigan National Guard had played a critical role in Detroit nine months earlier. He argued that the Michigan National Guard, which was 98.7 percent Caucasian, represented the segregated majority and thus fostered the same prejudices as the larger society. Blumenson, Adam Yarmolinsky, and Roger Beaumont agree on the issue of race and the positive result that an integrated Michigan National Guard could have made. Whereas it is difficult to assess the impact that the integrated D.C. National Guard may have had on the rebelling citizens, *Washington Star* reporter Oliver Thomas noted that the presence of Negro soldiers was reassuring to him personally.[71]

No evidence suggests any violations of the Posse Comitatus Act by federal troops, and the factors that best explain why forces were successful in the nation's capital may also illustrate why the 1878 statute was not an issue. Success in part can be attributed directly to the "Five P Principle"--prior planning prevents poor performance. As a result of a poor showing in Detroit, and the subsequent recommendations of the Army Task Group and the Kerner Commission, the riot control components of the Army (active and National Guard) had conducted significant and focused training, implemented refined procedures, and developed plans that affixed responsibilities to designated units for riot control operations in specified cities.

In February of 1968 the Army initiated, by the direction of the Army Chief of Staff, the "Senior Officers Civil Disturbance Orientation Course" (SEADOC).[72] From February 1968 to April 1969 the Army trained over 2,000 active and reserve commissioned officers (lieutenant colonel and above), 982 National Guard personnel, and 1,200 civil law enforcement officers. Additionally, the Regular Army took the lead in training the reserves, National Guard, and civilian law enforcement agencies in civil disturbance operations. The *Washington Daily News* noted the extensive training undertaken by the District of Columbia National Guard and the Metropolitan Police Department to prepare for any eventuality in the spring or summer of 1968, saying: Squads of policemen received extensive training in marksmanship, procedures for dealing with snipers without indiscriminate firepower--as done in Newark and Detroit in 1967--and training in crowd control, alert procedures, and establishment of a communications center. Key members of the District of Columbia National Guard were attending anti-riot training at the Military Police School located at Fort Gordon, Georgia.[73]

District Guardsmen had also undergone extensive unit training since the summer of 1967, engaging in twelve hours of riot control training prior to their annual field training and another seventy-two hours during Annual Training including: a twenty-four-hour training exercise for each unit in a realistic riot environment, twenty hours of staff training, and another twenty-eight hours of training during the period October to April. During the 21-22 October 1967 Vietnam demonstrations at the Pentagon, the Guard also performed eight hours of actual riot duty. The entire unit had undergone a thirty-two-hour riot-control refresher course only a month before King's assassination. The District Guardsmen additionally made detailed reconnaissance and coordination plans for all security missions assigned in contingency plans, which included public utilities, bridges, the National Guard Armory, Camp Sims, and the police headquarters.[74]

Another aspect of planning and preparation that assured Army compliance with the Posse Comitatus Act and contributed to the success of federal troops was their familiarity with the riot area, local police, and National Guardsmen. The operations plan for Washington (OPLAN Cabin Guard) assigned specific units to specific police precincts. In February and March of 1968 officers of each of these units toured their assigned precincts with Washington police officials.[75] An account in the *Washington Daily News* elaborated on the fact that federal forces were no strangers in the District: "some troops knew the names and faces of the policemen they'd be working with, and the neighborhoods where they'd be stationed."[76] The importance of the familiarity between the Guard, local police, and the Regular Army cannot be overstated. A lack of understanding by local police and politicians of the roles, responsibilities, and constraints imposed on federalized forces which proved to be a great source of frustration in Los Angeles in 1992, was not evident in Washington in 1968. Local political officials and police understood that the military's mission during any eventuality was to restore order to a level that would allow civilian officials to resume control of the city. Arrests, search and seizures, and detention remained the responsibility of police and federal law enforcement agencies.[77]

The violence and lack of restraint of the Guardsmen seen in Detroit and Newark during the summer of 1967 was almost nonexistent among the professional soldiers that guarded the streets of Washington. The Army's training after Detroit had created units that were well-prepared, with strong professional-soldier traditions and training in the latest riot-control techniques, emphasizing restraint in the use of physical force. The soldiers' restraint was reciprocated by the populace. According to a *Washington Evening Star* reporter who was also a soldier in the District of Columbia National Guard, "I was struck by something no one had suggested was possible during all of our civil disturbance training--the friendly attitude of people living under what almost amounted to military occupation. People gave us coffee and food, greeted us on the streets with a 'how're you doing?' Kids, hundreds of kids, pointed to us and waved, and we waved back."[78] The troops of the 82d Airborne Division received a little rest and relaxation as they were entertained by students from Richmond, Virginia.

The Army's success in Washington was also the direct result of preparation for the Southern Christian Leadership Conference Poor People's Campaign originally scheduled for 22 April 1968 in Washington. The units assigned to Task Force Inside, all already stationed within the Washington metropolitan area, had undergone a series of field training and command post exercises in preparation for crowd control during the Poor People's Campaign. This preparation and Task Force Inside's high level of preparedness was one more reason the violence in Washington was quelled after only three days.

General George C. Marshall's World War II-era statement that "We cannot train without planning and we cannot teach without preparation," epitomized the Army's post-Detroit civil disturbance efforts.[79] The Army and National Guard had redeemed themselves and contributed significantly to the increased readiness of civilian law enforcement agencies. Perhaps the role of federal troops in quelling the Washington riots of 1968 was best described in a 17 April 1968 memorandum from the Under Secretary of the Army to the Army's Chief of Staff. Under Secretary David McGiffert wrote:

> With the withdrawal of troops yesterday from Washington and de-federalization at midnight of the D.C. National Guard, the direct participation of Federal military forces in controlling the recent civil disorders has ended. I want to take this occasion to express my appreciation and congratulations to you and to all the personnel of the active Army and of the National Guard who played a part in this effort. The task was a difficult one; the response was magnificent. The extensive work which had been done in the six months previous to these disorders to improve training and to perfect planning paid tremendous dividends. Even more important, the disciplined and restrained approach adopted by the military forces contributed very significantly to bringing the disorders rapidly under control without substantial loss of life and without creating a legacy of bitterness which could only serve to stimulate further unrest. The citizens of our country can be rightly proud of this achievement.[80]

After the fiasco in Detroit the entire Army--Regular and National Guard--adopted a philosophy of restraint. Even in Chicago in 1968, where Mayor Richard Daley instructed police to shoot arsonists and looters on sight, federal troops did not fire a shot. The Army Chief of Staff's selection of General Ralph E. Haines as the Task Force Washington commander proved to be a very prudent choice. Haines worked closely with civil authorities. Fostering a good working relationship with District city officials, while staying abreast of the military situation, Haines proved equally adept at handling the inquiries of senators and congressmen. Following his assignment in Washington, Haines was selected as the Commander-in-Chief, U.S. Army Pacific Command. He served his final tour of duty as the Commanding General of the United

States Continental Army Command (USCONARC)--the command responsible for civil disturbance operations and planning.[81]

The Army's role in quelling the civil unrest that shook the very foundation of Washington, D.C., in 1968 though not flawless, was a monumental success. Not only did the Army quickly restore order to the city, but it also served as a calming presence. The Army's performance also reconfirmed its reliability in a role performed with scattered success since the 1790s. April of 1968 found the military fully capable of fulfilling its oath to support and defend the Constitution against all enemies, foreign and domestic. Once again, the Army had proven itself to be, as Political Scientist Samuel Huntington noted, "the country's general servant, well-disciplined, obedient, performing civil functions."[82]

## CHAPTER 4

## *FROM KING TO KING: 1969 TO 1991*

*Studies of past and present riots show that the immediate cause of the riot is a failure of social control. These failures are of two sorts, undercontrol and overcontrol. In the condition of undercontrol, law enforcement personnel are insufficiently active. The dissident group, noting the weakness of the authorities, seizes the opportunity to express its hostility. The inactivity of the police functions as an invitation to act out long-suppressed feelings, free of social consequences of illegal behavior.[1]*

This chapter examines the affect of the systematic dismantling of the role of civil disturbances, as "race" became less and less the urban issue, and the nation's aversion to Vietnam—especially amongst college students—took primacy. This chapter examines violence at Kent State University in 1970; reviews the first-ever clear violation of the Posse Comitatus Act at Wounded Knee, South Dakota in 1973; and examines the 1980 Miami Riot—which in many ways mirrored the 1992 Los Angeles Riot.

After its success in Washington in 1968, the Regular Army performed varied and diverse domestic duties. However, National Guardsmen, under state control, performed the lion's share of civil-disturbance missions. Federalized forces deployed to the nation's capital three times for crowd control during Vietnam War protest rallies from 1969 to 1971. None of these incidents, however, were categorized as major disturbances. Thus, the Army's major focus during each of the Vietnam moratoriums was basic crowd control.

On one occasion, as the Department of the Army Civil Disturbance Directorate prepared for an anti-war demonstration in 1969, it received the task of protecting the South Vietnamese Embassy from the radical New Mobilization Committee. The mission went to the Army's premier civil disturbance unit, the 503d Military Police Battalion from Fort Bragg, North Carolina. This duty, however, would violate the Posse Comitatus Act. Recognizing that the Marine Corps was not constrained by the Act, the Civil Disturbance Directorate transferred the mission to the 2d Marine Civil Disturbance Regiment.[2] Shortly after the demonstration, the Department of Defense implemented DOD Directive 3025.12, which placed Posse Comitatus-like restrictions on the Marine Corps and Navy.

In March of 1969, President Richard M. Nixon exerted his constitutional authority by directing that the military develop contingencies to assist the U.S. Postal Department in moving the mail during the nation's first major postal strike. The Army developed plans for Operation Graphic Hand, which called for the use of Regular and Reserve soldiers, sailors, Marines, and airmen in New York, Philadelphia, Chicago, and Boston to sort and move mail. Table 7 depicts the joint service augmentation forces for Operation Graphic Hand.

| TABLE 7: Operation Graphic Hand, 1969 | | | | |
|---|---|---|---|---|
| **CITIES** | **ARMY** | **NAVY\*** | **AIR FORCE** | **TOTAL** |
| New York | 1,100 | 900 | 500 | 2,500 |
| Boston | 400 | 300 | 300 | 1,000 |
| Philadelphia | 500 | 300 | 200 | 1,000 |
| Chicago | 500 | 500 | 500 | 1,500 |

Source: Continental Army Command/Army Strike Command, Annual Historical Summary, FY 1970, (Fort Monroe, Virginia: Headquarters USCONARC, 28 February 1972), 133. Located at the Center of Military History, Washington, D.C. *U.S. Marines are included in the naval figure.

Execution of Graphic Hand by Army troops occurred only in New York City. All told, "28,100 men--both Active and Reserve component--were used in the New York City area."[3] Soldiers deployed with riot control equipment and munitions, but no confrontations occurred between military forces and striking postal employees. More than 1,000 troops delivered mail to over 500 businesses and firms within New York's financial district. The remaining forces processed and sorted mail, and worked at counters in local post offices. Troops, however, did *not* deliver mail to residential areas.

Although the United States experienced 4,330 domestic bombings and 35,129 bomb threats during 1969 and 1970, Lieutenant General William McCaffrey, the military director for civil disturbance planning and operations, minimized any future role for federal troops. In September of 1969, McCaffrey prepared an assessment outlining the Army's response to the U.S. civil disturbance threat. In his memorandum McCaffrey concluded that federal intervention in civil unrest was unlikely and that local police and the National Guard--under state control--were sufficient to handle any eventuality. He also noted that the military's training requirements for civil disturbances had been increased and instructional doctrine revised. The general also observed that federalized troops had not participated in riot duty at all during 1969, and he stated that police departments were much better prepared to respond to a riot than they had been in the past. Table 8 bears out McCaffrey's contention of a better trained military force.

Whereas General McCaffrey's report contended that sixty-six cities were identified in April 1969 as being vulnerable to civil unrest, he noted that thirty-seven of these locales had well trained and properly equipped special purpose riot control units. His memorandum recommended that the Army continue to provide civil law enforcement authorities with films and other instructional materials, but recommended that the Army reduce its quick reaction force from two brigades to one, due to the lessening threat.[4] McCaffrey's September 1969 memorandum was the first major step towards freeing active-duty forces from the onerous task of suppressing civil disturbances, and his recommendation to reduce the quick reaction force from two brigades to one was approved by the Army Chief of Staff on 6 October 1969.[5]

In May of 1970, a force of 4,300 Regular Army soldiers and Marines was sent to New Haven, Connecticut, to quell an expected disturbance during the trial of Black Panther Party leader Bobby Seale. Units deployed "with 264,854 rounds of small-arms ammunition, 12,084 riot control grenades of various types, and 696 pounds of bulk CS [tear gas] riot control agent."[6] They anticipated hostile confrontation between

Black Panther supporters and military forces, but the violence expected in New Haven did not occur.

| TABLE 8: Annual Training Requirements for Civil Disturbance Operations | | | |
|---|---|---|---|
| Subject | Hours of Training | Hours for Refresher Training | Hours for Individual Preparatory Training |
| Introduction | 1 | 0 | 0 |
| Policies and Legal Considerations | 1 | 0 | 1 |
| Military Leadership Responsibilities and Discipline | 2 | 1 | 1 |
| Evolution of a Civil Disturbance | 1 | 0 | 1 |
| Control Measures and Application of Force | 2 | 1 | 1 |
| Riot Control Agents and Munitions | 2 | 2 | 1 |
| Formations | 4 | 4 | 1 |
| Communication Training | 2 | Integrate or conduct concurrently | 0 |
| Anti-looting and Anti-sniper Measures | 4 | 2 | 1 |
| Arson and Protection of Firefighters | 2 | 1 | 1 |
| Civil Disturbance Operations in Built-up Areas | 4 | 1 | 0 |
| Practice Exercise (FTX) | 8 | 4 | 0 |
| Totals | 33 | 16 | 8 |
| Source: Continental Army Command, Appendix XV, Training in Civil Disturbance Operations, 22 October 1968. Located at the Center of Military History. | | | |

The results of actions by the Ohio National Guard at Kent State University on 4 May 1970 were less fortuitous. On this fateful day Ohio Guardsmen fired on students, killing four and wounding nine others. In the years that followed several interpretations evolved describing what happened on 4 May. Skeptics forwarded theories of conspiracy, arguing that the Guard's actions were deliberate and irresponsible. Conversely, the leaders of the National Guard minimized the event and focused on the selfless service of their soldiers, asserting in their after action report that there were no problem areas or recommendations for improvements in future operations.[7] In short, the Guard expressed no official remorse for its actions. The Regular Army tried to distance itself from the disaster, seeing that the Guard had violated the Army's doctrine, but the Regular Army took actions to ensure that the nation would not experience another Kent State tragedy.

Writers and scholars examining the events at Kent State have presented the incident as one of the great mysteries of the twentieth century. The conundrum surrounding the affray between Guardsmen and students centers on a simple question: "Why did the soldiers fire their weapons into a crowd?" Several books have all attempted to answer this question. The authors of these books postulate machinations of collusion and treachery on the part of the Ohio Guard. Each volume subscribed to the notion that Guardsmen conspired to teach the assembled students a lesson for their blatant disregard for authority and felonious actions against the agents of law and order.[8]

Conversely, many private citizens, as well as the senior leadership of the National Guard, argued that the Ohio Guardsmen's actions were justified. Guard leaders believed that the students determined their own plight on that fateful day. According to an article published in *The National Guardsman* one month after the incident, "the Guard as a whole--and those involved at Kent as well--were supported verbally by thousands of Americans who have felt their lives and property endangered by the rising tide of violence and by the drift towards possible revolution."[9] A *Newsweek* poll taken shortly after the violent encounter bore out this contention. The survey noted that 58 percent of Americans blamed the students for what transpired at Kent State; 11 percent faulted the Guard; while 31 percent of those polled had no opinion.[10] Even more surprising were the letters to the editor that appeared in the Cleveland *Plain Dealer* newspaper. For example, Mrs. Donald Ramsayer of Canton, Ohio, placed the ultimate blame on the students. She argued that the "National Guard did not invade the campus. They came to enforce the law." Likewise, R. Robert Koch of Lakewood, Ohio, argued that his "sympathies are with the parents of the dead and wounded and with the Ohio National Guard, which reacted exactly as any reasonable individual should have expected under the circumstances."[11]

In a statement released one week after the incident, the president of the National Guard Association, Major General James F. Cantwell, stated: "Distorted, hysterical recollections of what took place, offered by distraught eyewitnesses, cover only fragments of the sequence of events leading up to the deaths, and are no substitute for facts." He argued that these distortions unjustifiably brought out "terms like 'trigger-happy,' 'poorly trained,' 'young and immature,' and other equally damning terms that have been applied to Ohio troops and the entire National Guard," but Cantwell claimed that the facts proved otherwise.[12] He contended that from January of 1968 to May of 1970 the National Guard was called out 191 times to help civil authorities restore and maintain order during civil disturbances. The General noted that in that time not "more than one or two fatalities" could be attributed to the National Guard. Cantwell concluded that "no element among law enforcement agencies has been more insistent than the Guard in protecting the rights of all citizens to peaceful, orderly protest."[13]

Major General Winston P. Wilson, the Chief of the National Guard Bureau, testified before the Senate Armed Services Committee three days after the violence at Kent State University. General Wilson urged the committee to keep in mind that all persons on the green [field at Kent State University], whether or not confronting the police and Guardsmen, were law breakers in violation of the Governor's (and the University's) ban, in violation of the riot act, and for some in violation of the Ohio code in knowingly assaulting, striking, or wounding a law enforcement officer or member of the organized militia.[14]

General Wilson further stated that all Ohio National Guardsman had received the Army's prescribed training and annual refresher training. He also noted that the unit responsible for the shooting at Kent State--Company A, 143rd Infantry--had "received riot training far in excess of, and perhaps equal again, to the Department of the Army requirements."[15] Wilson concluded his testimony with the assurance to the committee that every man in the unit was struck by rocks or bricks, and that twenty-six Guardsmen were treated at local hospitals and two additional soldiers were hospitalized during this tragic incident.

An article published in the June 1970 edition of *National Guardsman* supported General Wilson's assertion. With respect to the violent actions carried out by the students, the article stated that, "troops had been pelted with rocks, with chunks of concrete--some with sections of reinforcing rod protruding--and even with sections of reinforcing rod hurled like javelins."[16] All told, "forty-six Guardsman later received treatment for injuries including smashed teeth and severe bruises."[17]

To better understand what transpired at Kent State, a review of the chronology leading up to the violent confrontation is required. Following a television address to the nation by President Nixon on 30 April, in which he tried to explain the U.S. invasion of Cambodia, anti-war groups and students on college campuses protested throughout the nation. Due to rising tensions between local police and protesters in Kent, Ohio, the local mayor requested that the governor send in a contingent from the Ohio National Guard. According to an article in Cleveland's *Plain Dealer*, Ohio Governor James Rhodes responded by sending 600 Guardsmen from the 1st Battalion, 145th Infantry and the 2d Squadron, 107th Cavalry. This contingent was augmented by "41 campus police reinforced by Kent and Ravenna police, sheriff's deputies from Portage counties, and about 20 state highway patrolmen."[18]

According to the National Guard's liaison officer at the university, "approximately 250 to 300 students assembled at approximately 6:20 p.m." These students, according to the report, "carried all types of weapons including guns."[19] During the evening of 2 May an unruly crowd of students congregated at the university's ROTC building and began hurling rocks, flares and burning rags into the building. Within a short time, flames engulfed the structure. When firefighters arrived, the angry mob threw rocks at them and attempted to cut the fire hoses. Sheriff's deputies escorted the firefighters and split the crowd in two with tear gas. Upon the National Guard's arrival at the scene, the troops were met by a barrage of rocks thrown by students, but after a sweep through the campus, Guardsmen had effectively quashed that night's unrest.

On 3 May, during a news conference, Governor Rhodes stated that his solution was to "eradicate the problem," saying "we're not going to treat the symptoms."[20] Why did Governor Rhodes believe that it was so important to dig in his heels at Kent State? Perhaps he, like many other governors across the nation, had tired of the radical student movement. After all, Rhodes had already utilized the Guard to quell student protests in Akron and Columbus during his tenure as governor. After the governor's comments, the commander of the Ohio National Guard contingent, Major General Sylvester DelCorso, asserted: "We're going to employ every weapon possible" and "use any force that's necessary, even to the point of shooting."[21] The statements by the governor and the general set the tone for the next confrontation between soldiers and students.

During the morning of 4 May, 850 Ohio Guardsmen converged on Kent State, assuming complete control of the situation from campus and local authorities. By noon a crowd of approximately 2,000 students congregated on campus at a gathering area known as the Commons. As the Guard attempted to disperse the crowd, violence ensued. The beleaguered soldiers fired tear gas into the assembled masses only to have the canisters thrown back at them by disconcerted students. National Guardsmen carried loaded rifles the entire time that they were in contact with the crowd. Although carrying loaded rifles was considered to be a gross violation of the guidelines of Army civil disturbance doctrine, it was not unusual for Guardsmen to deploy this way. Journalist Michael D. Roberts quoted Brigadier General Robert Canterbury as stating that, "it was standing operating procedures for the Ohio National Guard to carry loaded weapons."[22] Following the incident at Kent State, the President's Commission on Campus Unrest noted that Annex F (Pre-employment Briefing of the Ohio National Guard) to OPLAN 2 (Aid to Civil Authorities) the rules of engagement paragraph f.(1) stated that "rifles will be carried with a round in the chamber in the safe position."[23] Thus, it was standard practice for the Ohio National Guard to have their weapons locked and loaded during riot duty, despite the fact that such a step was contrary to *Field Manual 19-15.*[24]

As the soldiers' line of advance halted at the football practice field, leaders of the Guard conversed behind the forward elements of troops. Conspiracy theorists argued that the decision to fire upon the students was made during this meeting of the unit's leadership. However, the Guard officers actually decided that the Guardsmen would return to their original position across campus. Upon arrival at the area near Taylor Hall the soldiers appeared to turn almost simultaneously and began firing upon the crowd. Twenty-eight soldiers acknowledged firing a total of sixty-one rounds during the thirteen-second volley. Photographs presented in the President's Commission on Campus Disorders depict Brigadier General Robert Canterbury, the Assistant State Adjutant General, behind the National Guardsmen's wedge formation as they moved throughout the campus on 4 May 1970. From Canterbury's vantage point on the field, he would have been well aware of the situation that confronted the Guardsmen. Canterbury was only one of a few people who could have made the claim: "In view of the extreme danger to the troops at this point, they were justified in firing."[25]

The events transpiring on 4 May 1970 have been scrutinized by writers, scholars, military leaders, government officials, and a presidential commission. Many questions have been raised and the results of interviews and investigations have resulted in numerous publications. Not often examined are the photographs that captured the sequence of events on 4 May. It has been said that a picture is worth a thousand words, and such is the case for the series of photos taken as events unfolded at Kent State. First, the pictures revealed that most of the actions conducted by the Ohio Guardsmen occurred while they wore protective (gas) masks. This seemingly minor revelation is critical, as the protective mask severely degrades the depth perception and peripheral vision of the wearer. Wearing a mask also significantly limits one's hearing and muffles voice projection. As a result, visual hand-and-arm signals and the actions of recognized leaders provide the *example* that soldiers are likely to emulate in the absence of verbal commands. According to General Canterbury "no verbal commands to fire" were ever given by him or any other officer at Kent State.[26] This statement is probably true. The noises of an angry crowd focused on agitating the Guardsmen coupled with the severely muffled voices of officers in protective masks, makes it highly unlikely that the assembled troops could have heard a command to fire--even if it were given.

La Rochefoucauld wrote in *Maxims* that "Nothing is as contagious as example, and we never perform an outstandingly good or evil action without it producing others of its sort."[27] Example, as shown in the photographs, may best explain what caused the Ohio Guardsmen to fire upon the students at Kent State University. It does not matter which source one consults, as the numerous volumes on Kent State all depict the identical photographs taken by Howard E. Ruffner, John P. Filo, and John A. Darnell, Jr. However, for quality of print and photograph resolution Peter Davies' volume, *The Truth about Kent State*, provides the best pictures.

Photographs 50, 51, and 52 in Davies' book clearly display a soldier in the prescribed standing firing position with his M1911A1 (.45 caliber) pistol in front of the formation.[28] From the perspective of a soldier in formation behind this unidentified person these actions are of the utmost importance. In an environment where hearing and peripheral vision are significantly impaired, line of sight and the actions or example of the leader becomes the best method of communication. Although the donned protective mask provides anonymity, a soldier recognizes that the .45 caliber pistol is almost exclusively the weapon of a commissioned officer or senior noncommissioned officer.[29] William A. Gordon identified the person holding the pistol as First Sergeant Myron Pryor.[30] Photograph 52 in Davies' book clearly shows Pryor out front in one of the prescribed stances for engaging a target with a .45 caliber pistol. This photo, as well as photo 51, shows that other soldiers appear to emulate the example of Pryor as they began to level their weapons and engage the students to their front.

First Sergeant Pryor stated that the individual depicted in the picture could have been him. In 1970, he also stated emphatically that he did not fire his weapon.[31] The photographs, however, undermine Pryor's claim. The John A. Darnell photograph, shown as picture 47 in the report of the President's Commission on Campus Unrest, and as photo 52 in Peter Davies' volume--which is magnified for the cover of Davies' study--bears out this conclusion. Picture 52 shows, without question, that the soldier identified as First Sergeant Pryor did in fact fire his weapon. The picture depicts that the slide group on the weapon is retracted and locked to the rear, with the barrel of the weapon exposed.[32] This position is achieved only when all rounds within the ammunition clip have been exhausted.[33] In other words, Pryor's weapon could not have been depicted as shown in the photograph unless it had been fired and his clip emptied. The slide group on this automatic weapon would remain as seen in the photo-graph until the operator releases the slide stop, which releases the slide forward. Figure 5 provides a graphic illustration of the .45 caliber pistol and its component parts. Thus, the photographs show that First Sergeant Pryor provided the example that proved to be the non-verbal order to fire upon the students at Kent State University. Contrary to Pryor's con-tention that he did not fire, the evidence provided by photograph 52 of the Davies study indicates that he did.[34] The question that remains, how-ever, concerns the number of rounds that Pryor expended. Additionally, judging by the cant of the first sergeant's weapon illustrated within pho-tograph 58, he appears to be inserting another clip into his weapon.[35] In picture 59 the slide stop has been released, making the weapon again capable of firing.[36]

**Figure 5: M1911A1 (.45 Caliber) Pistol**

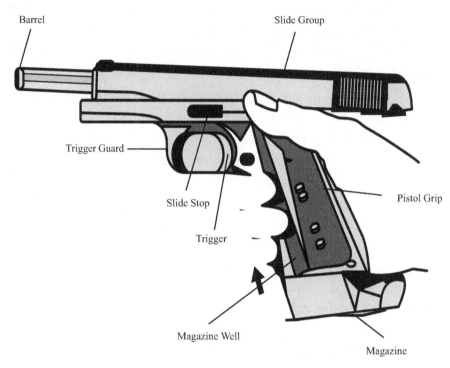

Barrel                Slide Group

Trigger Guard

Slide Stop                Pistol Grip

Trigger

Magazine Well

Magazine

Source: Department of the Army Technical Manual 9-1005-211-12: Operator and Organizational Maintenance Manual Including Basic Issue Items and Repair Parts and Special Tools List, Pistol, Caliber .45, Automatic, M1911A1, (Washington: Headquarters, Department of the Army, Government Printing Office, 1968), 3-5.

Another question that deserves examination is: What caused the violent confrontation between soldiers and students on 4 May 1970? Perhaps President Richard Nixon best explained the situation with his statement: "When dissent turns to violence it invites tragedy."[37] The numerous studies recapturing the incident created the impression of helpless students who were the victims of a barbarous assault by the Ohio National Guard. A contrasting impression came from the authorities. According to Kent Police Chief Donald Swartzmiller, "many of his men were hit by rocks--four badly enough to require medical attention."[38] Likewise, Major Arthur E. Wallach, commander of a National Guard detachment at Kent State, contended that "many Guardsmen were struck by rocks as they marched across the campus commons to push demonstrators out of the area."[39]

Even one of the original conspiracy theorists, journalist Joe Eszterhas, quoted Kent State student Brian Fisher in an article as saying: "There were students on all sides of them [Guardsman], with rocks and bricks being thrown at them."[40] Likewise, journalist William Hickey argued that local and national media coverage of the incident had been nothing short of "a blatant assault on the National Guard with no regard for the particular circumstances its members faced that fateful day."[41] Hickey further contended that the various television shows discussing the events gave the false "impression that a troop of National Guardsmen invaded the campus without cause, provoked the students into a protest action, and then fired into their ranks at will."[42]

During the three decades after an American tragedy unfolded in the small town of Kent, Ohio, National Guardsmen continued to seek a societal reevaluation of the incident. Many critics of the National Guard's actions focused only on the shooting. What many of the antagonists missed was the violent actions of the students. According to a retired Maryland National Guard officer, John F. Kutcher, "college disorders frequently were worse than the racial disturbances."[43] Likewise, the former National Guard Bureau Chief, Major General Francis S. Greenlief agreed with Kutcher. Greenlief contended that student antiwar riots were often more violent than the civil rights disorders. Greenlief argued that "in the civil rights disturbances the target usually was property, while the students were more inclined to attack people."[44] The former president of the National Guard Association, Major General James F. Cantwell, provided a perspective that had only been captured casually in the many volumes published on Kent State. Cantwell noted that, "National Guardsmen... bear the scars on their souls, as well as their bodies, from hundreds of encounters with lawless violent elements in our society. We [at the National Guard Bureau] can't help wondering if our critics would have reacted as harshly had four Guardsmen been killed by thrown missiles, as they easily might have been."[45]

Suffice it to say that the aforementioned positions--albeit one-sided--present a valid concern. This perspective is, however, contrary to the conclusion of the President's Commission on Campus Unrest that "the Kent State tragedy must mark the last time that, as a matter of course, loaded rifles are issued to Guardsmen confronting student demonstrators."[46] It is unlikely that proponents of the two contrasting views--the pro-Guard faction and the pro-student supporters--will ever reach an understanding over the controversies of Kent State.

Surprisingly, in the aftermath of an incident which proved to be an enormous embarrassment for the National Guard, the state of Ohio Adjutant General's Department did not appear to view the incident Kent State confrontation as even remotely significant. In the AG's annual report for fiscal year 1970, a solitary sentence referred to an event which resulted in American soldiers firing indiscriminately upon college students. The report's only mention of Kent State contended: "The disturbance ended when the National Guard troops acting in self-defense fired their weapons killing four students and wounding several others."[47] Remarkably, the Ohio National Guard's official after action report concluded with the following: "Problem Areas and Lessons Learned: None." "Recommendations: None."[48]

This conclusion is absolutely astounding. Only one month before the release of this after action report, Ohio National Guardsmen shot and killed four college students and severely wounded nine others. How could these actions not warrant significant discussion of problem areas, lessons learned, and recommendations by the Ohio National Guard? This blatant oversight is more than likely the result of basic human error, as the report was probably written and staffed in advance of the Kent State tragedy.

While the Guard minimized its mistakes and the President's Commission viewed them as "unnecessary, unwarranted and inexcusable," the Department of the Army was somewhat bewildered by the Guard's actions.[49] The Guard had undergone all directed training by the Department of the Army's Civil Disturbance Directorate. In a memorandum Major General Charles Gettys, the acting director for civil disturbance planning and operations, noted: "There is no evidence available to this Directorate that indicates that the training of the National Guard is deficient."[50] Gettys further stated that the Guard's problems at Kent State were attributable to their failure to follow federal policies concerning force options and rules for the application of force.

Certainly, the Ohio National Guard's actions violated the Army's intent of avoiding the appearance of an invading alien force. The Department of the Army, according to the *New York Times*, "disavowed any federal ties to the Ohio Guard at Kent State."[51] This article was careful to specify that Ohio's governor was in charge of the Guard at Kent State, not the President. Herein lies the major issue of this tragedy, which will continue to be important so long as the National Guard exists. A *Newsweek* article published two weeks after the Kent State tragedy captured the key question of the debate from a federal perspective: "Who Guards Against The Guard?" As the article reminded readers, "National Guard units are really militias under the command of the governors in each of the nation's 50 states."[52] Only when a Guard unit is brought under the control of the federal government (federalized) is it constrained by the Posse Comitatus Act, and governed by *Field Manual 19-15* and the Garden Plot Contingency Plan and its rules of engagement.[53] Albert Brien, writing in the *Boston University Law Review*, argued that "in spite of federal training and funding, when mobilized by the governor, Guardsmen must conform to individual state regulations…[54]"

In the aftermath of the Kent State tragedy, the Army Chief of Staff, acting as the Department of Defense executive agent for civil disturbances, focused his attention on written policies regarding the use of force. It became the Army's intent to ensure that the civil disturbance doctrine clearly delineated its applicability to *any military force* performing this critical mission. The Army concluded that the existing federal guidelines were sound, but changed some wording to prevent misinterpretation. The Ohio Guard's performance at Kent State had revealed a great chasm between its responsibilities under state control and the significant limitations existing under federal authority. As a result of this revelation, significant actions were taken by the doctrinal proponents at the Military Police School to clarify the Army's views regarding nonviolent means for quelling a civil disturbance. The 1972 modifications shown in Table 9 depicts the numerous changes to *FM 19-15* that were the direct result of the Guard's poor performance at Kent State University. Although the events at Kent State involved only Ohio National Guardsmen, the legacy of their actions had a significant impact on Army doctrine, and further clarified the military's civil disturbance mission.

| TABLE 9: Field 19-15: Civil Disturbances | | | |
|---|---|---|---|
| Edition | Changes to Manual | Weapons Utilized | Social Events |
| March 1968 | • Organization and leadership techniques reworked<br>• Added anti-looting and anti-sniping sections<br>• Added appendices on<br>  – riot control formations<br>  – staff officer checklists<br>  – mob behavior<br>• Integrated FBI Doctrinal Concepts into FM 19-15 | • Machine guns (not to exceed .30 caliber<br>• Shotguns<br>• Rifles with bayonets<br>• Chemical weapons<br>• Helicopters<br>• Masks | • 164 riots, summer of 1967<br>• Detroit riot of 1967<br>• Kerner Commission<br>• Army Task Study Group<br>• Black Panther protests<br>• Vietnam War demonstrations<br>• Protest by the Students for a Democratic Society |
| March 1972 | • New Chapter on Civil Disturbance Management<br>• "Disasters" dropped from manual title<br>• Added sections on<br>  – Mental Preparation of Troops<br>  – Urban Demonstrations<br>  – Agitators and Mob Action<br>  – Campus Disorders<br>  – Labor Disputes<br>  – Protection of Federal Property<br>• Term "Group Behavior" changed to "Collective Behavior" | • M16A1 rifles with bayonet and lock plates (stops auto fire)<br>• Shotguns<br>• Riot batons<br>• Machine guns (carried but not displayed)<br>• Armored Personnel Carriers<br>• Helicopters<br>• Bullet proof vests<br>• Masks | • Kent State University Unrest (1970)<br>• Vietnam Moratoriums<br>• President's Commission on Campus Unrest |
| October 1975 | • Deleted sections on:<br>  – Campus Disorders<br>  – Labor Disputes<br>  – Protection of Federal Property<br>  – Urban Demonstrations<br>• Added section on Fire Fighting Operations<br>• Added chapter on Riot Control Agents | • Hand held mace<br>• Shotguns<br>• Masks<br>• Riot batons<br>• M16A1<br>• Helicopters | • Bombs explode at Pentagon<br>• Wounded Knee standoff (1973)<br>• 30 National Guard humanitary missions<br>• President Nixon signs Vietnam Peace Agreement (1973) |
| November 1985 | • Totally Revamped<br>• Added section on Federal Invention and Aid, Causes and Locations<br>• Added sections on Civil Disturbances in Civilian Communities and on Department of Defense Installations<br>• Provided chapters on<br>  – Information Planning<br>  – Threat Analysis<br>• Added sections on Funding and Military Resources and Coordination of Civil/Military Efforts<br>• Added sections on<br>  – Weapon positions<br>  – Commands<br>  – Cadence<br>  – Water as a riot control agent<br>• Added chapters on<br>  – Riot batons, offensive and defensive techniques<br>  – Extreme Force Options<br>  – Apprehension and detention operations<br>• Added Glossary of:<br>  – Acronyms and abbreviations<br>  – Related publications, films, circulars, forms, manuals, and training aids | • Body shields<br>• Riot batons<br>• Ring Airfoil System on M16A1<br>• Shotguns<br>• Rifles<br>• Machine guns | • Varied National Guard deployments to assist in:<br>  – Humanitarian relief operations<br>  – Civil disturbances<br>  – Labor disputes<br>  – Prison riots<br>  – Political conventions |

The Department of the Army attempted to fulfill its desire to apply *FM 19-15* to *all* armed forces, whether under federal or state control. It should be noted that the training requirements outlined in Table 8 were the *only* ones imposed by the Department of the Army on all National Guard units, but the Adjutant General of each state assured compliance, *not* the Regular Army. Additionally, as of 1997 no mechanism existed to ensure that Guard units under state control adhered to federal guidelines. A National Guardsman under state control can possess the same authority as a local police officer. The Department of the Army, acting as the Department of Defense's executive agent for civil disturbances, was careful to emphasize after Kent State that *FM 19-15* was the standard operating procedure for any military unit involved in riot duty, but its guidelines could not be enforced until units were federalized.

The Kent State experience, much like the Guard's actions in Detroit in 1967, called into question the lack of legislative oversight for the Guard while its units acted under the auspices of a state governor. Kenneth Pye recognized the need for legislative action at the state level, observing that "the current pattern combines broad powers of governors to use Guardsmen, no clear statement of their powers, no legislative oversight, and limited judicial capacity or inclination to restrain executive action."[55] Pye urged that state legislatures "remove the incentive to use Military forces except as a last resort."[56] The Kent State tragedy traumatized America. Who should bear the nationally embarrassing burden of responsibility for Kent State? Columnist James J. Kilpatrick's all-encompassing rhetorical commentary, although negligent in not affixing any responsibility to the National Guard, very well demonstrates that the students, staff, and faculty of Kent State University were equally remiss and irresponsible. "Who bears the blame for these deaths," Kilpatrick asked?

> Not the Guardsmen, who were the instruments of the state. I suggest that a terrible responsibility lies upon the heads of student revolutionaries who have kindled the wild torches of unreason... upon college

> administrators who failed for years to act on val-
> id student complaints, and then reacted wrongly to
> them... Upon faculty members who abdicated their
> high responsibility to provide examples of maturity
> and restraint... upon the apathetic, nonparticipating
> students who were too timid to stand up for their
> rights.[57]

In September of 1970, the Directorate for Civil Disturbance Planning and Operations, formerly called the Army Task Study Group, was re-designated as the Directorate of Military Support (DOMS). By the end of fiscal year 1971 all active Army, Marine Corps, and Army National Guard units assigned civil disturbance missions (Garden Plot forces) had "conducted initial training programs which included forty hours of unit training and an additional eighteen hours of training for commanders and staffs." Additionally, "each Army service school incorporated into its curricula the appropriate civil control training applicable for that branch of service."[58]

During the last month of fiscal year 1970, the Army Chief of Staff appointed a study group to evaluate the civil disturbance mission through fiscal year 1975. The group produced a report, published in April 1971, which concluded "that the use of Active Federal military forces for the control of civil disturbances was extremely unlikely during that period." The report further noted that "the Army could no longer justify retention of a large number of brigade-sized Garden Plot units or inclusion of Reserve or provisional units in Garden Plot forces."[59] The study group's findings led to the dismantling of the Army's civil disturbance apparatus. The Regular Army's final deployment for potential unrest prior to May of 1992 occurred in May of 1971. On that occasion 10,000 federal troops deployed to Washington, D.C., for crowd control during a nonviolent Vietnam protest march.[60]

The Continental Army Command did not participate in any major civil disturbance operation during fiscal year 1972. This marked the first year that active duty forces had not deployed for riot duty since James Meredith entered the University of Mississippi in 1962.[61] According to an Army report, in August of 1972, "CONARC relieved all Army Reserve units from Garden Plot missions" and significantly "reduced the over-all civil disturbance force structure from 20 Brigades and 18 Task Force Headquarters to 10 Brigades and 9 Task Force Headquarters."[62]

One year later the 27 February 1973 seizure of the village of Wounded Knee, South Dakota, by members of the militant American Indian Movement caused reverberations around the nation. During the two and one-half month stand-off, the Department of the Army provid-ed equipment, advice, and support for the Department of Justice, which spearheaded the Federal Government's efforts. Although military units were not utilized, Army involvement was apparent, seen in the high den-sity of military equipment evident--jeeps, trucks, and a few armored per-sonnel carriers. Historian James Gardner contended that, "In the years since Wounded Knee, a clearer picture of the Army's involvement has emerged, primarily as a result of the litigation of Wounded Knee-related criminal offenses and the surfacing of questions regarding possible vio-lations of the Posse Comitatus statute by the Army."[63]

Wounded Knee presented a tangled web of issues with respect to the Army and the provisions of the Posse Comitatus Act. One of the ex-ceptions to the original act was the provision relating to the enforcement of laws on Indian lands. According to *Farrow's Military Encyclopedia*, "the President may direct a military force of the United States to be em-ployed in the apprehension of such Indians" accused of committing any crime and fleeing into the Indian country.[64]

Absent at Wounded Knee were local and state law enforcement agencies, as well as the National Guard, agencies that have traditional-ly served as buffers between the Army and the populace and helped to maintain the image of the Regular Army as an unaggressive interven-ing force. With no such buffers and significant media coverage of the standoff, the Army focused on steering clear of formal involvement in the conflict. According to James Gardner, a 3 March 1973 memoran-dum from the Department of the Army, Director of Military Support (DOMS) highlighted the Army's concerns. The memo noted that "Army involvement resulting in loss of life and injury would reflect badly upon the Army... every confrontation between the Indians and the federal forces has both national and international coverage. The federal forces should not be the aggressor... The object of the exercise is not to create martyrs."[65]

In an effort to keep troops out of the crisis, the Army emphasized its role in support of local and state law enforcement agencies. The provisions of Posse Comitatus forbid military forces from assisting in the enforcement of civil law, unless specifically authorized by a presidential proclamation of a state of domestic emergency. The larger issue at hand for the Army, however, centered upon the legal distinction between advice and assistance in civil law enforcement. When the Army provided military advisors, who took an active advisory role, without a presidential proclamation at Wounded Knee, it violated the Posse Comitatus Act.

The absence of any state and local law enforcement agency involvement, coupled with the real possibility that the Army might eventually be called upon to end the standoff, caused the military liaison officers to adopt an active advisory role. Army personnel maintained continuous contact with the Federal Bureau of Investigation and U.S. Marshal Service and regularly participated in tactical decisions.

In the aftermath of Wounded Knee, the Army sought judicial clarification of its involvement. The Southwestern Division of the U.S. District Court in Bismarck, North Dakota, ruled that the Army had acted within the congressional intent of the law. The court also concluded that the actions of the Army liaison officers were passive and thus acceptable. In arriving at that conclusion, the court provided a description of specific situations that could be considered as passive actions:

The mere presence of military personnel under orders to report on the necessity for military intervention; preparation of contingency plans to be used if military intervention is ordered; advice or recommendations given to civilian law enforcement officers by military personnel to deliver military material, equipment or supplies, to train local law enforcement officials on the proper use and care of such material or equipment... ; aerial photographic reconnaissance flights and other like activities.[66] The court's decision significantly expanded the criteria for using the military without violating the Posse Comitatus Act. Beginning in the early 1980's, Congress would pass a series of statutes under Title

10 of the U.S. Code that facilitated the use of the military in drug inter-diction missions.[67]

Two months after the stand-off ended at Wounded Knee the Army activated the U.S. Forces Command (FORSCOM) at Fort McPherson, Georgia. FORSCOM replaced the Continental Army Command. In 1975, after a three-year absence from civil disturbance operations, FORSCOM proposed to the Army Chief of Staff that the military elim-inate the requirement to maintain units for Garden Plot deployments. The proposal also requested a reduction in the number of cities covered by Garden Plot contingency plans. In January of 1977 the Department of the Army responded to FORSCOM's 1975 proposal by expunging "the requirement for specific planning for civil disturbance operations in all cities, with the exception of Washington."[68]

Although sixteen years would pass before federal troops were or-dered into Los Angeles in May of 1992, three days after the verdict hand-ed down in the Rodney King beating trial, the National Guard contin-ued to deploy under state control within America's cities. From 1973 to 1991 National Guardsmen responded to over 269 civil disturbances, 75 labor disputes, 18 campus disputes, 26 prison uprisings, 5 political con-ventions, 731 humanitarian relief operations, and more than 6,000 drug interdiction assignments.[69]

Although state governors dispatched the Guard on many deploy-ments, few could be considered major operations, but one significant use of the National Guard occurred in Miami, Florida, in May of 1980. The Florida Guard deployed to quell racial violence following the acquittal of four local police officers accused of murdering a local African-American insurance agent. Like the situation in Los Angeles twelve years later, the venue for the Miami trial was moved to ensure a fair trial for the accused officers. After the officers were acquitted, many of Miami's African-Americans responded with violence. Although the Florida Guard was hailed by some for playing an instrumental role in quelling the distur-bance, the Guard's performance was insignificant at best.

After the turbulent sixties, the Regular Army and the National Guard ushered in the 1970's having shown great promise in handling domestic disturbances in 1968 and 1969. Despite the failure at Kent

State, the Army's domestic civil disturbance plan (Garden Plot) and the civil disturbance doctrine (*FM 19-15*) were sound. Also, Army troops were trained according to the minimum guidelines for civil disturbance training outlined by the Continental Army Command.[70] Yet the Florida National Guard put in a lackluster performance in Miami in 1980. Perhaps the Duke of Edinburgh's statement to the cadets at the Royal Armed Forces Academy best explains what occurred after the civil disturbance apparatus was dismantled. His Royal Highness stated: "There will always be a strong tendency to assume that any future war will start where the last one left off. We should learn our lessons from what went wrong at the beginning of the last war, and not from what went right at the end of it."[71] The same false sense of security helps to explain what happened in Florida.

The 1980 Miami race riot may be more important for what it was not than for what it actually was. Certainly, the uprising that followed the wrongful death trial of Arthur McDuffie led to several days of violence, fifteen fatalities, and significant damage to the city, but there was little positive legacy of the event for the National Guard, the Army, and the nation as a whole. If one examines the lessons of this local tragedy and evaluates the mistakes made by the city of Los Angeles and the California National Guard after the Rodney King trial verdict, it becomes apparent that any lessons learned were as localized as the Miami riot itself. The Los Angeles Police Department and the California National Guard would repeat the same mistakes in 1992 that were made by the Miami Police Department and the Florida National Guard in 1980.

Numerous parallels existed between the situations in Miami and Los Angeles. In 1980 the violent protest in Miami resulted from the not-guilty verdicts for four white Miami police officers accused of beating to death a local African-American man. In Los Angeles, civil unrest followed the not guilty verdict for four white Los Angeles police officers accused of beating African-American motorist, Rodney King. In both situations, there was a change of venue and both juries were without African-American representation. In both cases, after the defendants were acquitted, racial violence ensued and the state governors mobilized the National Guard. In both instances, the location of ammunition-storage facilities some distance from the battalion headquarters slowed the deployments and the deploying Guardsmen required refresher training prior to being sent into the cities. To the Florida National Guardsmen's credit, they captured these significant lessons in their after action report. Los Angeles could have benefited from examining the 1980 Miami experience. Indeed, all National Guard units should have paid closer attention to the Florida after action report.

Authors Bruce Porter and Marvin Dunn describe a confused and untrained Florida Guard in 1980. According to Porter and Dunn, the Florida National Guard had not been involved in a major civil disturbance since the 1968 Republican convention in Miami. Additionally, any edge that the Florida Guard may have gained during the years when annual civil disturbance training was mandated by the Department of the Army certainly was lost by 1980. Miami's domestic disturbance plan had four phases. First, on-duty police officers would be switched from one assignment to another; second, off-duty police officers would be called in; third, outside police agency assistance would be sought; and finally, a request for the governor to send in the National Guard would occur. Within the plan the number of law enforcement personnel on duty would increase in stages, as the situation required. Although it was a sound plan, according to Porter and Dunn, the riot quickly escalated "to such magnitude that the early phases of mobilization made so little difference as to be meaningless."[72]

When the Guard arrived on 17 May, only eight hours after violence erupted, the situation was out of control. The Guard did not reach its peek strength for another three days. Due to 12-hour shifts and the requirement to maintain a reserve, out of the 3,900 Guardsmen deployed to Miami, only 1,500 were available to perform riot duty. The maximum number of Guardsmen on duty at any time was only 750.[73] Local officials had no plans for deploying the Guard upon arrival. Thus, Guardsmen were on hand, but not on the streets. Tactical plans had not been developed to saturate volatile areas of the city. In other words, local officials and police did not make the best use of the more than 3,900 National Guardsmen sent to Miami to assist them.

Basically, Governor Bob Graham had the Guard form a ring around the perimeter of the Miami area known as Liberty City. According to the Florida National Guard after action report, Governor Graham directed that the "Guardsmen perform perimeter security, escort duties with law enforcement and fire department personnel," and man check points.[74] The Guard also protected public buildings and enforced the 8:00 p.m. to 6:00 a.m. curfew.[75] Not surprisingly, a review of the *Miami Herald* and the *Miami Daily News* during the period of 17 May to 1 June 1980 revealed numerous photographs of Guardsmen on duty, but offered little evidence that the Florida National Guard played an integral role in quelling the riot. Perhaps the statement by an anonymous Guardsman, that "they're [local residents] the ones that have contained the unrest--not us [Florida National Guard]," best defined the Guard's role in Miami.[76]

The *Kerner Report* revealed that within each twenty-four-hour period of rioting, generally a lull takes place between 3:00 a.m. and 9:00 a.m., followed by the resumption of rioting.[77] The Florida Guard was not visible when people returned to the streets on 18 May because the governor had ordered the troops to deploy to the perimeter of the riot area. He feared that the poorly trained Guard would make matters worse. Thus, the rioters seized the opportunity to express their hostility again.[78] According to Porter and Dunn, the "Governor instructed that they [the Guard] had to be accompanied by the police officers even on the perimeter." In other words, police were required to "guard the Guards." [79] Troops were used essentially for sentry duty. Although their participation in isolating, containing, and dispersing the rioters was minimal, the Florida Guard was credited with playing a key role in quelling the unrest. In the aftermath of racial violence in Miami, 15 were people were killed, 300 injured, and over 200 million dollars in property damage occurred. *U.S. News and World Report's* assessment reads like the *Kerner Report* of 1968--unemployment amongst blacks in the Miami area was 13.5 percent, amongst black teens it was 32.6 percent.[80]

In retrospect, the Florida Guard was credited with showing restraint and with employing chemical weapons instead of conventional munitions. Not a single civilian injury was directly attributed to the actions of a Florida Guardsman. Although the Guard's performance cannot be described as commendable, the Miami riot, if studied, could have provided the Los Angeles Police Department and the California National Guard with many valuable insights as it prepared for its very similar situation in 1992.

# CHAPTER 5

# DISCERNING THE DIVIDE

*"I welcome you to the city of Angels, where the impossible always happens."* [1]

Mayor Norris Poulson's contention about the city of Los Angeles, California, where the impossible had proven possible time and again was apropos. Despite the city's great ethnic diversity and wealth, the economic policies of President Ronald Reagan's administration and well-publicized instances of police brutality contributed to the volatile atmosphere that led to what *Historic Preservation* called "the worst civil disturbance to hit any American city in this century."[2] Unfortunately for the city and its residents, the initial response by the local police and the California Army National Guard was inadequate to thwart the violence that followed the Rodney King trial verdict. The riot also revealed that the constraints of the Posse Comitatus Act and the lack of training for riot duty had significantly reduced the effectiveness of federal forces.

This chapter examines the origins and background of the 1992 Los Angeles riot and zeroes in on several issues from the 1960's that remained ever-present two and one half decades later:  heavy-handed tactics and unchecked violence by police officers.  Police brutality continued to be the friction point leading to riots within America's urban centers.  Likewise this riot demomstrated that the contraints of the Posse Comitatus Act on employing Federal Forces made their value more psychological than physical.

## Prelude to Violence

The seeds of dissent for a riot in Los Angeles had taken root long before the brutal beating of African-American motorist Rodney Glen King by four Los Angeles police officers in March of 1991. Once hailed as the city of new beginnings, Los Angeles was the first of the great cities in the United States to explode in racial violence during 1965. In August that year, violence erupted in the neighborhood known as Watts, after two white police officers apprehended Marquette Frye, an African-American male suspected of driving while intoxicated. After seven intense days marked by massive arson, looting, and the death of thirty-four people, the violent outbreak ended. All told, 1,300 police and 13,400 National Guardsmen deployed for ten days to restore order. A report to President Lyndon B. Johnson estimated that "10,000 Negroes" participated in the riots out of "650,000 Negroes [who] live[d] in that area, which means that less than 2% of the Negro residents actually rioted."[3]

In the aftermath, Governor Pat Brown appointed a commission headed by former CIA director John A. McCone to examine the underlying causes of the riot. President Lyndon Johnson also appointed a federal commission headed by U.S. Attorney General Ramsey Clark to investigate the causes of the violence. The McCone report attributed the unrest to a lack of jobs, poor educational opportunities, public resentment of the police, a disappointing anti-poverty program, publicity of violence nationally, and the 1964 repeal of the Rumsford Fair Housing Law in California.[4]

A closer examination of Watts revealed the same squalor and substandard living conditions that existed in other major cities plagued by violence during the 1960s. Ramsey Clark's report to the President assessed causal factors and listed vignettes of riot participants and local residents. Clark's report also offered a comprehensive list of solutions that he thought would negate the possibility of future violence within the Watts community. The causal factors of violent unrest in Watts were not difficult to find. One resident argued that, "Watts is Los Angeles' dumping ground. We carry the burden of poverty, crime, vice, the immigration of poor and disadvantaged for the entire city." Another frustrated resident complained, "We can't borrow money, buy homes, or obtain insurance."[5] Clark's report also revealed that "in 1961 in the South Los Angeles area, the overall death rate was about twenty-two percent higher than that for the remainder of the city."[6] Death rates among infants in Watts were 40 percent higher than that of other Los Angeles communities. Watts, like many urban ghettos of the 1960s, was largely Negro (87 percent), had limited sources of employment, and was densely populated with "16,400 people per square mile."[7] Moreover, the median educational attainment for African-Americans stood at only 9.5 years and the unemployment rate of 29 percent was amongst the highest of any American city.[8]

To Daryl Gates, a commander with the Los Angeles Police Department in 1965, the living conditions in Watts were not so bad. In his book *The Chief*, Gates viewed the area through the comparative lens of a Northeastern ghetto. He argued that the single-family dwellings with manicured lawns that were normal in Watts indicated a pretty good life, especially when compared with the concrete and overcrowded slums of Detroit or Washington, D.C. Unfortunately, Gates' myopic view lacked an understanding of the long-repressed emotions that had built up in Watts.[9]

As an anonymous Watts citizen observed, "A lot of us are beginning to feel that riots are all they understand. This is the only way to talk to downtown."[10] This statement not only reflected the attitude of many Watts residents, but also appeared accurate. Following the riots in 1965, the federal government responded to the city of Los Angeles with several programs for economic renewal. Millions of dollars were channeled into the area by government agencies and private corporations. Major companies such as Goodyear, Max Factor, Firestone, and Bethlehem Steel opened plants in the city and offered jobs and a piece of the American dream to many Angelenos. However, according to *U.S. News & World Report*, many of the major companies that came to Southern California in the mid-sixties had ceased operations in the area by 1991, causing "Los Angeles to face its worst recession since World War II, with the loss of nearly 200,000 jobs in 1991 alone."[11] Moreover, defense-industry budget reductions and a decline in both the construction and finance industries exacerbated an already troubled situation.

A major finding in the McCone Commission report was the existence of "a deep and longstanding schism between a substantial portion of the Negro community and the [L.A.] police department." The report noted that "Police brutality is a recurring charge."[12] The confrontational relationship between the police and the city's African-American populace had begun long before the 1965 riot. In the 1950s, under the

watchful eye of Chief William Parker, the department focused on elim-
inating internal corruption and turned away from the national norm
of community policing. Parker structured the LAPD as a highly professional, paramilitary, and corruption-free force. Detective Joe Friday
and the television series "Dragnet" helped to promote the department's
tough but professional crime-fighting image.[13]

During the second half of the twentieth century, according to the
official post-mortem on the 1992 Los Angeles Riot, *The City in Crisis*,
two struggles existed within the Los Angeles Police Department: one
the fight against corruption, and the other seen in the tensions between
police and the local populace. Each new police chief entered his role as
the city's "top cop" with a mandate to undo, modify, or improve upon
the foundation laid by his predecessor. Chief Parker died of a heart attack in 1966, replaced by Tom Reddin. Supported by the findings of the
McCone Commission, Reddin entered the job with a mandate to change
the focus of policing from crime fighting to crime prevention, and he
sought to depart from the insularity of the paramilitary model and return to a model of community policing.[14] Reddin remained in the job for
only two years, replaced by Ed Davis in 1968.[15]

In an attempt to bring the public and the police together, Davis
embraced community-based policing. According to Jesse Brewer, former Assistant Chief of Police and President of the Los Angeles Police
Commission, "the philosophy behind community-based policing was
to assign police officers to one geographic area in the city where they
would develop a relationship with the people that they served. Officers
would meet with their assigned community leaders once a month."[16]
Community relations officers served as liaisons between the police and
neighborhood organizations. Senior lead officers monitored conditions
within assigned areas, joining community watch groups and conducting
crime prevention meetings with local residents.

The concept of team policing decentralized authority and created
smaller autonomous policing units. The overall focus of Davis' efforts
was the return of the "cop on the beat," someone who was both a friend
and a fixture within the community. Daryl Gates served as Davis' assistant chief, and according to Bernard Parks, Deputy Chief of Police, for

the city of Los Angeles "Daryl Gates implemented team policing and community based policing for Ed Davis."[17]

In 1978 Gates became the city's "top cop," and under his leadership the department reverted to Parker's paramilitary model of policing.[18] The new chief took pride in having a department that was assertive, tough, and professional. He advocated a model of policing in which aggressive crime- fighting was the principal focus. To Gates' credit, he shaped a well-disciplined, highly trained, and technically advanced force, one that favored specialized units over the concept of the traditional cop on the beat. As Figure 6 depicts, the chief also developed a force that looked very much like the local community, but despite the outward appearance that the force resembled Los Angeles' ethnic divisions of society, Gates' paramilitary philosophy isolated the department from the community that it was obligated to protect and serve.[19]

*Figure 6: Demographics of the LAPD Versus the City of Los Angeles*

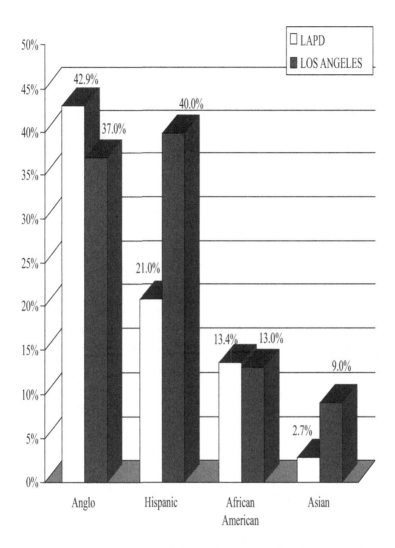

Source: Data extracted from the Report by the Special Advisor to the Board of Police Commissioners on the Civil Disorder in Los Angeles. *The City in Crisis.* (Los Angeles: Office of the Special Advisor to the Board of Police Commissioners City of Los Angeles, 1992).

Gates had joined the Los Angeles Police Department in 1950 and served initially as Chief Parker's driver. He absolutely idolized Parker, save for Parker's penchant for heavy drinking. Gates became Parker's protégé, and according to Gates, Parker nurtured his growth as an officer in those early days. Gates asserted that, "my unofficial lessons began each morning as he [Parker] slid into the front seat."[20] During this tutelage Gates began to comprehend the special bond that united police officers, and he later claimed that "misunderstood [by society], the police banded together and like a true minority, developed instinctively a minority's mentality: Us Against Them."[21] This mentality would evolve into a destructive and counter-productive system of loyalty and allegiance within the LAPD. It fostered a "code of silence" among police officers in which the chief would give his unwavering support to his subordinates--good and bad.

Numerous well-publicized instances of strong-armed tactics by the LAPD helped to reinforce the "Us against Them" mentality within Los Angeles. One such highly publicized incident occurred in 1979--the shooting death of Eula Love, a thirty-nine-year-old African-American woman. During this incident two police officers shot the irate, knife-wielding woman eight times. Deputy Chief of Police, Bernard Parks called the episode a "defining moment that led to standardization of procedures on how the department used deadly force."[22] Chief Gates, much to the chagrin of the media and local minority community, "found the shootings to be in line with department policy."[23] Gates' decision not to punish the officers only reinforced the animus that had long existed between the police department and the city's African-American community.

Other well-publicized episodes of police brutality against African-Americans in Los Angeles further strained the long standing adversarial relationship. One such incident was the death of Long Beach State football star Ron Settles. Settles died while in the custody of the LAPD's Foothill Division after being arrested on a traffic violation.[24] In June of 1982, Chief Gates was reprimanded for allegedly saying that, "When the chokehold is applied to African-Americans the veins or arteries do not open up as fast as they do in normal people."[25] Gates' response was undoubtedly an attempt to offset criticism that the department received for inflicting sixteen African- American fatalities during the 1970's by employing the carotid chokehold.[26] Other examples of overwhelming and inappropriate force used by the LAPD included the 1988 deployment to curb gang violence and a 1990 confrontation with striking janitors. In April of 1988, the police department sent over a thousand extra-duty patrolmen, elite tactical squads, and its special anti- gang task force into South Central Los Angeles. This extraordinary force arrested over 1,400 African-American youths. In the months that followed the operation, according to the Webster Commission's Report, "88 LAPD officers wielding shotguns and sledgehammers engaged in a drug raid on four apartments… which caused extensive property damage and yielded only two minor drug arrests."[27] In June of 1990 a confrontation with more than 400 striking janitors resulted in the arrest of more than 40 demonstrators, and injury to sixteen.

The videotaped beating of Rodney King in March 1991 served as the *coup de grace* to the abusive tactics of officers within the city's police department. The video taken by a local resident, George Holliday, served a dual purpose. First, it was the catalyst for the appointment of an independent commission to review the Los Angeles Police Department. This commission was headed by Warren Christopher, the former Assistant U.S. Attorney General in President Johnson's administration, and subsequently U.S. Secretary of State under President Bill Clinton. Second, the video created the popular expectation that the officers of the Los Angeles Police Department would finally be held accountable for their actions. The beating of Rodney King brought demands for the resignation of Daryl Gates from Mayor Tom Bradley and other city officials, as well as from numerous local and national civil rights leaders.

The findings of the Christopher Commission proved conclusively that the physical abuse imposed on Rodney King was not an anomaly, but an example of a much larger problem. The report revealed that the "Us against Them" siege mentality among police was pervasive and reinforced by the leadership of the department. For example, between 1986 and 1990 there were 8,274 public complaints against police officers. Of these complaints 3,419, or 23.7 percent, were complaints regarding police brutality.(See Figure 7)

*Figure 7: Types of Allegations in Complaints by the Public Against LAPD Officers, as Classified by the LAPD*

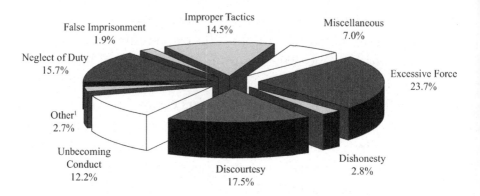

Source: LAPD Complaint Database. There were 8,274 total complaints against the LAPD from January 1986 through December 1990. Complaints listed as "Other" included: Unlawful Search (1.43%), SexualMisconduct (.34%), Use of Narcotics (.31%), Discrimination (.24%), Improper Relations (.15%), Insubordination (.11%), Alcohol (.07%), Firearm Discharge (.01%)

Yet, of the 3,419 complaints that were lodged against the LAPD, only 102 or 3 percent were sustained. (See Figure 8) An even more alarming finding was the fact that police officers were more likely to be punished for conduct that embarrassed the department (drug use or theft) than for conduct reflecting improper treatment of citizens.

*Figure 8: Disposition of Allegations of Excessive Force or Improper Tactics*

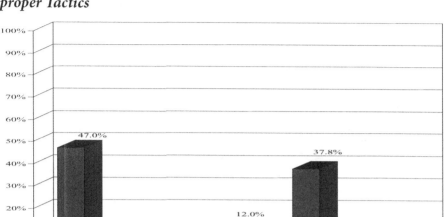

Source: LAPD Complaint Database. There were a total of 3,419 allegations of excessive force or improper tactics from January 1986 through December 1990.

## The Verdict: Los Angeles Erupts in Violence

By 29 April 1992, at approximately 3:00 p.m. Pacific Time the lines were drawn, when the twelve jurors (ten Caucasian, one Hispanic, and one Asian) returned to the jury box in the Simi Valley, California, court room. The jury would either support the accused officers' contention that the Rodney King apprehension was "careful police work," or they would render the seemingly clear-cut guilty verdict.[28] The 81 seconds of explicit videotape appeared to be proof positive that the police used excessive force to apprehend Rodney King.

The time that the verdict was announced was almost as important as the verdict itself. The normal shift change within the police department occurred at 3:00 p.m. Pacific time, but the department's leadership did <u>not</u> hold over all or part of the day shift. They could have doubled the department's available manpower, which would have greatly enhanced its ability to thwart potential violence. To Mayor Bradley, "it was an air of invincibility and professional arrogance that led Chief Gates to allow the day shift to depart at that critical juncture."[29] According to Chief Gates, "the city council had denied his pre- verdict request for payment of overtime for police officers." The chief argued that "the council was concerned that a significant show of force by the LAPD might be interpreted by the local populace as provocation for a violent confrontation."[30]

At approximately 3:07 p.m. all eyes focused on the jury foreman as he prepared to announce the verdict on the various charges. Perhaps South Central Los Angeles Congresswoman Maxine Waters described it best when she said, "my heart sank when I heard the staccato notes of 'not guilty' again and again on count after count for one defendant after another."[31] Even President George Bush observed, "Viewed from outside the trial, it was hard to understand how the verdict could possibly square with the video." The President further noted that "civil rights leaders . . . were stunned and so was I . . . and Barbara and so were my kids."[32] *Los Angeles Times* reporter Robert Connot placed the violent reaction to the verdict in perspective when he asserted that "just as the Watts riot was a symptom of a social malaise in the United States, so the 1992 riot is a manifestation that the disease, while it has undergone major mutations, remains unchecked. Its name: Alienation."[33]

The reaction to the verdicts across the country quickly changed from one of shock and disbelief to one of dismay, anger, and rage. Violence followed the Rodney King verdict in eleven states and thirteen cities across the United States. (See Figure 9) In the city of Los Angeles the initial reaction of shock was subsumed by rage and violence within an hour of the verdict. Crowds assembled in South Central Los Angeles and at Parker Center (Police Headquarters) to protest the verdict. The first incident of looting occurred at the intersection of Florence and Normandie streets at 4:15 p.m.-- one hour and five minutes after the jury acquitted the four officers. According to *The City in Crisis*, (hereinafter the <u>Webster Report</u>), "events at this intersection reached their peak at approximately 6:45 p.m., when cameras captured live several young African-American males dragging Reginald Denny, a passing motorist, from his truck and beating him close to death."[34]

*Figure 9: National Violence After the Rodney King Trial Verdict*

Source: "Violence in Other Cities," Los Angeles Times, 2 May 1992, A5.

Concurrent with the beating of Denny, the violence spread to other parts of the city. As pandemonium prevailed, the same euphoric, carnival-like atmosphere that existed in Washington in 1968, occurred in South Central Los Angeles. Protesters attacked firefighters responding to calls, and one firefighter was hospitalized early in the evening after being shot while on duty. As late as 7:00 p.m. outbreaks of violence were largely confined to one area--along 77th Street Southwest, but within the next hour fires and violence began to spread. The first riot-related fatality, the shooting death of eighteen-year-old Louis Watson, occurred at approximately 8:15 p.m.[35]

Allen Grimshaw's concept of "undercontrol," may best explain the quick escalation of violence during the initial stages of the riot. Grimshaw contended that a correlation exists between a lack of physical presence by law enforcement personnel and outward expressions of hostility by dissidents. He asserted that antagonists view a lack of police action and presence as an invitation to act out long-suppressed feelings. The LAPD initially responded to violence by removing officers from the streets. If the department's intent was to avoid potential provocation of local citizens, their actions had the opposite effect, for the LAPD's withdrawal from the riot area led to increased violence, which necessitated the mobilization of the California Army National Guard (CAANG) and eventually the deployment of federal forces.

The CAANG was not prepared to respond immediately to Governor Pete Wilson's request to quell the Los Angeles riot. The Guard had asked the California Office of Emergency Services (OES) twelve days before the trial verdict if it would be needed if the four defendants were acquitted. According to Mayor Bradley, Chief Gates believed that "the LAPD could respond to any eventuality that might evolve if the accused police officers were acquitted."[33] Thus, the Guard was assured that its physical presence would not be necessary in Los Angeles. OES, however, instructed the Guard to "be prepared to airlift mutual aid police officers and equipment to the area of operation" and "transfer civil disturbance equipment assigned to the CAANG when required."[36]

The Guard informed the Air Guard of its airlift mission and began lending its organic riot equipment, such as body armor, body and face shields, to state and local law enforcement agencies. When placed on alert by the governor, the California National Guard had to borrow riot gear from the Wyoming and Arizona National Guard to replace equipment loaned to local law enforcement agencies. Thus, when the Guard was alerted for immediate mobilization and deployment to Los Angeles it was not equipped to perform riot duty.

Assessing blame for this mistake is difficult. Certainly, the Guard was correct in responding positively to the OES request for transferring vital equipment to local law enforcement personnel. Moreover, Guard officials had anticipated the possibility of mobilization and sought clarification of their role if the accused police officers were acquitted, only to be reassured that local law enforcement personnel were sufficient to handle any eventuality. Therefore, the office of Emergency Services must bear the greatest responsibility for the problems, but regardless of the circumstances, the Guard can never be excused from its constitutional requirement to respond to a state governor's request to restore order. Although extenuating circumstances existed, the California National Guard remains ultimately responsible for its failure in 1992.

A major criticism leveled against the Guard focused on the time it took to deploy its forces throughout the city. To this charge representatives of the Guard compared its 1992 mobilization to their response in 1965. During the Watts riot, the unit was already assembled and undergoing annual training when it was ordered to deploy over 13,000 troops within thirty-six hours. In 1992, a dispersed CAANG was criticized for not having troops on the streets of Los Angeles within twelve hours, drawing the response from the deputy adjutant general of the California Guard, Brigadier General Daniel Brennan, that "You don't normally call up a military unit and have them deployed and ready to go in 24 hours. They wanted us in 12. The expectations were a little unrealistic. But you can understand the need, with buildings burning and people being killed."[37]

The commander of Joint Task Force Los Angeles, Lieutenant General Marvin Covault, echoed Brennan's sentiments, arguing: "the California National Guard is not a rapid reaction force. They should not have been criticized for the rapidity of their deployment."[38] Major General Daniel Hernandez, the commander of the 40th Infantry Division California National Guard, agreed with Covault's contention; saying "the criticism of the Guard was not well founded." According to Hernandez "the Mutual Aid Agreement specified that the Guard is expected to take 24 to 72 hours to deploy."[39] When a frustrated Mayor Bradley realized during the first 48 hours of rioting that the window of opportunity to quell the riot with local and state assets had passed, he asked Governor Wilson to request federal troop assistance from President Bush.

Unlike the 1965 riots, which were confined to the Watts area, the 1992 riot spread "over a 32-square-mile area from Hollywood Hills to Long Beach."[40] The numerous flash points and the distances between them created a logistical and communications nightmare for deployed troops. As the riot erupted in South Central Los Angeles, LAPD supervisors had made a series of critical mistakes. Not only had the police leadership failed to anticipate the outrage spawned by the not guilty verdicts, but they also proved unable to stop the looting crowds. The situation was further exacerbated by an absence of leadership within the department. At a critical time, Chief Gates was attending a social engagement, although he later argued that his physical presence at Parker Center "was not necessary." He contended instead that the impotence of the department was "based largely on key subordinates posturing for his job." According to Gates, senior leaders within the LAPD recognized that he--as a lame-duck chief-- would be the scapegoat, and thus they chose not to act decisively during the crisis.[41]

In the field, police lieutenant Michael Moulin, of the 77th Street Precinct, ordered the removal of his outnumbered officers from the Normandie and Vermont area, but as happened in 1965, the absence of a physical police presence may have led rioters to conclude that law enforcement officials would not intervene in their actions. A lawless free-for-all that left fifty-nine people dead and more than $785 million in property damages followed Moulin's fateful decision, with the preponderance of destruction occurring in the poorest sections of town.[42] (see Figure 10)

When Mayor Bradley realized that local law enforcement agencies required assistance, he requested National Guard troops from Governor Wilson at 9:00 p.m. on 29 April. The governor ordered the mobilization of more than 2,000 soldiers from the California National Guard after 9:45 p.m. At midnight the CAANG began mustering elements of the 40th Infantry Division (Mechanized) and 49th Military Police Brigade for duty in Los Angeles.[43] The first unit to arrive, the 40th Military Police Company based in Sacramento, deployed at 1:45 p.m. on Thursday, 30 April in the Lakewood section of Los Angeles. However, major problems continued to paralyze the deployment of the majority of Guard units.

Governor Wilson directed retired Army General William H. Harrison to review the CAANG's performance. The general was very critical of the Guard, arguing that, "the California National Guard bungled its initial deployment of 2,000 troops to Los Angeles because of a series of errors that could have been avoided." Harrison believed that Guardsmen should have been ready to disperse throughout the city before dawn the day after the verdicts, thus curtailing a significant amount of the violence and looting which occurred on 30 April. The general also noted that Guardsmen deployed to Los Angeles without "bullets, batons, protective shields, or the training required to fulfill their mission." He concluded "there were failures, absolute failures on the part of the Guard."[44] To make matters worse, once Guardsmen arrived in Los Angeles, they needed to conduct riot refresher training prior to their deployment throughout the city.[45] Neither General Harris nor critical newspaper accounts alluded to the fact that the state operated OEShad helped create the conditions for the Guard's failure before their efforts to quell the riots had ever begun.

*Figure 10: Map of the Riot Area*

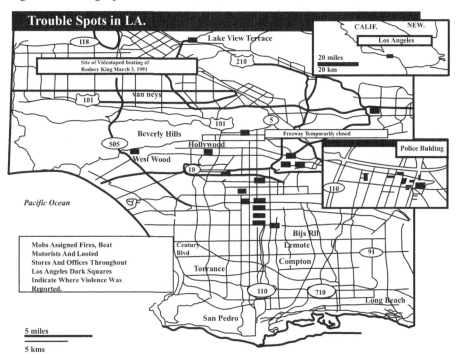

Source: *The Stars and Stripes* (European Edition) 1 May 1992, p.2.

The Guard suffered other sorts of delays as well. Virtually all of the troops initially activated were at their armories ready to go by 8:00 a.m. Thursday, but Governor Wilson argued that "police commanders apparently were slow to decide how to best use the troops." Wilson also cited delays while "guardsmen obtained necessary equipment, including ammunition."[46] Upon their arrival in Los Angeles, conflicts immediately arose over when and how they would be used. National Guard officers reported to the Los Angeles Sheriff's Office Incident Center to receive tasks from the OES, but confusion quickly arose over the types of missions the Guard would perform. Various officials within the police department, sheriff's department, and the California Office of Emergency Services gave 40th Infantry Division leaders contradictory information. Some officials told Guard officers that the 40th would be used immediately, while others informed the Guard's leadership that their units would not be needed until the next evening.

Believing that they would not be deployed until the next day, Guard commanders did not schedule ammunition airlifts from the consolidated ammunition holding facility at Camp Roberts in Paso Robles until 6:30 a.m. on 30 April. Camp Roberts was a poor choice for an emergency operation facility, located too far from major population centers to allow for the rapid distribution of ammunition. It also lacked any outdoor lighting, which prevented the loading of ammunition on the night of 29 April. Ten unit armorers also faced the daunting task of installing restricting plates on 2,000 M16A1 rifles. Commonly referred to as "lock plates," the gadgets modified the weapon to allow only semiautomatic fire. Brigadier General Daniel Brennan admitted that the Guard's response was also slowed by the state adjutant, Major General Robert Thrasher, who was reluctant to order troops not fully equipped or with full automatic weapons onto the streets.[47]

Additionally, the police were slow to task the Guard with assignments. As late as 11:00 p.m. on 29 April, Chief Gates still resisted Bradley and Wilson's decision to call-up the Guard, arguing that the LAPD could handle the situation.[48] Local police and sheriff's deputies were also confused and hesitant about how to employ the Guard. This indecision resulted in Guardsmen sitting around for hours waiting for tasks. Despite having over 1,000 troops prepared for duty by the late morning on 30 April, the Guard had no missions assigned until late that afternoon. At that time Guardsmen began taking positions at various flash points such as the area around the Los Angeles Memorial Coliseum, Koreatown, South-Central Los Angeles, and Watts.

Poor communications between civilian law enforcement officials and the National Guard created further confusion and also hindered the Guard's performance. While the CAANG believed the request was to have 2,000 troops in staging areas within eighteen hours of the initial mobilization, LAPD and LASO commanders assumed that this would also mean that the 2,000 troops would be available immediately for duty throughout the city, which was not the case.[49] The CAANG attributed this problem to the fact that the OES did not specify a time the Guard was expected to begin their operations in Los Angeles.[50] Although the first Guard units were employed in riot duty by 1:45 p.m. on 30 April, the full complement of 2,000 troops was not available for duty until twenty-nine hours after the initial call-up. A lack of equipment was the main reason for the slow deployment of the Guard. The 670th Military Police Company was available for commitment after the Los Angeles Police Academy supplied them with ammunition, but no other law enforcement officials assisted the Guard in this way.[51]

While the California Guard met most of its time schedules, civilian authorities were still dissatisfied with the Guard's slow response time. By Friday, 1 May, Governor Wilson and Mayor Bradley concluded that the Guard and local law enforcement agencies were incapable of handling the situation. Oddly, one source feeding Wilson's irritation with the CAANG was Chief Gates, who claimed that while Guardsmen may have been positioned in holding areas, they were not properly equipped to go onto the streets. In fact, at the time many units were already assisting law enforcement officials, while others were available and awaiting missions.

While the CAANG did not deploy 2,000 troops onto the streets within eighteen hours, by that point all troops were in forward staging areas, awaiting ammunition and instructions from local authorities. Many of the troops that were adequately supplied lacked any mission from local law enforcement as the absence of a mutual integration plan slowed the Guard's participation, and once troops deployed, they failed to slow the looters.[52] Desperate to regain control of Los Angeles, Mayor Bradley asked Governor Wilson to seek the assistance of federal troops at 6:00 a.m. on 1 May. After exhausting state and local resources, Wilson and Bradley, at the urging of former Assistant U.S. Attorney General

Warren Christopher, requested federal troops from President Bush. On the evening of 1 May, Bradley ordered a dusk-to-dawn curfew. However, the curfew did little to deter the vigor of the looters. Despite an increase in personnel strength to over 6,000 National Guard troops ready or almost ready for riot duty, a curfew, and a waning of enthusiasm on the rioters' part, Wilson and Bradley still wanted federal troops. Their deployment marked the first time in almost twenty years that a federal force was utilized for riot duty.

### The Creation of Joint Task Force Los Angeles (JTF LA)

The federal government had the advantage of time to prepare and plan for its role. At 3:00 a.m. on 1 May the 7th Infantry Division, located at Fort Ord, California, was alerted by Forces Command (FORSCOM) for a possible deployment to Los Angeles. At 6:30 a.m. the 1st Marine Expeditionary Force was alerted for deployment. Presidential spokesman Marlin Fitzwater announced at 10:30 a.m. on 1 May that the President had ordered federal troops to Los Angeles in case local authorities requested their assistance. He noted that 1,000 federal law enforcement officers from the FBI, the Border Patrol, the Bureau of Alcohol, Tobacco, and Firearms, the U.S. Marshal Service, the U.S. Park Police, and the Bureau of Prisons were also being sent to Los Angeles.[53]

A total of 1,838 troops from 7th Infantry Division's 2nd Regiment departed via air transport from Fort Ord at 4:30 p.m. on 1 May en route to the Marine Air Station in El Toro, California. Upon arrival, the contingent moved directly to a staging area at the Los Alamitos Armed Forces Reserve Center. All 7th Division soldiers had arrived in Los Angeles by 2:30 a.m. on 2 May. Concurrent with the Army's alert and mobilization, a force of 1,500 Marines convoyed from Camp Pendleton near San Diego, California, to their staging area at Tustin Marine Corps Air Station on 1 May. The contingent arrived at the staging area by 7:00 p.m. on 1 May.

President Bush issued Executive Order Number 6427 on 1 May at 8:45 p.m., Eastern Standard Time, activating federal troops for duty in Los Angeles and creating Joint Task Force Los Angeles.[54] All California

National Guard troops mobilized for the riots were ordered into federal service at 9:00 p.m. At 11:30 p.m. elements of the 7th Infantry Division and 1st Marine Headquarters units established Joint Task Force Los Angeles Headquarters. The major task of JTF LA was to "assume responsibility from the 40th CAANG Division for controlling civil disturbance operations. This entail[ed] repositioning forces in accordance with new boundaries established by the JTF Commander and integrating elements of the 7th Infantry Division (Light) and 1st Marine Expeditionary Force into the operation."[55] As figure 11 shows, the California National Guard's 40th Infantry Division maintained responsibility for over 75 percent of the riot area.

*Figure 11: Zones for Forces in Los Angeles*

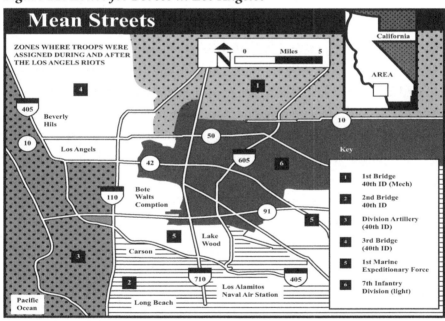

Source: "Mean Streets," *Army Times* 47 (18 May 1992), 15.

The JTF commander, Major General Marvin Covault, the commanding general of 7th Division, appointed the commander of the CAANG, Major General Daniel Hernandez, as the commander of

Army Forces (ARFOR) and likewise appointed Marine Corps Brigadier General Marvin Hopgood commander of Marine Forces (MARFOR). The first JTF LA mission was processed at midnight on 2 May.[56]

The appointment of General Hernandez as the ARFOR commander was a significant event in the history of federal intervention in civil disturbances. His appointment marked the first time that a Regular Army force was under the control of the National Guard. To General Hernandez, "the appointment made a powerful and positive statement for the California Guard. The appointment was indicative of the trust and confidence that General Covault had in the Guard's ability to handle the situation at hand."[57]

Government officials at all levels spent 1 May preparing for the mobilization of units comprising the joint task force. Department of Defense and Department of Justice personnel began the intricate process of employing federal troops in a domestic disturbance under the auspices of the "Garden Plot" contingency plan. First developed in 1968, Garden Plot was a response to the frequent call-ups the active component experienced during the late 1960s. The contingency plan established the stages of alert, procedures involved in mobilizing federal troops and their responsibilities once deployed. The Department of Defense designated the Secretary of the Army as its executive agent for planning and employing federal troops in domestic civil disturbances. Once the President and Attorney General decided to use troops, the Army became responsible for selecting the appropriate troops and the commanding general of the task force.

The chain of command for the federal intervention in Los Angeles was essentially the structure established during the late 1960s. The President, as the Commander-in-Chief of the armed forces, topped the wiring diagram, with the Secretary of Defense serving directly under the chief executive. As in the 1960s, the Secretary of the Army continued to perform duties as the DOD executive agent during riot control operations. A major difference in the hierarchical structure was the utilization of the Commander-in-Chief of Forces Command (CINCFOR) versus the Army Chief of Staff as the direct superior of the JTF commander. Additionally, the Department of Justice representative, known as the

"Senior Civilian Representative of the Attorney General" (SCRAG), co-ordinated the federal effort with state and local authorities. The SCRAG also doubled as the President's and Attorney General's representative in Los Angeles.

Under the 1992 force structure for riot duty, proximity and response capability were the primary determinants that decided which federal units would deploy to the riot area. In 1968 when Garden Plot was first developed, specific units where earmarked for a predetermined city-- proximity was not always a primary factor. JTF LA utilized the 7th Division and elements of the 1st Marine Expeditionary Force because they were stationed in California.[58] According to General Covault, "the Marines volunteered to head the JTF in Los Angeles, however, the role was given to the Army."[59] Once the decision was made that the 7th ID would be the primary Army unit deployed, General Covault assumed duties as the Joint Task Force commander. To the Army's good fortune, General Covault, as one of the original architects of the rapid response light infantry concept, and therefore was an appropriate choice for the job.[60] During the late 1960s the JTF would have normally been headed by a lieutenant general.

A "total force" concept was instituted and JTF LA liaisons were assigned to the Army and Marine staffs, the Department of Justice Senior Civilian Representative of the Attorney General, the police, and the sheriff's department. The Joint Task Force also received liaisons from the police, the sheriff's department, the FBI, and the Los Angeles Fire Department. The SCRAG was supposed to be one of the most important civilian relationships that the JTF LA developed. Garden Plot designated the SCRAG to be the JTF's primary liaison with law enforcement commanders, but that was not the case in Los Angeles.[61] FBI agent Buck Revelle served as the SCRAG for JTF LA, but according to General Covault "his lack of experience precluded him from receiving mission taskings from law enforcement agencies, prioritizing them, and then passing them on to the JTF J3 (operations officer)."[62] Conceptually, the JTF LA and other federal agencies should have responded to the missions as set forth by the SCRAG,[63] but General Covault noted that

"Revelle allowed the experts [senior military leaders] to conduct these functions."[64]

In Los Angeles federal troops performed three missions: protecting specific sites, maintaining an area after a police action, and supporting firefighters. The JTF LA J3 (operations section) evaluated the missions and then passed them to ARFOR and MARFOR headquarters units to task out to subordinate units. Subordinate brigade-sized units' boundaries were designed to replicate civilian boundaries to facilitate close coordination between civilian law enforcement agencies and the military.[65]

The process of command and control changed significantly as the federalized force assumed control. If procedures seemed slow when the National Guard was under state control, they became even more sluggish and bureaucratic after federalization. The Forces Command and Sixth Army After Action Report (AAR) outlined many of the complexities inherent in the federalization of a state force. Chief amongst these challenges were the restrictions imposed by the Posse Comitatus Act. The AAR stated that the JTF LA commander spent an inordinate amount of time educating civilian police and political leaders on the legal limitations of employing federal forces in civil disturbance operations. General Covault stated that "civilian authorities asked military forces to assume missions that were clearly in the realm of [local or state] law enforcement."[66] To offset this problem, according to the AAR, the JTF created screening criteria for accepting a mission from local officials. This screening "for appropriateness by the JTF, often took as long as three hours." Even more critical was the fact that the "response by Army and Marine Forces could take up to 12 hours."[67] State and local authorities, when considering the fluidity and volatility of a riot environment, would undoubtedly find the twelve-hour response time unsatisfactory.

Moving the federal troops from their home station to the Los Angeles area was a relatively smooth process. Regular Army troops and active component Marines arrived without incident. However, they did not deploy onto the streets of Los Angeles for 72 hours after their arrival. According to *Army Times* reporter Greg Seigle, "active duty soldiers, who get no riot-control training, had to take a three-day crash course..."[68] A 72-hour refresher course during a riot is clearly unacceptable, although

140

it is significant that fifty of the fifty-nine fatalities occurred before the federalized force deployed throughout the city of Los Angeles on 4 May 1992. Eighteen of these fatalities occurred while Army troops underwent refresher training. What Los Angeles needed were troops capable of executing riot control duty immediately upon arrival. The volatility of a riot allows little time for on-the-spot training.

Federal troops could not avoid being affected by the violence they witnessed within the city. In their mission to assist local law enforcement agencies in restoring order, military personnel suffered casualties. On 2 May, three soldiers were injured in a traffic accident when a civilian ran a stop light and hit their military vehicle. A fourth soldier was wounded when his .45 caliber pistol discharged as he re-holstered the weapon. All four soldiers were treated at civilian hospitals and released.

Federal troops also became involved in several violent confrontations that produced civilian casualties, including the first U.S. civilian killed by a soldier or Guardsman during riot control duty since the 1970 incident at Kent State University. The initial confrontation occurred at 10:30 a.m. on 3 May. After a two-car accident, Guardsmen fired five shots at a man who had fired upon them while fleeing from a crime scene. The LAPD arrested the man without any casualties. At 7:00 p.m. Marines from the 1st Light Armored Infantry Battalion were fired upon from a moving vehicle but sustained no wounds. At 7:50 p.m. a civilian attempted to drive through a barricade manned by members of the National Guard. The driver, Victor Rivas, twice attempted to run down the Guardsmen manning the barricade without success. On the third attempt, two Guardsmen fired fourteen rounds at the car striking Rivas twice in the head. He was pronounced dead later that night at the hospital. Investigations by the CAANG and LAPD found that the Guardsmen had acted appropriately.[69]

The final incident occurred on 3 May when Marines accompanied Compton police officers and LASO deputies called to a residence to investigate a domestic squabble. The two police officers were injured when one of the occupants of the residence fired several shotgun blasts through the door. According to an Intelligence Summary, the "Marines laid down a base of fire [53 rounds] and pulled the officers to safety."[70]

141

Why were the Marines enforcing the law in what seemed to be a clear violation of Posse Comitatus? First and foremost, the Marines were not subject to the provisions of Posse Comitatus. At the time only the Army and the Air Force were constrained by the statute. Perhaps a better question is why the Marines accompanied the two police officers. Unfortunately, these questions were neither posed nor answered in the after action reports. Major General James Delk, the commander of troops for the California National Guard, asserted during an interview, "that they did what they've been trained to do."[71] General Hopgood, the MARFOR commander, likewise contended that for a Marine hearing the phrase "'cover me' meant "laying down a base of suppressive fire."[72] In other words, they acted in accordance with their training, although General Covault attributed the Marines' actions to what he called "the Beirut Syndrome,"[73] a reference to the passive action by Marines during the terrorist bombing of the U.S. Embassy in Beirut, Lebanon. Quite likely, given the same conditions, an Army soldier would have responded in a similar manner.

Other incidents occurred on 5 May, the first shortly after midnight when two shots were fired at a CAANG patrol. No one in the patrol was injured, and the suspect was able to flee the scene. Much later, at 9:55 p.m. Guardsmen fired at a suspect after witnessing him run down an LAPD officer with his automobile. The suspect was hit in the buttocks by one of the two shots fired and was arrested when he attempted to get away on foot after abandoning his car. Later that evening several shots were fired at a 7th Division patrol in downtown Los Angeles. The infantrymen did not return fire and the suspect was detained by LAPD officers. By the 6th of May the JTF Chief of Staff, Colonel John Ryneska, determined that the need for federal troops no longer existed. In his daily situation report, Ryneska lamented that his troops were "being further drawn into the law enforcement/security role… At a time when we should be weaning the public away from our resources, mission requirements are going off the chart." The colonel concluded that "law enforcement officials at every level encourage and support increased military involvement," and several issues arose that kept federal troops in place longer than seemed necessary.[74] Realizing that the military was seen as "a free security force,"

Colonel Ryneska's main concern was that local officials, and fearful Los Angeles residents, were becoming too comfortable with the military's assistance. From 4 May forward Ryneska's primary goal was to decrease federal troop involvement in street missions and to pull them back to staging areas to begin moving them out of Los Angeles.[75]

Slowing down the defederalization process were the constant disagreements among local officials. Ryneska saw Governor Wilson's criticism of the CAANG leadership for its slow deployment of National Guard forces; and Sheriff Bloch's criticism of the LAPD's response "as making 'no sense.'"[76] Their lack of trust led civilian officials to depend on the only neutral entity assisting with the riots, the active duty Marines and soldiers. Interagency squabbling in the local media also played a role in keeping the federal force on the job. Mayor Bradley, Governor Wilson, Chief Gates, Sheriff Bloch, and many of their key subordinates used the press to air their complaints. On 7 May Governor Wilson agreed to release the 7th Division and the 1st Marine Expeditionary Force, only after the Secretary of Defense had already ordered them to their home stations by Friday, 9 May. The 40th Division was returned to state control, ready to respond in the event a violent flare-up occurred.[77] As it turned out, no additional violence took place. Federal law enforcement officials, such as the FBI special weapons and tactics team and U.S. marshals, remained in the area for rapid response as well. By the evening of 9 May only the JTF LA command group remained, and they rapidly prepared to conclude task force activities.

## *Conclusions*

Breakdowns in leadership and a lack of preparedness at all levels characterized the early stages of the response to the 1992 riots. The Los Angeles Police Department must bear a heavy-weight of criticism for its failure to act forcefully and promptly when the riots started, and the California Office of Emergency Services committed a serious error when it informed the National Guard that it would not be needed. Nevertheless, Guard leaders might have tried to anticipate the role they would play if major unrest occurred. As a result of these misjudgments, the Guard received the lion's share of the criticism for its uncoordinated response. While the Guard's deployment time was initially extended by a lack of ammunition and shortages of necessary riot equipment, once the situation was rectified over 1,000 Guardsmen waited in staging areas while unprepared local law enforcement agencies tried to decide how to use them.

The Guard should have displayed better planning and more decisive leadership. Although it was a serious error to initially order troops into action without the M16 locking plates, Guard commanders were not at fault for the biggest impediment: a lack of specific, legal missions from local law enforcement officials. To alleviate such problems in future local law enforcement agencies and the National Guard will require better coordination. The LAPD did not develop a plan that fully integrated the National Guard, and the first Guard unit to deploy within the city was able to do so only because the Los Angeles Police Academy provided it with ammunition. No evidence of other such assistance can be found.

A second policy area also requires further evaluation. Federal troops did not disperse throughout the city until seventy-two hours after their arrival, and by the time federal troops deployed to Los Angeles the riot had ended. Mayor Bradley ended the curfew that same day, indicating that he recognized that the riot was over. When federal troops began performing riot duty, local police and the National Guard under state control had already performed the yeoman's portion of the task at hand. The Marines and the Regular Army covered a very small portion of the riot area. General Delk, of the California National Guard, was careful to point out that "the mission of federal troops was the maintenance of law and order, not the restoration of it."[78] In other words, federal troops were not in Los Angeles to quell the riot, they were there to prevent it from reoccurring. Finally, save for a few challenges to the soldiers' authority by a few extremists, the vigor and enthusiasm of the rioters had waned significantly by the third day of the disturbance.

According to Chief Gates, "one of the main benefits of using federal troops is financial," and from the point of view of the city and the state, Gates was absolutely correct. [79] Once federal troops were authorized in Los Angeles, the Federal Government was responsible for financing the operation. Conversely, a point that Gates did not address, was the psychological advantage and peace of mind that the troops provided to local residents.

The 1992 riots and Joint Task Force Los Angeles demonstrated the need for a much deeper commitment by the military and local law enforcement agencies across the nation to better preparedness when facing the prospect of a civil disturbance. The Los Angeles riots illustrated that riot control training is a perishable skill. Whatever edge the federal civil disturbance apparatus had gained during the late 1960's and early 1970's was clearly lost by 1992. When the military answers the call to duty, much work and coordination is required by all involved. Local law enforcement agencies must develop comprehensive civil disturbance plans that clearly define how and when National Guard and federal troops will be used.

More importantly, the Los Angeles riot revealed that civilian officials did not fully understand that the Posse Comitatus Act significantly limits their flexibility and options in the use of troops. According to General Delk, "the limitations were so severe that a federal force would probably never be invited back to Los Angeles under similar circumstances."[80] Moreover the National Guard must communicate to civil authorities what can be expected with regard to reasonable deployment times for military units. Frustrated civilian officials repeatedly expressed a lack of understanding when the Guard was not ready in a few hours, unaware of the 18 to 24 hours of prior notice normally needed to alert and muster troops for deployment. They tried to hold the Guard to standards that were higher than that of an active duty rapid deployment force.

A greater understanding by local authorities of the roles and responsibilities of federal troops is also necessary. The FORSCOM and Sixth Army after action report contended that local authorities tended to view the military as an extension of their authority. Many times during the riot, civilian law enforcement officials were frustrated by the severe limitations placed on federal forces.[81] Whereas all evidence points to compliance by Regular Army troops and Marines, there were several instances of noncompliance by the federalized National Guard. One prime example was the 4 May incident when a National Guardsman accidentally shot himself while holstering his .45 caliber pistol. In this instance the Guardsman was at the highest level on the arming order, level 6, calling for a loaded pistol in the individual's hand, implying that the soldier was in imminent danger, but that was not the case when the soldier accidently shot himself.

## The Riot in Retrospect

After the smoke had cleared and the embers and tempers had cooled, the city of Los Angeles began the difficult process of rebuilding. The police and the military had played a role in quelling the riot, but perhaps not as significant a role as they should have. The riot had proven once again that the quiet riots of gang violence and drive-by-shootings that were occurring within the nation's inner cities were capable of turning overnight skirmishes into mass protest. Despite praise from many local residents for actions during the riots, the performance in Los Angeles revealed that the ability of the federal and state government to respond effectively to a domestic crisis was in doubt. Although not stated in any military after action report, the lessons learned during previous riots had not been applied in Los Angeles in 1992.

The riot response showed that a seamless transition from the previous era of riot duty had not taken place. Guard units, local police, and local and state governments operated within a vacuum. In both the Los Angeles riot of 1992 and the 1980 Miami riot, the trigger was a violent reaction to highly publicized cases of police brutality followed by a change of venue for the trial and not-guilty verdicts. As in California, the Florida National Guard's deployment was also slowed by the placement of its ammunition in a distant centralized storage facility. Moreover, the Florida Guardsmen required refresher training upon their arrival in the riot area. Additionally, both states lacked plans for the employment of the National Guard.

The Los Angeles riot and the performance of local police, the National Guard, and the federalized force demonstrated that the skills necessary to quell civil unrest effectively are complex and highly perishable. A major lesson that evolved from Kent State was that Guardsmen should not deploy with loaded weapons, but many California Guardsmen deployed with chambered rounds in 1992. Fortunately for all concerned, great restraint was demonstrated by the Guard during the riot. According to Generals Hernandez and Delk, "the Guard only fired twenty-two rounds during the entire deployment," indicating that a few lessons of earlier deployments persisted.[82]

## CHAPTER 6

## *Looking Forward Through the Past*

> *Progress, far from consisting in change, depends on retentiveness. When change is absolute there remains no being to improve and no direction is set for possible improvement: and when experience is not retained, as among savages, infancy is perpetual. Those who cannot remember the past are condemned to repeat it.*

## Training and Doctrine

This chapter provides a retrospective look at the continued valued of using troops domestically during riot control duty. It examines training for the role; how doctrine evolved over time; and it considers wheter the Posse Comitatus Act is a statute, a statue, or a shield through an examination of its continued relevance currently. Finally, this chapter examines the myth of the madding crowd and reveals that the doctrine created in the 1940s has tremendous relevance today.

Throughout American history, the United States military has been an extension of the society that it supports and defends. George Washington's call-up of troops from three states to quell unrest in Pennsylvania during the Whiskey Rebellion of 1794 demonstrated how the military was intended to be used domestically, and it provided an early opportunity for the newly formed central government to use its military muscle to enforce the law of the land. Federal forces controlled by a single commander received explicit instructions from the Commander-in-Chief, who also issued the order to the rebels to cease, desist, and disperse. After accomplishing its mission, the quelling force departed the area. The procedures utilized in 1794 are virtually the same methods that would be used today, but what separates the past from the present are the significant technological advancements in communications, weaponry, and command and control measures.

Whereas the procedures for employing a federal force have remained consistent throughout U.S. history, restrictive measures such as the 1878 Posse Comitatus Act, have turned local pleas for federal assistance into a bureaucratic labyrinth that places military leaders in a position where they must constantly interpret the law. In the case of the 1992 Los Angeles riot, Posse Comitatus was more of a subterfuge under which the intervention of federal troops was more symbolic than functional. The original purpose of the statute was twofold. First, it prohibited a military presence at polling locations during all elections after 1878. More importantly, it exempted the military from duty under the auspices of the 1854 Cushing Doctrine, which required *all males* over the age of 15 to assist local sheriffs and marshals upon demand.

The Posse Comitatus Act served a very specific purpose in 1878, to limit the use of the military within the U.S. In the late twentieth century, however, local political figures and law enforcement officials expected federal troops to play a much larger role in quelling the Los Angeles riot in 1992. But the provisions of the Act prohibited the military from making arrests, detaining suspected criminals, and conducting searches and seizures. The sizable military forces deployed in 1992, although appreciated, proved incapable of meeting the expectations of the local leadership.[2]

A riot is a fluid, volatile, violent, and very uncertain event. The 1992 Forces Command (FORSCOM) and the 6th Army After Action Report (AAR) described numerous instances where local law enforcement officials requested support from Joint Task Force Los Angeles only to be refused under the limits of Posse Comitatus. According to the report, many of the requested missions were inappropriate, rejected because they placed soldiers and Marines in law enforcement roles. To rectify this situation, the JTF commander provided "mission acceptance criteria and required that every mission be revalidated daily."[3] At times, however, the consequence of this decision has negated the purpose and intent of deploying military forces to a riot area to assist local law enforcement personnel in restoring order.

The AAR noted that federalized forces were unable to respond to the request of civil authorities as rapidly as local law enforcement officials expected,[4] noting that the total time it took the military to process a request could take upwards of fifteen hours--three hours to screen and up to twelve hours to respond.[5] State and local political officials quite reasonably believed that if the situation were desperate enough to warrant federal intervention, they could expect the deploying force to play a major role. Yet, even when the situation might seem dire, the provisions of Posse Comitatus prevent federal troops from enforcing civil law.

In Los Angeles in 1992, there was great variation with respect to compliance with the statute. Occasionally the federalized National Guard and Marine Corps focused more on the mission of ending the riot, while the Army, ultimately concerned with its domestic image, often found itself interpreting the law more strictly. During the Los Angeles riot, the Marines participated in an incident that would have clearly violated the Posse Comitatus law had the Marines been constrained by the Act. The fact that they were not constrained sent a very confusing message when federal forces were deployed and one service appeared to be an unconstrained asset, while the other proved to be a severely constrained one. Kenneth Pye recommended in 1982 that "the Posse Comitatus Act be amended to limit the use of Naval and Marine forces in the same manner as the use of Army and Air Force forces is limited."[6] If the Act is to be continued, Pye's conclusion is logical.

In light of the military's past performances, including within the George Floyd murder riots, three feasible courses of action are worth considering. First, the Act could be repealed, as its original purposes are no longer at issue. Or, it could be amended to allow the suspension of the "law enforcement" prohibitions during riot control operations. This would maximize the potential uses of the federal force and provide local authorities and police with greater flexibility during a crisis. Finally, the Posse Comitatus Act could remain unchanged. If no revisions are made, the Marine Corps should assume primary responsibility for the domestic disturbance mission, providing the government with the greatest flexibility in putting down civil disturbances.

The Marine Corps has participated in most federal civil disturbance missions since 1968, and experience would not be an issue, because any units given riot-control assignments would be trained for the mission.

However, this course of action would require providing the Marines with the necessary riot-control equipment such as helmets with protective face shields, riot batons, and locking plates for rifles--items which are not organic to Marine Corps units.

Prior to the outbreak of violence in Detroit in July of 1967, the Army's response to riot control was reactive. Although doctrine and the Steep Hill planning contingencies existed, the system for creating a task force to quell civil unrest was essentially ad hoc. Unit deployments to designated cities and transportation arrangements upon arrival were not planned in advance. Before 1967, military forces lacked detailed written instructions for the task force commanders. After the Detroit riot, the Army remedied many old problems and focused on organization, planning, and detailed instructions for all involved in riot duty.

Following 1967, the Army task force performing riot duty received specific directives for the commander, his staff, officers and soldiers alike. Civil disturbance guidelines allowed little room for individual initiative and flexibility. The commander received his directives within a seven-page "Letter of Instruction" (LOI) that specified the mission, task organization, location for establishment of the command post, options for how troops were to carry individual weapons--bayonets fixed or unfixed, sheathed or unsheathed, weapons in the ready position or at sling arms on the shoulder. The task force commander also received guidance regarding the arming of weapons, use of riot-control agents, and the Rules of Engagement for the use of force. Instructions were also outlined on methods for dealing with snipers, civilian detention, search and seizure procedures, cooperation with civil authorities, communications, and reporting procedures. Finally, the LOI designated the task force operational name as Task Force Detroit.[7]

During the latter part of the 1960s every officer, warrant officer, and enlisted soldier participating in riot-control operations received a laminated card which listed eight special orders requiring strict compliance. The orders demanded that individual actions reflect positively on the Army, requiring maximum restraint in the use of force and full cooperation with local police. In 1992, soldiers and Marines received the same special orders that were used in 1968, but deploying forces also received a list of questions that would most likely be asked by the media. Responses to the inquiries were provided to the soldiers as well.[8]

Doctrinal development presents yet another challenge to the future of the civil disturbance mission. In the aftermath of the 1967 Detroit riot, Major General Charles P. Stone noted that, "what was needed was different emphasis on training, imaginative employment or techniques, better leadership, and better command and control."[9] Stone's words ring true today. The 1985 edition of *Field Manual 19-15: Civil Disturbances* incorporated the lessons of the 1960s and 1970s, but the Army did not anticipate the changes in weapons and urban life that have occurred since 1985.

First written in 1945, *Field Manual 19-15* is both comprehensive and detailed, and has been updated five times. It outlined required procedures to disperse a crowd, provided schematics on riot-control formations, described sniper control techniques, and listed preferred weapons for specific situations. *FM 19-15* also provided specific commands for soldiers to recite as they dispersed a crowd. It even recommended procedures for separating agitators from onlookers. Although thorough, the Army's 1985 version of *FM 19-15* bore significant similarities to the original version published forty years earlier. Although the later editions of *FM 19-15* were more comprehensive than the earlier versions, the basic focus of the manual was crowd control. Whether consisting of Pennsylvania farmers who refused to pay an excise tax on whiskey in 1794 or an unruly mob that hurled stones at National Guardsmen at Kent State University in 1970, the basic tendencies of the crowd remained constant. Crowds tended to mass; they generally lacked significant mobility; and they were armed with rocks, sticks, and only occasionally, firearms. Crowd control was the scenario for which civil disturbance doctrine was written.

In Los Angeles in 1992, a totally different domestic adversary appeared. The 1992 rioter operated independent of massed crowds, and he was sometimes better armed than the forces deployed to control him. In a few instances, individual rioters' actions appeared suicidal, with no regard for their personal safety. The Forces Command and Sixth Army After Action Report (AAR) captured this critical lesson, stating:

152

*In the 1960s civil disturbance operations were oriented on crowd control. The anti-Vietnam demonstrations required forces to be proficient in crowd control techniques. Today, the environment is similar to peacekeeping operations or MOUT [Military Operations in Urbanized Terrain]. Crowd control is less important while anti-sniper and peacekeeping operations are of increased importance.*[10]

The author of the after action report entry lacked a clear understanding of military operations in urban terrain, for the use of MOUT doctrine would be misplaced in an American city during a civil disturbance. MOUT is a tactical operation that invariably includes the fire support of automatic and direct fire weapons, movement across open and well defended areas, an assault on the identified objective, and the reorganization of the assault force upon completion of the mission.

If the Marines had used MOUT operations, according to *FM 90-10: Military Operations in Urban Terrain*, when they assisted the Compton police officers, the assault phase would have proceeded as follows: the two Marines would have knocked the apartment door open with automatic fire and thrown a hand grenade into the room. After the grenade detonated, one man would have "quickly enter[ed], spray[ed] the room with automatic [weapons] fire, and take[n] up a position where he could observe the entire room."[11] This is not, however, what the military's role should be during a civil disturbance. MOUT doctrine supposes an aggressive and extremely violent operation. Its purpose runs counter to the Army's need to avoid being viewed as an alien invading force, a goal that has defined federal intervention for much of the twentieth century.

Although *FM 19-15* is not obsolete, it needs to be revised to incorporate the lessons of the 1992 Los Angeles riot. The military should have a doctrine that is less focused on crowd-control techniques and more focused on the variety of domestic threats that federal forces are likely to encounter, especially within the American inner city. The major civil disturbances of the late twentieth century, such as in Los Angeles, indicated that troops must be equally concerned with terrorists and street gangs. They must also be capable of discerning the difference between a curious onlooker and a hardened criminal. As has always been the case, discipline and restraint must continue to be the hallmarks of civil disturbance doctrine.

The Army's long-standing contingency plan, Garden Plot, continues to provide the continuity that makes employment of federalized forces possible--especially with the great time lapses between deployments. Although specific units are no longer earmarked for riot duty in designated cities, the basic focus of the plan remains intact. When Garden Plot was first introduced in 1968, specific units were allocated to specific cities. The catalyst for this action was consecutive summers--1965, 1966, and 1967-- during which increased domestic violence occurred. According to Army Brigadier General (Retired) Douglas Kinnard, the primary focus of the original plan was the capability of deploying 10,000 troops to twenty-five cities across the United States simultaneously.[12]

Since Garden Plot's introduction, the operational phases of the plan remain unchanged--deployment, employment, and redeployment. At present, the Commander-in-Chief Forces Command (CINCFOR) is "tasked to maintain, train and equip a QRF [Quick Reaction Force] consisting of a TF HQ [Task Force Headquarters] and one brigade."[13] Critical to understanding Garden Plot is the fact that it is a reactive versus a proactive system. Presently, a single brigade is designated as the Division Ready Brigade within each of the three corps that comprise the Continental United States Army (CONUS). In other words, the XVIII Airborne Corps located at Fort Bragg, North Carolina, I Corps located at Fort Lewis, Washington, and III Corps located at Fort Hood, Texas, will have one brigade prepared-- without training--to conduct civil disturbance operations.[14] Although this was the plan in 1992, refresher training of deploying forces was required.

In 1993 the Army and the Marine Corps published a joint service manual approving refresher training as an acceptable solution for preparing federalized forces. *FM 100-19, FMFM 7-10: Domestic Support Operations*, placed the role of federal troops during civil disturbances in perspective with the statement that:

*Training for war is the Army's top priority. With the exception of the training required in OPLAN Garden Plot, the Army does not normally do specific training for domestic support missions until after a mission is assigned. Most domestic support missions can be accomplished by a disciplined force, proficient in its war fighting tasks, as described in its mission- essential task list (METL).*[15]

For the Army, discipline, regardless of whether a unit has been trained for riot control, is the key to success in quelling civil disturbances. However, *FM 100-19, FMFM 7-10* makes it perfectly clear that, from the perspective of active-duty forces, riot duty and domestic operations are a National Guard function.

Another area in civil disturbance operations that has remained consistent since the 1967 Detroit riot concerns the application of force and rules of engagement. The JTF commander is authorized to use non-deadly force to control a disturbance, apprehend or detain persons who have committed crimes, and act to prevent crimes. However, Garden Plot states that "the degree of force used must be no greater than that reasonably necessary under the circumstances."[16] In other words, deadly force is not authorized for the purpose of preventing activities such as looting or curfew violations, as these occurrences do not pose a significant risk of death or serious bodily harm to anyone.

The 1992 Los Angeles disturbance demonstrated that riot training is absolutely necessary for military units. During the mid-1970s, the Regular Army breathed a collective sigh of relief in finally ridding itself of primary responsibility for domestic riot control duty. This action not only affected readiness for the duty, but it also undercut Army resources and funding. The edge gained by active-duty forces and National Guardsmen in the aftermath of the 1967 Detroit fiasco--focus, dedicated resources, and priority--was lost by the time the Florida National Guard deployed in May of 1980 to quell the Miami race riot. The need for refresher training by active-duty units in Los Angeles illuminated the lack of readiness of forces for riot-control duty.

The post-Los Angeles After Action Report (AAR) contended that units had not trained for civil disturbances because this peacetime mission was not considered a part of the unit "mission essential task list" (METL). The AAR said "civil disturbance training received a low priority until units are imminently involved in a riot, or until higher Headquarters orders civil disturbance training."[17] George C. Marshall noted that "training is the cornerstone of readiness."[18] Marshall's contention, although provided in the context of preparation for a major war, is apropos with respect to the civil disturbance mission as well.

The questions that warrant an answer after the 1992 riot must be: Do federal forces need to be involved in civil disturbance operations; or should sole responsibility rest with state and local assets--including the National Guard? What role will the dwindling military budget and the significant reduction in personnel strength which has led to the disbanding of units like the rapid reaction 7th Infantry Division play in the military's ability to participate in future domestic riots? If federal forces are utilized, should there be a societal expectation that they be prepared to answer duty's call? Or should they be afforded the opportunity to undergo refresher training, as was the case in Los Angeles? Additionally, should the National Guard undergo a Department of Defense-mandated program similar to the Civil Disturbance Orientation Course developed in January of 1968? Is the issue training, or simply deterrence through physical presence? The latter appears to be closer to the Army's position.

The U.S. military has demonstrated time and again the correlation between training and readiness. The federal response in Washington after the assassination of Dr. Martin Luther King, Jr., exemplified this association. During the nineteenth century no standard system of riot training existed. During the latter part of the century, several states developed state-specific doctrine, but standardized doctrinal training procedures for the Army did not exist. During World War I, the development of War Plan White provided focus and required coordination between the military and specified local governments, but coordination is not synonymous with training. Fortunately for the Army during those years, the lack of the need for federalized forces to quell civil unrest neither mandated nor necessitated a priority or requirement for training.[19]

During the 1950's and 1960's the Army's approach to this mission continued to be ad hoc, based largely on need. Training was on-the-job and the learning curve was based largely on unit continuity and maintenance of unit personnel. The lessons learned during the 1967 Detroit riot identified the need for developing a training program that included active military, National Guard and civilian law enforcement personnel. The federal government's response included SEADOC, reconnaissance and liaison between local law enforcement, firefighters, and military forces earmarked for specific cities. The post-Detroit solution also included demonstrations by military police units throughout the nation on techniques for crowd control. The most practical solution is for all National Guard units to undergo a requisite number of hours of civil disturbance training each year. A system that closely resembles the system utilized during the 1970's would suffice.[20] In addition, active duty units currently designated as members of the Division Ready Brigade (DRB) should undergo a requisite number of hours of training during their cyclical duty. If this system had been in place prior to the Los Angeles riots, the need for refresher training would not have existed.

All training lends itself to professionalism, whether a soldier participates in a Battle Command Training Program exercise, a real world or contingency mission, field training, or a command-post exercise. All such activities contribute to readiness and confidence in self, unit, and the larger organization. William Hazlitt perhaps makes the case best with his statement: "as is your confidence, so is your capacity."[21]

The major riots described in this study have demonstrated that active-duty forces must always be prepared to perform civil disturbance duty. The oath for individuals as they enter into military service states: "I will support and defend the Constitution of the United States against all enemies, foreign and domestic."[22] Likewise, the Constitution provides the President with the legal authority to utilize active forces in domestic disturbances. Clearly, the Regular Army has never relished this potentially unpopular role, but circumstances sometimes require the use of federal forces. Skeptics may contend that twenty years between massive urban episodes of violence does not, and should not, necessitate any great changes within the current system. After all, the system at present has doctrine in *FM19-15* and a contingency plan in Garden Plot, both of which provide structure. However, sound doctrine without trained forces can be as detrimental as no doctrine at all.

Perhaps what is needed is a compromise. One of three courses of action could be adopted by the proponents of the civil disturbance mission. First, units should undergo civil disturbance training while in the Division Ready Brigade cycle. This training would ensure that a unit deploying to quell a riot is prepared to execute the mission upon arrival in the staging area. A second alternative would relieve the Army from the role and make the Marine Corps responsible for the civil disturbance mission when active-duty forces are required. This course of action avoids the constraints of Posse Comitatus and would provide the nation with a highly trained rapid deployment force for domestic contingencies. Finally, a third potential course of action would give the National Guard sole responsibility for quelling domestic unrest. The advantages of the third course are proximity, knowledge of local areas, and familiarity with firefighters and police officers. With these three possible courses of action, it is imperative to remember that it is the intent of the federal government to use active-duty forces only as a last resort. Thus, the National Guard would seem best suited to assume responsibility for this important role.

The National Guard is also fully capable of handling this mission without being federalized. Contrary to the brow-beating that the 40th Infantry Division received during and after the 1992 Los Angeles riot, it was very effective in bringing the riot under control before the Regular Army and Marines arrived in Los Angeles. As Major General Daniel J. Hernandez, observed, "the mission of the Active Duty forces in Los Angeles was maintaining the peace, not quelling the riot."[23]

Guardsmen continue to train to support local and state officials during emergencies throughout the nation. A joint exercise in between the Maryland National Guard, civilian police and firefighters provided an excellent example of this. According to Jody J. Elwell, the Maryland Guard redefined their standard operating procedures after examining the lessons- learned from the Los Angeles riots. Elwell noted that, "by training . . . closely with local police and firefighters, we will trust and respect each other's strengths and know limitations."[24] The cooperative training between the triad of civil disturbance forces (military, police, and firefighters) that proved successful in Washington after the assassination of Martin Luther King, Jr. will significantly improve the readiness posture of the forces in Maryland and in other states.

Likewise, a similar training opportunity occurred in New Orleans in 1995. Maria LoVasco highlights the mock riot training that occurred between the Louisiana National Guard's 1st Battalion, 141st Field Artillery and the New Orleans Police Department. Realistic training not only hones the skills necessary during riot control duty, but it also builds close ties between local police and the National Guard. According to LoVasco, "the training gave the soldiers an eye-opening look at how ugly and dangerous working riot control can be."[25] Just as the nation's armed forces must be prepared to meet its foreign adversary, so too must they prepare to face the domestic enemy.

Doctrine presents yet another challenge to the future of employment of military forces domestically. In the aftermath of the 1967 Detroit riot, Major General Charles P. Stone noted that, "what was needed was different emphasis on training, imaginative employment or techniques, better leadership, and better command and control."[26] The Joint Doctrine that's currently in use for Homeland Defense is replete with great "buzz words" like defeat, deter, and dissuade, but the doctrine lacks the specificity that military leaders will require to navigate the legal framework that constrains them domestically. What is needed domestically is an Emergency Plan White-like document that is comprehensive, detailed, prescriptive, and rehearsed by military and civil authorities periodically. This new doctrine has to be created for all conceivable scenarios in which a military force would deploy within American cities. NORTHCOM is heading in the right direction in providing military assistance in support of lead federal agency, providing military civil support including domestic disaster relief operations that occur during wildfires, floods, hurricanes, earthquakes, in support of counter-drug operations and consequence management assistance, and during biological, chemical, nuclear, and terrorist threats. NORTHCOM's Task Force Civil Support has already played a viable and instrumental role with several American cities during weapons of mass destruction exercises.

Doctrine will be inclusive of all of the military services and their National Guard and Reserve components will not only be required, but demanded as America continues to prosecute it's Global War on Terrorism (GWOT). Just as the nation's armed forces must be prepared to meet its foreign adversary, so too must they prepare to face the domestic enemy. In an interview with the men's lifestyle magazine *Cigar Aficionado*, General (retired) Tommy Franks -is quoted as saying that "if the United States is hit with a weapon of mass destruction that inflicts large casualties, the Constitution will likely be discarded in favor of a military form of government."[27] Hence, he's stating that we'll be under martial law—precisely the type of conditions that were advocated within Emergency Plan White.

## Posse Comitatus Act in Retrospect

The Posse Comitatus Act has existed within the United States for more than 142 years. Why has this statute-comprised of forty-nine words and written with as loose a construction as the U.S. Constitution itself endured the test of time and evolved to a doctrine and concept as great as any law affecting the military? Perhaps the reason for the Act's endurance is the fact that it did not disrupt the president's constitutional powers or any act of Congress that predated the statute. Moreover, the Act has been so whittled from its original form that it hardly resembles the statute proposed by J. Proctor Knott in 1878. Decades of study have channeled my focus towards three fundamental questions: (1) Is the Posse Comitatus Act (PCA) a statue--a likeness sculptured model, or a cast; (2) Is PCA a statute, a decree, something laid down or declared as fixed or established, a law enacted by the supreme legislative branch of a representative government; or (3) Is it a shield, a protective device with which the military can hide. These questions became more pressing after my examination of the 1992 Los Angeles riots. Research has revealed that the statute's original purpose—to overturn the Cushing Doctrine and to keep soldiers out of local law enforcement—has been met.

From its inception, the Posse Comitatus Act has been defined by some level of ambivalence and confusion, especially if the Act is evaluated through the prisms of the stakeholders—federal legislators, jurists, and the executive branch of government. It appears that the most decisive volley by legislators was in 1878 when the Act was proposed by J. Proctor Knott and passed by Congress. Since that time, Congress has whittled away the Act to the extent that only the forty-nine basic words that were proposed at its inception are all that remains consistent.

History reveals that with each new domestic demand for a readily available manpower pool, and with each apparent violation of the statute by that same pool of active armed forces, Congress creates a new exception to the original Act. For example: during the San Francisco earthquake of 1903 (Emergency Intervention); after the assassination of Bobby Kennedy 1968 (augmented Secret Service protection for candidates); violations of the PCA by lending military equipment and by the presence of military advisors at Wounded Knee, South Dakota (Congress granted these authorized exceptions in 1980); the War on Drugs (Congress approved direct military support of counter-drug operations); and the Stafford Act (detailing the military's role during natural disasters).

One month after September 11, 2001, as the Global War on Terror began, Sen. John Warner, the ranking member of the Senate Armed Services, asked the Secretary of Defense in a memorandum dated October 11, 2001, "should this law [PCA] now be changed to enable our military to more fully join other domestic assets in the war against global terrorism?[28] DoD's response, not surprisingly, came from its general counsel, Mr. William J. Haynes, ll, who asserted: "There are a number of reasons that the Department of Defense has been reluctant to accept law enforcement missions: (1) a longstanding distaste on the part of the citizenry for the use of the military as a police force; (2) a lack of formal training on the part of most service members to engage in domestic police activities involving functions such as arrest, execution of warrants, searches and seizures, and the protection and preservation of evidence; (3) an unwillingness with the military to permit service members to undertake extensive law enforcement training because such training may well interfere with a service member's ability to train for our warfighting mission; and (4) a significant concern that the addition of a law enforcement mission to the many high demands already shouldered by the Armed Forces in defending the country will degenerate or destroy the ability to accomplish those already existing demands.[29]

Jurists, on the other hand, have never convicted anyone for violating the statute, but have occasionally granted exclusion to assailants based on clear violations of the Act. Whereas it is difficult to assess the seeming reluctance by the court to establish a precedent, it is irrefutable that the Act has indeed been violated and no one has been prosecuted. It appears that the only entity that has remained constant with respect to maintaining the PCA is the Department of Defense. DOD has appeared as shrewd as the master poker player, playing the "it's a violation of PCA card" often times as a matter of convenience rather than a matter of principle. Lt. Col. Donald Currier was absolutely correct in his assertion that "PCA provides DOD with a convenient shield to protect it from missions that it does not want."[30]

Throughout American history, the United States military has been an extension of the society that it supports and defends. George Washington's call-up of troops from three states to quell unrest in Pennsylvania demonstrated how the military was intended to be used domestically. The Whiskey Rebellion of 1794 provided an early opportunity for the newly formed central government to use its military muscle to enforce the law of the land. Federal forces were controlled by a single commander, who had received explicit instructions from the Commander-in-Chief. The President issued the order to the rebels to cease, desist, and disperse accomplishing its mission, the quelling force departed the area. The procedures utilized in 1794 are the same methods that would be used today, except now requests for federal forces are now directed to NORTHCOM. What separates the past from the present, however, are the technological advancements in communications, weaponry, restraint, professionalism, and command and control measures.

As was the case in Los Angeles in 1992, the Posse Comitatus Act, has turned local pleas for federal assistance into a bureaucratic labyrinth that places military leaders in a position to interpret the law. Posse Comitatus, in most cases during the twentieth century, has been more of a subterfuge under which the intervention of federal troops proved more symbolic than functional. The original purpose of the statute was twofold. First, it alleviated a military presence at polling locations during all elections after 1878. Second, and more importantly, it eliminated the military from duty under the auspices of the 1854 Cushing Doctrine, which required *all males* over the age of 15 to assist local sheriffs and marshals upon demand.

The Posse Comitatus Act served a very specific purpose in 1878, but what role does it serve at present? Local political figures and law enforcement officials expected federal troops to play a much larger role in quelling the Los Angeles riot in 1992. However, due to the provisions of the Act, which precluded the military from making arrests, detaining suspected criminals, and conducting searches and seizures, the sizable military force-although appreciated--proved incapable of meeting the expectations of the local leadership.[31] The consequence of this decision negates the purpose and intent of deploying military forces in that situation—to assist local law enforcement personnel in restoring order. State and local political officials quite reasonably believed that if the situation were desperate enough to warrant federal intervention, they should expect the deploying force to play a major role. Although the situation might seem dire, the provisions of Posse Comitatus prevent federal troops from enforcing civil law. In Los Angeles there was great inequity with respect to compliance with the statute. Occasionally the federalized National Guard and Marine Corps focused more on the mission of ending the riot, while the Army found itself asking the question: "Am I in violation of Posse Comitatus?"

The Army—previously the lead federal agency for domestic interventions—and its doctrine, policies, and rules of engagement have had Posse Comitatus-like restraints, as well as passive and supporting roles to local authorities embedded within their doctrine, policies and rules of engagement. Only during a few occasions when the federalized force deployed in accordance with the Insurrection Act was a local populace subjected to its military in a law enforcement role.

It appears that NORTHCOM has the right answer within the post-9/11 era, that "PCA gives us the authority it needs to do our mission, yet it constrains us when we should not be acting." Likewise, the post-9/11 era finds the nation using the National Guard in Title 32 status (under the control of state governors) as first responders domestically—which I agree is the best solution. National Guardsmen under state control have full policing powers and are not constrained by PCA. More importantly, proximity, experience and knowledge of local areas, and familiarity with firefighters and police officers only enhances the argument of why the Guard should be the military's first responders to any domestic crisis.

Suffice it to conclude that PCA is all the aforementioned: a statue that memorializes or symbolizes a time past; a statute that provides a subtle and yet real reminder that the President in his role as Commander-in-Chief may be constrained by Congress; and a shield that allows some filtration between the local and state governments and the federal government—nothing more, and nothing less. Finally, PCA, even as a legal and structural impediment to progress, has prudential value to our nation, and thus should not be rescinded.

## The Myth of the Madding Crowd

Dr. Martin Luther King, Jr. called riots "the voices of the unheard," while Henry David Thoreau argued in 1849 that "Individuals should not permit governments to overrule or atrophy their consciences, and they have a duty to avoid allowing such acquiescence to enable governments to make them agents of injustice."[32] Until the riots which followed the murder of George Floyd in Minneapolis, Minnesota in May of 2020, the United States had not deployed a federalized force for riot duty since the Los Angeles riots of 1992, but there were countless near misses where local and state police were called in to restore calm—and on a few occasions state governors alerted and deployed the national guard.

Cities such as Ferguson, Cincinnati, Charlotte, and New York breathed life into the "Black Lives Matter Movement." The racial violence in Charlottesville, Virginia, during the summer of 2017, coupled with national anthem protests by NFL players should serve as apt reminders that the post-Obama era America is not synonymous with a "post-racial America." Our nation must continually be concerned with the dynamics unfolding within the crowd, as the crowd remains the unknown variable whenever it assembles. Since the Whiskey Rebellion, the dynamic and volatility of the crowd has remained constant. It gathers after a catalyzing event—the slain body of 18-year-old Michael Brown lying prostrate in the middle of the street in Ferguson, Missouri, for hours, as the internal fluids of life ebbed from his body. To the police, leaving Michael Brown's body in-place was standard protocol in preserving the sanctity of a "crime scene." To those gathering, Michael's lifeless, cloaked body served as the outward symbol of a history of tumultuous relations between local African-American citizens and Ferguson police. The forensics of what happened between Michael and a local Asian store owner earlier that day; and the confrontation between police officer Darren Wilson and Michael Brown were secondary to the convergence of public opinion that was taking root as the crowd amassed.

Likewise, we witnessed in Ferguson the dynamic of the crowd change over the hours that Michael's body lay covered in the middle of Canfield Drive. As articulated in Army doctrine from the 1960s, the crowd was initially a "casual" crowd, unorganized and without common purpose. As Michael Brown's mother arrived on the scene, and wasn't allowed access to his remains, that crowd started become "cohesive"—that is, held together by common interest. When Michael's stepfather arrived on the scene, the crowd became "expressive," with well-defined leadership. One can readily recall televised images of inflammatory language from police in riot gear, and antagonistic and provocative tactics by police on an armored vehicle. These lapses of restraint, coupled with the changing dynamics of the crowd, set the conditions for the increasingly "aggressive" crowd, with Michael Brown's stepfather emerging as the strong leader with significant influence on the emotions of the crowd.[33] Moreover, we can never forget the profound and most alarming phenomena within the crowd—what Collective Behaviorists call "anonymity,"-- the damage wrought by the notion that you as an individual are not responsible for what you do as a member of a crowd.

Additionally, we must address media coverage and examine the role that media play in fueling discontent. Whereas our nation's media no longer routinely speak about the so-called crowd, or about riots as we as a nation have known them in the past, sensationalism continues to drive coverage during times of crisis. Moreover, they report immediately, without forensics and without filters. Reporting in the current instantaneous context is tantamount to the rumors, milling, and keynoting of old, which helped escalate the mood of the crowd from casual to aggressive. With global 24-hour coverage, national news has become local news--and vice versa.

Finally, we must never forget that leaders set the tone at all levels within our democracy. The politics of anger, coupled with the pollution of public discourse that has become routine seriously degrades all notions of civility within our national construct. The volatility that we are witnessing during this "Age of Trump" is rekindling a tinderbox of emotions that many thought had been eradicated in the 1960s and 1970s. The President must be the grand arbiter of our democracy—not the parochial and polarizing figure that President Donald Trump has demonstrated to date. Perhaps the Prophet Muhammad said it best with his words: "Four things support the world: the learning of the wise; the justice of the great; the prayers of the good; and the valor of the brave.[34]

# CHAPTER 7

## *Conclusion*

*It was the best of times, it was the worst of times, it was the age of foolishness, it was the epoch of belief, it was the epoch of incredulity, it was the season of light, it was the season of darkness, it was the spring of hope, it was the winter of despair, we had everything before us, nothing before us,... the period was so far like the present period, that some of its noisiest authorities insisted on its being received, for good or evil, in the superlative degree of comparison only.[1]*

This chapter considers the Kerner Report fifty years later and asks the question: "Who's policing the Police?" Causal trends for riots continue to find police at the epicenter of the cause versus catalyst debate of why people riot. Likewise this chapter examines what we have learned over the history of this vital domestic role for the U.S. Military.

Charles Dickens's opening lines for *A Tale of Two Cities* epitomize the dichotomy that separates the 4 April 1968 assassination of Martin Luther King, Jr., and the so-called Trump Era within the United States of America. This period captures the full splendor of hope afforded to African-Americans in the 1960s by the Civil Rights Movement and Lyndon Baines Johnson's "Great Society." The Sixties were, as Todd Gitlin titled his book, "years of hope and days of rage." When viewing the 1960s, African Americans recall the monumental strides of the Civil Rights Movement; an eloquent orator and focused advocate in Martin Luther King, Jr.; and a sympathetic ear in the White House. The Sixties represented the dismantling of the tripartite system of oppression--political, economic and social--and the earnest beginnings of black enfranchisement. The Sixties witnessed the death of Jim Crow and a final end to the long night of physical, political, social, economic, and educational slavery. The Sixties with its tumult, physical violence, and overt racism in Dixie; its series of long hot summers and urban uprisings and riots in the North and Southwest; and its quagmire in Vietnam, epitomized Dickens's prophetic paradox.

The 1980s, with its twelve-year run of Reagonomics, captured the true essence of this perfect paradox. According to historian Alan Dawley, "policies under President Reagan widened the gap between rich and poor. The removal of state regulations in the 1980s precipitated an orgy of speculation and the biggest rash of business failures since the 1930s."[2] During the Reagan-Bush years it was very easy to feel good about being American, without really understanding why. Materially and economically, the federal government was dismantling Johnson's "Great Society" brick by brick. The uprising in South Central Los Angeles in April of 1992 was indicative of the facade that had been created during a Cold War that found America increasingly attempting to solve the ills of the world, but negligent in correcting its domestic travails.

The 1990s opened with tremendous promise, with the post-Gulf War United States of America being elevated to the world's first hyper-power. With the collapse of the Soviet Union, coupled with the tearing down of the Iron Curtain, and the overwhelming victory in the first Persian Gulf War, the United States had truly become what is described in Matthew 5:14: "You are the light of the world. A city that is set on a hill cannot be hidden,"[3] America was ideally positioned as that shining City on a Hill for the rest of the free world.

Although the United States had not committed a federalized force for riot duty from 1992 until after the protest associated with the May 25, 2020 murder of George Floyd in Minneapolis, Minnesota, our nation has witnessed significant civil unrest over the past quarter of a century— with the precipitating incidents remaining consistant with those reported in the 1968 *Kerner Report*: "grievances about police practices." [4]

## Who's Policing the Police?

Interesting is the fact that our social consciousness is often shaped by local and national news coverage. As a student of riots, especially those resulting from heavy-handed policing—like Rodney King, Freddie Gray, Michael Brown, Keith Lamont Scott, Sam DuBose, Walter Scott, and George Floyd, I, like many others within our nation, harbored suspicion, but most often concluded: "this is an isolated incident;" "this cannot be widespread;" and my training and conservative bent found me most often siding with the police in cases receiving national attention. Conversely, as a trained historian, my research reminds me that police forces have often served as visible and ever-present human demarcation lines--enforcing the rule of segregation, disenfranchisement, and racial separation. Playwright August Wilson in his 1985 play "Fences," reminds us that: "fences are designed to keep people out; but they also keep people in." These words have rung true throughout our nation's history with respect to police forces and minority communities. This pseudo, undeclared mission of keeping people both out and in, also defines the longstanding animus existing between the African-American community and the police. History is replete with examples of abuse, heavy-handed policing practices, profiling, and the view that the primary mission of law enforcement is to protect the majority population from minorities.

The Mapping Police Violence Website lists every fatality attributed to law enforcement, with a comprehensive look at the "when," "what," "where," and "how" for each fatality. An assessment of the data from 2013 through 2019—a period of seven years--reveals that what national news provides as isolated occurrences, are really widespread within our nation. Indeed, the data shows that 7,919 Americans were killed as a result of an encounter with law enforcement officials from 2013 through 2019. When one juxtaposes the reality that the United States has nearly 327 million citizens, 7,919 deaths over a seven-year period may not appear so dire. However, the forensics and the deeper meanings within each number may reveal disturbing truths, if we are desirous of avoiding the next major riot.[5]

Considering that we live in an era of police wearing body cameras confronting a population armed with video-capable mobile phones—this data is troubling for sure. As a veteran who served our nation faithfully for 31 years—the last six years as a General Officer--with two combat deployments, I know that it might be considered sacrosanct to compare casualties of war with fatalities attributed to police. I am not attempting to be inconsiderate or insensitive by comparing the deaths of those felled by police with service members who gave the last full measure of devotion to our nation during combat. That said, as a modern and advanced society, ALL Americans should be alarmed by the sheer numbers—especially when one considers the horrors and expected carnage of war. To be sure, police collectively are responsible for the deaths of more Americans than the combined losses of US Service Members in Iraq and Afghanistan during the Global War on Terror—6796. Again, in seven years, police have killed over 1100 more Americans than the combined totals of American Service Members who where killed during seventeen years of war in Iraq and nineteen years of war in Afghanistan. Incidentally, of the 7,919 Americans who were killed by police, according to the Mapping Police Violence (MPV) Database, only 686 where declared as **JUSTIFIED**—a mere 8.6%.[6] Police have killed an additional 781 Americans in 2020—226 since the May 24th death of George Floyd. As of August 30, 2020, there have been only 12 days in 2020 where police did not kill someone.

According to the Mapping Police Violence Database--which provides, dates, names, race, city and state, and a description of what transpired, the forensics of the case, and how the matter was adjudicated—44% of Americans killed during an encounter with the police were Caucasian, 25% were African-American, 17% were Hispanic, .014% Asian, .014% Native American, .005% Pacific Islanders, and the race/ethnicity of 10% was Unknown. Likewise, the oldest person killed during an encounter with the police was 107 years old, with another (107) being over the age or 70, with (70) being under the age of 15—(10) were under the age of 7, with (3) of the decedents being only 1 year old.[7]

The usual retorts that the assailant had mental health issues, or they were on drugs was also examined. A closer examination of the forensics reveals several critical factors. First and foremost, they demonstrate that the "audio" of what allegedly transpired and led police to shoot in the moment, doesn't always square with the "video" that's revealed in the aftermath. Of the 7919 Americans who were felled by police during the years 2013 to 2019, 1464 had known mental health issues, while only 296 were confirmed to have had drugs or alcohol in their system. A whopping 4747 had neither mental health issues or drugs or alcohol in their system, while the status of 1122 was unknown on the MPV Database.[8]

With respect to the issue of being Armed, quite a different story is revealed. Of the total number of fatal encounters with the police, 3997 of the assailants had a gun; 1143 had a knife, machete, or an axe, 3 had chainsaws, and two had a bayonet. Of the entire database, 5421---or 68% of the assailants where in possession of a weapon. The preponderance of alleged assailants killed during an encounter with police were killed by gunshot wounds (7059—89%).[9]

What happens to police officers after a fatal shooting of an American Citizen is perhaps the most startling revelation of all. When viewing the data, I was reminded of a verse of scripture that was frequently quoted by the Reverend Dr. Martin Luther King, Jr., during his speeches and sermons, from the Biblical teachings of Amos, the third of the minor prophets in the Old Testament. In the fifth chapter and the 24th verse of Amos, the prophet states: "But let justice roll down like waters and righteousness like an ever-flowing stream."[10] If one considers that only 686 of the 7919 were declared "justified;" that only 79 officers were convicted of a crime, with 4464 still pending an investigation.[11] Suffice to say that the legal system for our protectors has not rolled down like waters and righteousness like an ever-flowing stream. Quite to the contrary, both justice and righteousness for alleged police indiscipline appears to be constipated.

Martin Luther King Jr. often stated that the moral arc of the universe is long, but it bends toward justice, and so it must if we are to remedy what most believe are isolated events which bear the names of its victims: Eric Garner (2014, New York City), Akai Gurley (2014, New York City), Tamir Rice (2014, Cleveland, OH), Michael Brown (2014, Ferguson, MO), LaQuan McDonald (2015, Chicago), Freddie Gray (2015, Baltimore), Eric Harris (2015, Tulsa), William Chapman, II (Portsmouth, CA), Sam DuBose (2015, Cincinnati), Jeremy McDole (2015, Wilmington, DE), Ricky Ball (2015, Columbus, MS), Jamar Clark (2015, Minneapolis), Jordan Edwards (2015, Dallas), , Walter Scott (2015, Columbia, SC), Rekia Boyd (2016, Chicago), Keith Lamont Scott (2016, Charlotte), Terence Crutcher (2016, Tulsa, OK), Alton Sterling (2016, Baton Rouge, LA), Philando Castile (2016, St. Paul, MN), Breonna Taylor (2020, Louisville, KY), and George Floyd (2020, Minneapolis,

MN). These are not martyrs, as their deaths are not aligned with a belief system. Yet their deaths illuminate the reality that the moral arc does not always bend towards justice, hence those voices of the unheard rise in protest and American cities bear witness to the reality of the mood of the madding crowd as it has changed from casual to aggressive.

So, what can be done, what are the potential solutions and remedies? In fairness to law enforcement, I acknowledge that our society is more violent and police officers are subjected to greater dangers at present, but danger is an occupational hazard of policing. This reality doesn't negate the requirement for discipline and restraint? Would a possible mistake, or a premature or accidental discharge by an officer be considered so egregious if officers and police departments simply stated: "We made a mistake?" I believe the answer is no, if the department is swift in its investigation, transparent in its communications with the locality, and is fair and just in disciplining their own. The tendency to circle the wagons within our police departments must cease. The "Us against Them" mindset must stop, and bad cops who plant evidence, who abuse their power, and who have a record of violence against the very citizens that they are sworn to protect must be purged from police forces, prosecuted, and made an example of, if "protect and defend" is to become more than a convenient slogan within our police forces.

It's appreciated that police officers at best work with a partner, and at worst, work as individuals--unlike the military who work within a larger framework of a squad (11 people), platoon (33 people), or a company (132 people). Within the military's larger construct, safety and security are much less an individual consideration. The pack or the tribe mentality within the military adds both strength and confidence within military units, and unlike police forces they are accustomed to working in large teams. It is difficult to evaluate a person's actions when all of their senses are heightened—which could cause "overreaction" resulting in accidental discharge or prematurely firing of a weapon. A simple fix in police training could be to mandate--and enforce--a policy of keeping one's finger outside of the trigger guard until the officer is absolutely ready to fire their weapon. Perhaps this simple remedy would have precluded Officer Rusten Sheskey from shooting Jacob Blake seven times in the back in Kenosha, Wisconsin on 23 August 2020. Placing one's finger inside of the trigger guard would mean that the situation has escalated in such a way that deadly force is warranted. Pistols are not the most accurate weapon—especially when one is afraid and adrenaline is pumping. Where one points with a pistol may not be where they'll actually hit, thus every shot fired from a handgun could be fatal if it hits the assailant. Our police forces require greater use of nonlethal means. Finally, individual accountability for officers should be at a higher standard if they are to enjoy the trust of the populace which they serve. Police "circling the wagons" and stubbornly defending their own in this age of a 24-hour news cycle, body cameras, and cell-phone videos has changed the landscape-- and it's irreversible.

Likewise, I would encourage a Kerner Commission-like study of policing within the United States of America. This study could consider hiring practices, screening criteria for employment, the use of force within police departments, best practices, and the use of nonlethal means—especially during minor crimes and offenses. Moreover, this Kerner-like Commission should also unmask the concept of sovereign immunity that is granted to police officers under the legal principle of Qualified Immunity—which insulates police officers from civil suit. A bad attitude by a citizen engaging the police should not equate to a death sentence at the hands of police.

## What Have We Learned

This volume has examined the causal factors of racial riots, and the use of federal troops to quell civil unrest. In evaluating how the Army can best serve the public during riots, it's clear that further study is required on riot prevention. Much of what may be necessary to end the quiet riots that are pervasive in America's urban centers is stored away within the *Report of the National Advisory Commission on Civil Disorders*-- the *Kerner Report*. The Kerner Commission provided in its March 1968 report many hard truths that it believed were essential to achieving racial and domestic harmony within the United States. Perhaps no statement within the report was more prophetic than its contention that:

> We have uncovered no startling truths, no unique insights, no simple solution. The destruction and the bitterness of racial disorder, the harsh polemics of black revolt and white repression have been heard before in this country. It is time now to end these things [riots], time to end the destruction and the violence, not only in the streets of the ghetto but in the lives of people. It can be done if we will it to be done. Much is at stake--for all of us.[12]

Perhaps no statement within the report proved more alarming than the assertion that, "What white Americans have never fully understood--but what the Negro can never forget--is that white society is deeply implicated in the ghetto. White institutions created it, white institutions maintain it, and white society condones it."[13]

How does one evaluate American race relations since the 1968 release of the *Kerner Report*? Truly great strides in U.S. race relations have been made, but there is much work that remains. One need only travel to any of the concrete bastions of hopelessness that we call the inner city to realize that the *Kerner Report* highlights much that America can still draw upon as a society. The squalor that the report described in 1968 remains a constant fixture within overcrowded ghettoes that serve as prisons to the minds, hopes and dreams of the poor. The report argued that two societies existed within America and the country's leaders focused on the political record since the Civil Rights Act of 1964. *Kerner* asserted that more effort is necessary, and America sought scapegoats, assessed blame, and retreated to the parochialism of partisan-politics which pitted Republican proponents of self-help against the Great Society Democrats.

Yet there was evidence of bipartisanship. Many Republican and Democratic leaders argued that the Kerner Commission blamed everyone but the rioter and the underclass, who were partly responsible for their own plight. What about this contention? Andrew Hacker asserted that "it is white America that has made being black so disconsolate an estate."[14] Poverty coupled with powerlessness creates vicious cycles that are not easily broken. America is, and has always been, race conscious. Even President Abraham Lincoln, according to George Fredrickson, believed in 1865 that the Negro could never achieve equality within the United States, and thus devised a plan to send the freed slaves to Liberia.[15] Some now argue that the nation has transformed from a race-conscious to a class-conscious society. There may be some truth to this contention, but race continues to be an issue. Michael Omi and Howard Winat argued that "the myth of steadily improving race relations is being dramatically exposed by the realities of the 1980s."[16] Omi and Winat further argued that, "the confrontations and reforms of the 1950s and 1960s altered the manner in which racism had operated, but these transformations were not far-reaching enough to prevent the subsequent reintroduction of various new forms of racism throughout the social fabric."[17]

John Hope Franklin reintroduced a term coined by W.E.B. Du Bois during the early 1900s--"the color line." Franklin argued that the color line was alive and well in 1993. He contended that, "it thrives because we have been desensitized to its significance over two centuries."[18] The most damning comments on the continued racial divisions in America are provided by Andrew Hacker, who argues that "a huge racial chasm remains, and there are few signs that the coming century will see it closed."[19] Hacker illustrated his contentions with social and economic data. For example, Hacker displayed that the median income for blacks was 39 percent less than whites in 1970, and 42 percent less than whites in 1990.[20] Likewise, Hacker noted that in 1990 there were 3.6 blacks in poverty for every one white American that was impoverished.[21] This figure becomes even more dismal when one considers that African-Americans constitute only twelve of every one-hundred Americans. In the area of unemployment, Hacker provided an even gloomier picture. Unemployment for blacks according to Hacker's figures was 6.7 percent in 1968, and 11.3 percent in 1990. During the same periods Hacker shows the unemployment rates for whites as 3.2 percent and 4.1 percent respectively.[22]

Does a true Protestant ethic, where hard work, frugality, responsibility, and deferred gratification, truly exist in America? If so, do all of America's sons and daughters have equal access to its promises? Harvard

Sitkoff"'s volume, *The Struggle for Black Equality*, attempts to answer these questions. Sitkoff tracked the plight of African Americans from slavery through 1992--although his focus was from 1954 through 1992. In his concluding chapter, appropriately entitled, "The Dream Deferred... The Struggle Continues," Sitkoff argued that each presidential administration since President Johnson's in 1968 played a major role in creating the racial polarization and distrust that is pervasive today. Sitkoff contended that America is returning to a time immemorial where two accepted societies existed within America. He credited all presidential administrations since Johnson, along with conservative Supreme Court appointments, with effectively dismantling the nation's second attempt at Reconstruction. One of Sitkoff's more critical assertions of the federal government's lack of concern with urban issues was "the government's willingness to rescue Kuwait and bail out the Chrysler Corporation but not to salvage African-American ghetto youngsters."[23]

America of the late 1990s was also filled with numerous examples of racially divisive issues. Attempts to repeal affirmative action serve as a case in point, including the Hopwood Decision and Proposition 209. This program, originally designed to afford equal opportunity to all--regardless of race, gender, and also sexual preference, is now being presented to society as a quota system. Is America as race conscious as it ever was? How did America respond when an Alabama high school principal canceled the prom to discourage interracial dating? What does our national consciousness make of the false imprisonment of more than two-hundred African-American men by a few Philadelphia police officers, which was discovered in 1995? Is it racism that allowed de facto segregation in public elementary schools in Calhoun, Georgia? Is it prejudice which allowed the alleged hanging of Antwan Sedgwick by two white Hampton, Virginia, police officers on 4 October 1995? Is it paternalism which allowed "60 Minutes" correspondent Andy Rooney to admonish all African Americans for what he believed to be their unanimous support for O.J. Simpson after the not-guilty verdict in October 1995? Certainly there are no definitive answers to these rhetorical questions. What about the University of Texas law professor who claims that it is his First-Amendment right to openly profess his aversion to African American and Latino admissions to the University of Texas Law School?

Suffice it to say that America's urban travails are not caused by a degraded Protestant ethic or a departure from the philosophy of Social Darwinism. The seeming return to times immemorial leads me to conclude that the observations of the National Advisory Commission on Civil Disorder from 1968 are of continuing value today. Barbara Ritchie carefully pointed out that the *Kerner Report* "was not intended as a cathartic outlet, its ultimate message is action."[24] Ritchie was absolutely right. The solution for America's urban ills cannot be solved exclusively with more quick-fix, band-aid solutions. Perhaps what is needed most is a retooling of the minds and hearts of America's sons and daughters. President Johnson stated in 1967 that:

> *The only genuine, long-range solution for what has happened lies in an attack--mounted at every level--upon the conditions that breed despair and violence. All of us know what those conditions are: ignorance, discrimination, slums, poverty, disease, not enough jobs. We should attack these conditions--not because we are frightened by conflict, but because we are fired by conscience. We should attack them because there is simply no other way to achieve a decent and orderly society in America.* [25]

President Johnson was right in 1967, and his assessment holds true in 2020: race still matters. We still tend to see things through different prisms based on background, experience, and what's been reinforced. And yes, there are still non-verbals which demonstrate that we have a long way to go as a nation. In an era after we've elected an African American to the highest office in our land—twice, our fears of one another have been heightened and our suspicions restored; the so-called age of Obama did not usher in a post-racial America. The present backlash harkens back to a time immemorial.

So what do we do about it? We simply have to talk, as moments are but snapshots in time. Some fuel discontent, some provide deeper meaning and context, and some change the landscape. The fabric that enjoins us as a nation is tremendously delicate and frays easily. The Neo-Nazi affray in Charlottesville in 2017 was one of those moments. Although President Trumps response shocked some and infuriated others--as it resurfaced a cancer that our nation believed it had eradicated. In my view it represented the promise of our nation, as the lion's share of the faces at that affray were Caucasian. If history has taught us any great lessons, it has revealed that it requires the clear majority populace of our nation to stamp out racism in this country; just as it will take good cops to ferret out the bad ones. Finally, Lady Justice must remove her blindfold that she might bear witness to our collective truth.

# *Epilogue*

*Those who do not remember the past are condemned to repeat it.*[1]

History is replete with examples of lessons-lost of the adverse impacts of heavy-handed policing. Over a thousand lives of American citizens are lost annually during encounters with police for misdemeanors. How does a traffic stop for an improper lane change result in someone's death? In all the cases that I have studied, I have not viewed the wanton violence that I witnessed when George Floyd encountered 19 year decorated police veteran Derek Chauvin. What appeared on video as a nonconfrontational apprehension of Floyd--who was suspected of passing a counterfeit twenty-dollar bill--resulted in imagery that I struggle to reconcile months later. Office Derek Chauvin—who had 18 previous complaints on his official record—literally murdered George Floyd in plain sight of onlookers, with officer Tou Thao in overwatch to protect his flanks.

On May 25· 2020 Derek Chauvin held his knee, with the full weight of his 6 feet, 200-pound frame on the neck of George Floyd for an uninterrupted 8 minutes and 46 seconds. A person's neck is designed to support the weight of the head and it protects the nerves that carry sensory and motor information from the brain down to the rest of the body. The neck is highly flexible and allows the head to turn and flex in all directions. The neck, however, is not a weight bearing part of one's body—except of course for that person's head. The neck is woefully incapable of withstanding the pressure that Officer Chauvin applied to hand-cuffed George Floyd for almost nine minutes.

This public execution of an unarmed African-American lacked the familiar utterances of "he was armed," or "I feared for my life." This time there were no echoes of mental illness, or whispers of drug or alcohol involvement. This occurrence was absent of all the usual trappings of why the situation escalated. This time the dastardly deed occurred during broad daylight, was caught on tape, and the officer had

179

three accomplices—whether wittingly or unwittingly. This execution lacked a judicial process with a District Attorney or Grand Jury to indict. Chauvin's street justice was absent a jury, but what Chauvin missed was that the jury was the entire world, and George Floyd became more than just another victim of yet another demonstrable case of police brutality. He became the symbol of a movement which said: no more to heavy-handed policing. But there was more, this time protesters not only demanded "Justice for George," but they demanded for an end to all vestiges and symbols of racism.

This time the movement demanded removal of the "stars and bars" from the Mississippi State Flag and demanded that the flag become unwelcomed at NASCAR events. This time the movement demanded that cities across the US—like Richmond, Virginia, the US Capital Building, and statues in locales around the world, which celebrated the "father's of oppression", be taken down. The time finally came when the Department of Defense sought approval to change the names of military bases which celebrated former enemies of the State like Fort Henry Benning, Fort Braxton Bragg, Fort Alexander William Campbell, Fort Thomas Jackson, Fort John Bell Hood, Fort John Brown Gordon, Fort Ambrose Powell Hill (AP Hill), Fort Robert E. Lee, Fort George E. Pickett, and Fort Leonidas Polk.

The protest which followed the murder of George Floyd revalidated the myths of the madding crowd and reminded us that who's in the crowd and the mood of the crowd has not changed from the first publication of *Field Manual 19-15* in 1945. We bore witness to the reality that the crowd still goes from casual, to cohesive, to expressive, to aggressive. The protest validated the truism that the military continues to play a vital and necessary role in riot control within the Continental United States. The George Floyd protests reaffirmed that a level-headed military has a calming effect on the crowd, as scenes of Soldiers standing in solidarity with the crowd, or Soldiers dancing the Macarena with crowds demonstrated the esteem that our nation has for its defenders.

Likewise, these protests revealed a host of "leader-lessons which cannot--and should not--be lost or overlooked. Lessons like the staged moment for President Donald Trump at St John's Church and Ashburton

House for a photo opportunity with his Bible held backwards and upside down. Shame on all who participated in that staged photo opportunity which violated the constitutional right to assemble of the protesters. Moreover, it's important that state and local leaders recognize their true powers when people assemble. Local leaders must know who's in the crowd, hence they must infiltrate the assembly. Nothing sets expectations and controls of a crowd more than imposing a dusk to dawn curfew during civil unrest. Night and the cover of darkness, favors the crowd—especially if it's been infiltrated by ne'er-do-wells and outside non peaceful agitators whose aim is violence, destruction, and looting. Police forces and military personnel should cordon off areas within the locale in an effort to control and contain the protest.

Likewise, city officials must use their own resources in plain-clothes to infiltrate the crowd, to isolate and segregate keynoters, people spreading rumors, and informal or formal leaders in a effort to regulate the temperament of the crowd. Civil leaders, under the advisement of military leaders, must consider closing places where people could assemble, banning the sale of firearms, ammunition, and alcohol and ban the sale of gasoline in containers. They must also consider the vital importance of securing federal facilities, establishing a vigorous patrol system, and creating a quick-reaction-force in an effort to maintain the psychological advantage. Finally, civil leaders must do all within their powers to avoid presenting the military as an invading alien force, but as the entity who'll help restore order, vice suppress the local populace.

Perhaps the greatest inhibitor of progress following the protest that accompanied the death of George Floyd was the President himself. His inflammatory language not only served as an accelerant domestically, but it ignited a tinderbox around the world. President Trump's insistence that the Insurrection Act of 1807 granted him authority to deploy federal forces at will is not without limits and conditions. As discussed within Chapter I of this volume, Article II, Sections 2 and 3, and Article IV, Section 4 clearly delineates the Presidents role as Commander-in-Chief of the military, charges the office with the faithful execution of laws, and guarantees every State in the Union a republican form of government—while requiring the federal government to protect the States against invasion.

Likewise, the Insurrection Act of 1807 empowers the President to deploy military forces to suppress civil disorder, insurrection, and rebellion. Before invoking these powers, however, the President must first publish a proclamation ordering insurgents to disperse, but this isn't executed in a vacuum by the President alone. These powers are conditioned upon the following provisions: first, the State must submit an application after it has exhausted all of its resources. Second, the insurrection must make it impracticable for the State to enforce the law; and finally, the State must be incapable of Governing itself and its citizens. None of these factors where present during the George Floyd protests.

Of note, the National Defense Authorization Act of 2007 had a short-lived amendment to the Insurrection Act to permit military intervention without State consent based on the Governor of Louisiana's refusal to ask President George W. Bush to intervene in Hurricane Katrina. This provision, however was repealed in January of 2008 when all 50 State Governors issued a joint statement against it.[2] Hence, President Trump's committing federal agents to American cities is operating outside of his constitutional authority.

Finally, we owe great thanks to the legions of well-intended peaceful protesters who took to the streets in support of someone that we know very little about. Thank you for being the voice for the silenced voice of George Floyd and countless others who suffered a similar demise. Thank you for standing up to the vitriol of a despot masked as the head of a democracy, who's focus on absolute power undermines the foundational ideals which led to the birth of our nation.

The Prophet Muhammed said it best when he stated: Four things support the world: the learning of the wise, the justice of the great, the prayers of the good, and the valor of the brave.[3] We, as Americans, must be learned, just, good, and brave--as the world is watching and taking their cues from us. So we must endeavor to have excellence, not as an act, but as a habit, as Aristotle so aptly advised. And as the late and great Ronald Reagan often said: "I still believe in that shining city on a hill." And so do I.

# *Endnotes*

## Preface

[1] Philip S. Foner, The Life and Writings of Frederick Douglass, vol. IV: Reconstruction and After (New York, 1955), 153.

## Introduction

[1]Paul S. Boyer, Clifford E. Clark, Jr., Joseph F. Kett, Neal Salisbury, Harvard Sitkoff, and Nancy Woloch, *Enduring Vision: A History of the American People.*, vol. 2, second edition, (Lexington, Massachusetts: D.C. Heath and Company, 1993), 1040.

[2]Army Troops in Capital as Negroes Riot: Guard Sent Into Chicago, Detroit, Boston; Johnson Asks a Joint Session of Congress, *The New York Times*, 6 April 1968, 1a.

[3]*Field Manual 19-15; Civil Disturbances and Natural Disasters* (Washington: Government Printing Office, 1968), 7-8. *FM 19-15* was originally published in 1945. Revisions were published in April 1952, September 1958, December 1964, March 1968, March 1972, October 1975, and November 1985.

[4]Eugene H. Methvin, *The Riot Makers: Technology of Social Demolition* (New Rochelle, New York: Arlington House, 1970), 105.

[5]Department of the Army, "After Action Report, 4-17 April Civil Disturbances," 13 August 1968, 12, File 103, Record Group 319, Records of U.S. Army Staff, National Archives, College Park, Maryland (henceforth RG 319, NA).

[6]James Gardner, "The Civil Disturbance Mission of the Department of the Army, 1963-1973," (Ph.D. dissertation, Princeton University, 1977), and Richard Guy Sedlack, "Riots as Disasters: An Exploratory

Case Study of Selected Aspects of the Civil Disturbance in Washington, D.C., April 1968," (Ph.D. dissertation, University of Maryland, 1973).

[7]Jean R. Moenk, "USCONARC-Participation in the Suppression of Civil Disturbances, April 1968," (Fort Monroe, Va.: USCONARC, October 1968), 14, copy located in File, USCONARC-2, Center of Military History, Washington, D.C.

[8]*Report of the National Advisory Commission on Civil Disorders* (New York: Bantam Books, 1968), vii.

## Chapter 1

[1] Robert W. Coakley, *The Role of Federal Military Forces in Domestic Disorders,* 1789-1878 (Washington, D.C.: Center of Military History/Government Printing Office, 1988), 347.

[2] It was never proven that the soldiers of all African-American 25th Infantry Regiment participated in the violence in Brownsville.

[3] Office of the Special Consultant to the Secretary of the Army, *Bicentennial of the United States Constitution: A Resource Guide, Supplement IV: 1991 The Adoption of the Bill of Rights* (Washington: Office of the Special Consultant to the Secretary of the Army, for the Bicentennial of the United States Constitution, 1991), 105-107. The state must exhaust all organic resources, such as the National Guard, state and local police, before it can request federal assistance.

[4] Coakley, *Role of Federal Military Forces*, 38.

[5] See ibid., "federalized" means to bring under the control of the Federal Government.

[6] During the Tariff Nullification controversy and Dorrs' Rebellion, Regular Army troops were alerted but never deployed.

[7] Coakley, *Role of Federal Military Forces*, 128.

[8] Critical in assessing the Army's role during the Civil War is the distinction that "martial law" was in effect in the cities and states seized by the U.S. military forces. Martial law (rule) refers to the temporary

government of the civil population by military forces as necessity may require. It exists only when and where a condition prevails in which the civil government has broken down and the courts are no longer properly and unobstructedly exercising their jurisdiction. Thus, martial law is born of necessity and ceases when the requirement ends.

[9] Coakley, *Role of Federal Military Forces*, 222.

[10] These statutes are now codified as Sections 592 and 593 of Title 18, United States Code.

[11] Allan R. Millett and Peter Maslowski, For the Common Defense: A Military History of the United States of America (New York: Free Press, 1984), 241-42, provides a brief introduction. See Joseph G. Dawson, III, Army Generals and Reconstruction; Louisiana, 1862 - 1877 (Baton Rouge: Louisiana State University Press, 1982), for how Lincoln's plan worked in one state.

[12] Joan M. Jensen, Army Surveillance in America, 1775 - 1980 (New Haven: Yale University Press, 1991), 29.

[13] See James Sefton, *United States Army and Reconstruction, 1865 - 1877* (Baton Rouge: Louisiana State University Press, 1967).

[14] Coakley, *Role of Federal Military Forces*, 342.

[15] Edward S. Farrow, *Military Encyclopedia: A Dictionary of Military Knowledge* (New York: Edward S. Farrow, 1885), 566-568. Also see H. W. C. Furman, "Restrictions Upon the Use of the Army Impose By the Posse Comitatus Act," *Military Law Review* 7(January 1960) 96, and Coakley, *Role of Federal Military Forces*, 344.

[16] The National Guard under state control is not subjected to the Posse Comitatus Act. The statute was amended in 1956 to apply also to the U.S. Air Force. Although the law does not mention the U.S. Navy or Marine Corps, Department of Defense (DOD) Directive 3025.12 places similar restrictions on these services. The Coast Guard and the National Guard are not affected by either Posse Comitatus or the DOD directive.

[17] Coakley, *Role of Federal Military Forces*, 345.

[18] Furman, "Restrictions Upon the Use of the Army," 97. To illustrate his contention, Furman points out that Hayes deployed U.S. troops to enforce the judicial process in New Mexico less than four months after signing the bill into law.

[19] See Paul Jackson Rice, "New Laws and Insights Encircle the Posse Comitatus Act," paper submitted in the Individual Studies Program located at the U.S. Army War College, 1983.

[20] On 7 July 1878, the War Department issued a general order enumerating the provisions of the Posse Comitatus Act. In addition to the Act and the exceptions, the Act also listed provisions relating to the enforcement of laws on Indian lands, the preservation of timber in Florida, and the protection of a discoverer of a guano island, his widow, heirs, executor, and administrator. See Farrow, *Military Encyclopedia*, 566, and Coakley, *Role of Federal Military Forces*, 345.

[21] Department of the Army, Army Regulation 500-50: Emergency Employment of Army and Other Resources--Civil Disturbances (Washington, D.C.: Department of the Army, 1956).

[22] Ibid. In this particular instance time is the critical factor. This exception is applicable when inaction by a local commander could result in a public crisis. Application by state officials must still occur. However, the local commander is not constrained by the time that it may take for the president to issue a proclamation and executive order.

[23] The congressional joint resolution resulted form the June 1968 assassination of presidential candidate Senator Robert F. Kennedy.

[24] Chapter VII of this study will evaluate the Posse Comitatus Act in light of the military's performance in quelling the 1992 Los Angeles riot.

[25] Jerry M. Cooper, *The Army and Civil Disorder: Federal Military Intervention in Labor Disputes, 1877 - 1900* (Westport, Conn.: Greenwood Press, 1980), 259.

[26] Jensen, *Army Surveillance in America*, 29.

[27] See War Department Emergency Plan White, 1946, 8, paragraph 4.f., Record Group 389, Records of the Provost Marshal General, file, 382-B, located in the National Archives, College Park, Maryland, (hereafter RG 389, NA).

[28] See Henry A. Bellows, *A Treatise on Riot Duty for the National Guard* (Washington, D.C.: Government Printing Office, 1920), 95.

[29] For more information on National Guard civil disturbance doctrine see Brigadier General Albert Ordway, *Drill Regulations for Street Riot Duty* (Washington, D.C.: James J. Chapman, Publisher, 1891);

Brigadier General Louis L. Babcock, *Manual for the Use of Troops: In Aid of the Civil Authority* (New York: George H. Doran Company, 1918); Edward S. Farrow, *Riots and Riot Duty* (New York: Edward S. Farrow, 1919).

[30] Ordway, *Drill Regulations*, 299-300.

[31] Ibid., 306.

[32] Babcock, *Manual for the Use of Troops*, 89.

[33] See Farrow, *Riots and Riot Duty*. The beliefs expressed by Edward S. Farrow within his volume are his own and were not consistent with the views of restraint advocated by the War Department during the period.

[34] Jensen, *Army Surveillance in America*, 178.

[35] Ibid. By the beginning of World War II the various Service Commands reported the status of local Negroes within their weekly intelligence summaries to the War Department. See Weekly Summaries from Headquarters Service Command, Enclosure 2 (Racial Situation) within the Racial Appendix, File 319.1, RG 389, NA.

[36] "Emergency Plan--White," Washington, D.C.: War Department, 8 June 1923, 11, File 383, RG 407, Records of the Adjutant General, located in the National Archives, Washington, D.C., (hereafter RG 407, NA).

[37] Ibid.

[38] See War Department, "Emergency Plan White, Basic, 1940," File 365, RG 407, NA. This plan superseded the 1923 plan.

[39] Ibid., 2.

[40] Ibid., 5.

[41] Bernard C. Nalty, *Strength for the Fight* (New York: Free Press, 1986), 91.

[42] See Bernard C. Nalty and Morris MacGregor, eds., *Blacks in the Military: Essential Documents* (Wilmington, Delaware: Scholarly Resources, Inc., 1981), for a full accounting of the inconsistencies of the Brownsville affray.

[43] Martin Binkin and Mark J. Eitelberg, *Blacks in the Military* (Washington, D.C.: The Brookings Institution, 1982), 16.

[44] For coverage of Brownsville see ibid. Also see Nalty and MacGregor, eds., *Blacks in the Military*, 60, and Richard Hope, *Racial Strife in the U.S.*

*Military: Toward the Elimination of Discrimination* (New York: Praeger, 1979), 15. For a full narrative accounting see also John D. Weaver, *The Brownsville Raid* (College Station, Texas: Texas A&M University Press, 1972).

[45] See U.S. Army Inspector General's Office, *The Brownsville Affray: Report of the Inspector General* (Washington, D.C.: Government Printing Office, 1908), and Ann J. Lane, *The Brownsville Affair* (New York: Kennikat Press, 1971).

[46] Robert V. Haynes. *A Night of Violence, The Houston Riot of 1917* (Baton Rouge, Louisiana: Louisiana State University Press, 1976), 1-7 and 10-24. Also see *Houston Post*, 20 August 1917, p. 1, for headline.

[47] William Tuttle, *Race Riot: Chicago in the Red Summer of 1919* (New York: Athenaeum, 1977), 4 and 65. See also Carl Sandburg, *The Chicago Race Riots, July, 1919.* (New York: Harcourt, Brace and Howe, 1919), 3-6.

[48] Ulysses Grant Lee, *U.S. Army in World War II Special Studies: The Employment of Negro Troops* (Washington, D.C.: Office of the Chief of Military History/Government Printing Office, 1966), 4.

[49] With respect to the so-called "Negro Problem," actions by the Army are shown in documents within RG 389, File 291.2 (Race Riots), and RG 407, File 291.2. These records are replete with examples of acts of violence against black soldiers by white soldiers, white military and civil police, and the white local populace in cities and towns outside of the military installations. For example, within File 291.2, RG 407, is a 12 August 1942 inquiry from Judge William Hastie suggesting that Negro troops be utilized in elite, amphibious, paratrooper, and commando units. Brigadier General I.H. Edwards, the Assistant Chief of Staff for the Army, responded "Negroes should be used to the greatest extent in shore and service elements." In a letter from concerned citizen, A.J. Burke to President Franklin D. Roosevelt, Burke described a brutal beating of a black soldier at a Fort Worth, Texas, restaurant by two white military policemen. Documents within RG 407 also recounted the shooting of Private Rubin P. Pleasant by a Montgomery, Alabama, bus driver on 27 March 1943. Likewise, RG 389 possesses weekly intelligence summaries from the various Army service commands--each highlighting the racial

situation throughout its region in the Racial Appendix. There was a pervasive tendency within these reports to depict the Negro as the perceived enemy. This view gives credence to Walter White's 1942 contention with respect to the Negro soldiers' perspective on fighting a foreign war. White stated, "The Army Jim- Crows us. The Navy lets us serve only as messmen. The Red Cross refuses our blood. Employers and labor unions shut us out. Lynchings continue. We are disfranchised, Jim Crow'ed, spat upon. What more could Hitler do than that?" See Walter White, "What more could Hitler do than the Army," <u>Annals of the American Academy of Political and Social Science</u> 223 (September 1942), 67.

[50] Memorandum for the Assistant Chief of Staff, G3, from Major General George V. Strong, Assistant Chief of Staff, G2, dated 17 June 1942, Subject: The Negro Problem in the Army, File 291.21, RG 407, NA.

[51] Ibid.

[52] Memorandum from Colonel Hayes A. Kroner, Chief, Military Intelligence Service, for the Assistant Chief of Staff, Operations Division 8 May 1942, Subject: Negro Civilians and Military Personnel Alexandria, Louisiana and Vicinity, File 291.21 RG 407, NA.

[53] Memorandum for the Provost Marshal General, from Lieutenant Colonel Palham D. Glassford, Instructor-Observer Group, dated 15 April 1942, Subject: Report on Race Discrimination and the Race Problems in IV Corps Area, File 291.21, RG 407, NA.

[54] Harvard Sitkoff, "Racial Militancy and Interracial Violence in the Second World War," in Roger Lane and John J. Turner, Jr., eds., *Riots, and Tumult: Readings in American Social and Political Violence* (New York: University Press of America, 1978), 315.

[55] Alfred McClung Lee and Norman D. Humphrey, *Race Riot (Detroit, 1943)* (New York: Octagon Books, Inc., 1968), 94. For further insights on the the 1943 Detroit race riot see ibid., 90-97.

[56] Ibid., 97.

[57] "U.S. at War," *Time* 41 (28 June 1943), 19.

[58] "Festering Tension: Detroit's Race Riots Ebb, but U.S. Problem Remains," *Newsweek* 22 (5 July 1943), 35.

[59] Thurgood Marshall, "The Gestapo in Detroit," in Joseph Boskin, ed., *Urban Racial Violence in the Twentieth Century* (Beverly Hills: Glencoe Press, 1969), 57.

[60] War Department Army Service Forces, Office of the Provost Marshal General, Memorandum for Director, Operations and Training Division, 16 October 1943, Subject: Plans for Action in Domestic Disturbances, File 370.6, RG 407, NA.

[61] See Chapter III of this study for an evaluation of the Army's 1967 performance in Detroit.

[62] Memorandum for the General Staff, Service Commands, and Defense Commands, from Colonel Frederick D. Sharp, Deputy Director of Army Intelligence, 10 July 1945, Subject: Domestic Racial Estimate, File 291.2, RG 389.

[63] Lee, *Employment of Negro Troops*, 349.

[64] Ibid.

[65] *FM 19-15*, originally published in 1945, underwent revisions in April 1952, September 1958, December 1964, March 1968, March 1972, October 1975, and November 1985. Highlights of the 1968, 1972, 1975, and 1985 editions will be discussed in Chapter V.

[66] The situation in Little Rock established a precedent in civil disturbance operations. This marked the first time that an American president had to usurp the authority of a state governor, Arkansas Governor Orval Faubus, who had violated a Supreme Court order. The governor had utilized the Arkansas National Guard to keep black children out of the Central High School. President Dwight D. Eisenhower federalized the Arkansas Guard and deployed troops from the 101st Airborne Division to enforce the Supreme Court desegregation ruling.

[67] See Provision 5297, Revised Statutes U.S. Code.

[68] See Office of the Chief of Military History Study 75 by Robert W. Coakley, Paul J. Scheips, and Vincent H. Demma, "Use of Troops in Civil Disturbances Since World War II, 1945-1965," 52-60.

[69] Ibid., 78. Of note: U.S. marshals deployed in civilian clothing with bullet proof vests. Oxford proved that the use of U.S. marshals was not an effective deterrent for the emotionally charged protestors.

[70] For unit specification and troop strength in Oxford see Coakley, Scheips, and Demma, "Use of Troops in Civil Disturbances Since World War II," 81.

[71] See Paul J. Scheips, "The Role of the Army in the Oxford, Mississippi Incident 1962 - 1963," Office of the Chief of Military History Monograph Number 73M, dated 24 June 1965, 281. See also Lewis Sorley's *Thunderbolt: General Creighton Abrams and the Army of His Times* (New York: Simon and Schuster, 1992), 157-65. Sorley focuses almost exclusively on the relationship between President John F. Kennedy, U.S. Attorney General Robert F. Kennedy and Major General Abrams.

[72] See Task Study Group and its recommendations and the establishment of the Department of the Army Civil Disturbance Committee. See Chapter III of this study, section "Army Plans for Future Disturbances." Historian Lewis Sorley may be overly optimistic of Abrams' contribution to the civil disturbance mission in *Thunderbolt* (p. 168). Sorley views Abram's message as the catalyst for revising *FM 19-15* and for revamping the Army's procedures for dealing with civil disorders, but does not provide conclusive evidence for this contention.

[73] See Paul J. Scheips and Karl E. Cocke, "Army and Operational Intelligence in Civil Disturbances Since 1957," Center of Military History Monograph, 1971.

[74] This operation was organized in Task Force Steep Hill XIII, a new standardized designation. During subsequent operations in the South, Steep Hill remained the operational designation, only the number would change.

## Chapter 2

[1] See transcripts from Warren Christopher Oral History; Accession Record Number 74-197, p. 12, located at the Lyndon Baines Johnson Library, Austin, Texas. (hereafter L.B.J. Library) The interview was conducted by Dr. Thomas H. Baker, University of Texas Oral History Project, on 18 November 1968.

[2] An after-hours night club which illegally sells alcoholic beverages is commonly known as a "blind pig."

[3] "An American Tragedy, 1967 -- Detroit, " *Newsweek* 70 (August 7, 1967), 18.

[4] Paul J. Scheips, "The Army and Civil Disturbances: Oxford and Detroit," in Garry D. Ryan and Timothy K. Nenninger, eds., *Soldiers and Civilians: Th U.S. Army and the American People* (Washington: National Archives and Records Administration, 1987), 185. The Michigan National Guard, 46th Infantry Division, National Guard, Guardsmen, and Guard are used interchangeably within this chapter.

[5] "An American Tragedy," 23.

[6] The unidentified Detroit citizen is quoted in Van Gordon Sauter and Burleigh Hines, *Nightmare in Detroit: A Rebellion and Its Victims* (Chicago: Henry Regnery Co., 1968), 219.

[7] See Warren Christopher Oral History, p. 12.

[8] The number of troops deployed varies with the source consulted. "An American Tragedy, 1967 -- Detroit", *Newsweek* 70 (August 7, 1967), 20, depicts Task Force Detroit troop strength as 4,700 while Paul J. Scheips and Karl E. Cocke, "Army and Operational Intelligence in Civil Disturbances Since 1957," Center of Military History Monograph, 1971), 65, contends that a little over 6,000 Regular Army troops deployed.

[9] "An American Tragedy," 18.

[10] Scheips, "The Army and Civil Disturbances," 187. See also Scheips and Cocke, "Army and Operational Intelligence in Civil Disturbances," 66.

[11] Samuel P. Huntington, *The Soldier and the State* (Cambridge: Belknap Press of Harvard University Press, 1957), 13.

[12] See William Serrin, "National Guard is Told: Shoot to Kill If Fired On, 8,000 Troops on Patrol with 5,000 Law Officers," *Detroit Free Press*, 25 July 1967, 5a., col. 1.

[13] Scheips, "The Army and Civil Disturbances," in Ryan and Nenninger, eds., *Soldiers and Civilians*, 187-188.

[14] See William Serrin, "Grim U.S. Troops Cool Riot Ardor," *Detroit Free Press*, 4a, col. 3.

[15] Lewis L. Zickel, "The Soldier and Civil Disorder," *Military Review*, 57 (May 1977), 69. See also Scheips, "The Army and Civil Disturbances," 187.

[16] For statistics see Scheips and Cocke, "Army and Operational Intelligence Activities," 65. See also Scheips, "The Army and Civil Disturbances," 189.

[17] Adam Yarmolinsky, *The Military Establishment: Its Impacts on American Society* (New York: Harper & Row, 1971), 186.

[18] Scheips, "The Army and Civil Disturbances," 188. See also Sidney Fine, *Violence in the Model City: The Cavanagh Administration, Race Relations, and the Detroit Riot of 1967* (Ann Arbor, Mich.: University of Michigan Press, 1989), 224.

[19] Charles P. Stone, "Lessons of Detroit, Summer 1967," in Robin Higham, ed., *Bayonets in the Streets: The Use of Troops in Civil Disturbances* (Lawrence, Kan.: University of Press of Kansas, 1969), 197.

[20] Ibid., 195. This paragraph is a brief synopsis of Stone's assessment of the status of riot control training within the Guard and the Army.

[21] *Report of the National Advisory Commission on Civil Disorders* (New York: Bantam Books, 1968), 6 (hereafter, *Kerner Report*). Of the 164 disorders reported during the first nine months of 1967, eight were major riots, thirty-three were serious, and 123 were minor.

[22] *Kerner Report*, vi. The Kerner Commission's membership included U.S. Representatives such as James C. Corman (Democrat of California), and William M. McCullough (Republican of Ohio); U.S. Senators Edward W. Brooke (Republican of Massachusetts) and Fred Harris (Democrat of Oklahoma). John Lindsay, Mayor of New York City, and Hubert Jenkins, Chief of Police in Atlanta, Georgia, gave their views on urban administration. Offering the view of labor and technology

were I.W. Abel, president of the United Steelworkers of America and Charles B. Thorton, chairman of the board and chief executive officer, Litton Industries, Inc., respectively. The group was rounded out by Roy Wilkins, executive director, National Association for the Advancement of Colored People, and Katherine Graham Peden, commissioner of commerce of the state of Kentucky.

[23] *Kerner Report*, vii.

[24] During telephonic interviews with Major General (Retired) Hugh Robinson (President Johnson's Military Aide) and Brigadier General (Retired) Douglas Kinnard (USCONARC Operations Officer) both gentlemen were unaware of a military response--either formally or informally to the *Kerner Report*. One could surmise that the military did not provide an opinion because the report stated only what was provided to the commission by the Army Task Study Group. See section of this chapter entitled "Plans for Future Civil Disturbances."

[25] Henry Hampton and Steve Fayer, *Voices of Freedom: An Oral History of the Civil Rights Movement From the 1950s Through the 1980s* (New York: Bantam Books, 1990), 398.

[26] Lillian Boehme, *Carte Blanche for Chaos* (New Rochelle, N.Y.: Arlington House, 1970), 2.

[27] Ibid., 222.

[28] Lyndon Baines Johnson, *The Vantage Point: Perspectives of the Presidency 1963-1969* (New York: Holt, Rinehart and Winston, 1971), 451.

[29] Memorandum from Joe Califano to President Lyndon Johnson, 28 February 1968, Subject: Summary and Recommendations on the Riot Commission Report, 6, located in the Papers of Lyndon Baines Johnson, President 1963- 1969, EXFG 690, Container Number 387, L.B.J. Library.

[30] Major General (retired) Hugh Robinson telephonic interview with author on 18 May 1996. General Robinson was President Johnson's military aide from 1965 to 1969.

[31] Memorandum from Harry McPherson, Special Counsel to President, for Joe Califano, 1 March 1968, Subject: President's Cold Reception to the Kerner Report, located in the Harry McPherson Collection, Box 32, file: riots (1), volume 11, L.B.J. Library.

[32] John V. Lindsay, The Commission Report--An Unanswered Challenge," *Harvard Review* IV (2nd Quarter, 1968), 18.

[33] See Michael Lipsky and David J. Olson, *Commission Politics: The Processing of Racial Crisis in America* (New Brunswick, N.J.: Transaction Books, 1977), ix. See also Kerner Report, 483.

[34] Gary Marx, "Two Cheers for the Riot Report," *Harvard Review* IV (2nd Quarter, 1968), 4.

[35] William Hazlitt, "Characteristics," in Arthur M. Eastman, ed., *The Norton Reader: An Anthology of Expository Prose*, 4th Edition (New York: W.W. Norton and Company, Inc., 1977), 898.

[36] See Herbert Hill, "Racial Discrimination in the Nation's Apprenticeships Training Programs," *Phylon* 23 (Fall 1962). See also Joanne Grant, *Black Protest: History, Documents, and Analyses 1619 to the Present* (New York: Fawcett Premier, 1968), 430.

[37] Hampton and Fayer, *Voices of Freedom*, 374.

[38] *Kerner Report*, 321.

[39] Ibid., 299.

[40] Tedd Gurr, *Why Men Rebel* (Princeton, N.J.: Princeton University Press, 1970), 24.

[41] Mark Perry, *Four Stars* (Boston: Houghton Mifflin Company, 1989), 176.

[42] Jean R. Moenk, "USCONARC--Participation in the Suppression of Civil Disturbances, April 1968," (Fort Monroe, VA.: USCONARC, October 1968), 14, copy located in File, USCONARC-2, Center of Military History, Washington.

[43] Department of the Army Message Number 826762, Deputy Chief of Staff, Operations, to Commanding General, United States Continental Command, 07162OZ August 68, Subject: Use of Military Personnel, Equipment, and Facilities During Civil Disturbances and Disorders, in File 103, Record Group 319, Records of the U.S. Staff, located at the National Archives, College Park, Maryland (hereafter RG 319, NA).

[44] Ibid.

[45] Department of the Army, Office of the Chief of Staff, Memorandum Number 000.5, For the Department of the Army Staff, dated 4 August

1967, Subject: Preparedness in Civil Disturbance Matters, File 103, RG 319, NA.

[46] Department of the Army, Office of the Chief of Staff, Memorandum Number 67- 316, Subject: Preparedness in Civil Disturbance Matters, File 103, RG 319, NA.

[47] Information provided by BG (Retired) Douglas Kinnard during telephonic interview with author on 23 May 1996.

[48] Moenk, "USCONARC -- Participation in Suppression", 23.

[49] Ibid.

[50] Department of the Army Civil Disturbance Plan, February 3, 1968, Annex I, Appendix 1, File 103, RG 319, NA. One may question the conventional wisdom of assigning the 5th Mechanized Infantry Division of Fort Carson, Colorado, to the nation's capital. The question was not one of distance, but one of phased deployment of a unit that would be mobilized as a reserve force. All military units within a 100mile radius of Washington, D.C., were assigned to Force Inside. According to Joan Moenk, "each CONUS Army was required to make preparations for providing three types of forces with varying reaction times: a company-size Immediate Ready Element with a strength of 150 to 200 men with a 6-hour reaction time; battalions of 600 to 800 men with a 12-hour reaction time; and brigades of 1800 to 2400 men ready to react within 24 hours." During civil unrest following Martin Luther King's assassination Task Force 5 deployed to Andrews Air Force Base, Maryland, for potential assignment to riot duty in Pittsburgh, Pennsylvania.

[51] Department of the Army Message Number 858668, From: Chief of Staff, To: Vice Chief of Staff, 060139Z April 68, Subject: Designation to Command Task Force Washington, File 103, RG 319, NA.

[52] Department of the Army, "After Action Report, 4-17 April Civil Disturbances," (Washington: Department of the Army, 13 August 1968), 6, File 103, RG 319, NA.

[53] Task Force Goblet Glass, District of Columbia National Guard After Action Report 5-16 April 1968, dated 14 May 1968, 2, Center of Military History, Washington.

[54] Memorandum For the Under Secretary of the Army, Subject: Federal Response to the Civil Disturbance Threat, dated 30 September 1969, 2, File 103, RG 319, NA. See also *Kerner Report*, 505.

[55] Ibid., 505.

[56] "A New Look at New Weapons to Cope With Riots," *U.S. News & World Report* 64 (January 1, 1968), 6-7. Weapons such as foam and foam sprayers, gas powered paint shooting pistols, cattle prods, and dart and injector weapons were not employed against rioters in Washington or Los Angeles.

[57] Lee and Humphrey, *Race Riot*, xxi.

[58] Ibid.

[59] Higham, ed., *Bayonets in the Streets*, 7.

[60] Martin Blemenson, "On the Functions of the Military in Civil Disorders," in Roger Little, ed., *Handbook of Military Institutions* (Beverly Hills, California: Sage Publications, 1971), 512.

[61] Ibid., 513.

[62] Ibid., 525.

[63] See *Kerner Report*, 499.

[64] Scheips, "The Army and Civil Disturbances," 189.

[65] Ibid., 187.

[66] Roger Beaumont, "The Embryonic Revolution: Perspectives on the 1967 Riots," in Higham, ed., *Bayonets in the Streets*, 208.

[67] William C. Cockerham and Lawrence E. Cohen, "Attitudes of U.S. Army Paratroopers Toward Participation in the Quelling of Civil Disturbances," *Journal of Political and Military Sociology* 7 (Fall 1979), 258. Although, Cockerham and Cohen's contention is true, Deputy Commander for Task Force Detroit, Major General Charles Stone provided the definitive reason for the calm experienced on the east side of Detroit. Stone asserted that, "eastern Detroit was initially occupied by the National Guard, and that the riot had really spent itself except for one short outburst on Wednesday afternoon, when the Regular Army forces were committed to eastern Detroit." See also Memorandum For: chief of Staff, U.S. Army, From: Major Charles P. Stone, 4 August 1967, Subject: Report of the Deputy Commander Task Force Detroit--Operations and

Observations, 13, located in the Combined Arms Research Library, Fort Leavenworth, Kansas (hereafter Major General Stone AAR, CARL).

[68] Cockerham and Cohen, "Attitudes of U.S. Army Paratroopers," 258.

[69] After troops were deployed in several southern communities during the 1876 elections, Congress enacted and President Rutherford B. Hayes signed the 1878 Posse Comitatus Act.

[70] Stone, "Lessons of Detroit," 191.

[71] Ibid., 192. See Major General Stone AAR, 8, CARL.

[72] General Throckmorton is quoted in Lewis L. Zickel, "The Soldier and Civil Disorder," *Military Review* 57 (May 1977), 69.

[73] *Kerner Report*, 503.

[74] Anthony Deane-Drummond, *Riot Control* (New York: Crane Russak and Company, Inc., 1975), 133.

[75] David Boesel and Peter H. Rossi, eds., *Cities Under Siege* (New York: Basic Books, Inc., 1971), 415.

[76] Bayard Rustin, "A Way Out of the Exploding Ghetto," *New York Times Magazine* (13 August 1967), 17.

[77] Boskin, ed., *Urban Racial Violence*, xii.

[78] Ibid., 104. Boskin offers no explanation of what he means by "the typical riot."

[79] Robert J. McNamara, "The Ethics of Violent Dissent," in Robert H. Connery, ed., *Urban Riots: Violence and Social Change* (New York: Academy of Political Science, 1968), 150.

[80] Louis H. Masotti and Don R. Bowen, eds., *Riots and Rebellion: Civil Violence in the Urban Community* (Beverly Hills, California: Sage Publications, Inc., 1968), 17. An article within the 26 July 1967 edition of the *Detroit Free Press* is perhaps the basis of Masotti and Bowen's contention that over 50 percent of the men assigned to the 82d Airborne Division were Negroes. The article contended that "A large number--perhaps 50 percent--were Negroes, simply because airborne units are prestige-laden." See Serrin, "Grim U.S. Troops," 4a, col. 3. See also Sidney Fine, *Violence in the Model City*, 223. Fine's contention "that twenty to twenty-five percent of the paratroopers were black" was probably a more realistic figure in 1967.

[81] Sitkoff, "Racial Militancy and Interracial Violence in the Second World War," in Lane and Turner, eds., *Riot, Rout, and Tumult,* 314.

[82] Ibid., 313.

[83] Robert Fogelson, "Violence as a Protest," in ibid., 331.

## Chapter 3

[1] *Report of the National Advisory Commission on Civil Disorders* (New York: Bantam Books, 1968), x (hereafter the *Kerner Report*).

[2] Ibid., vii.

[3] Ben W. Gilbert, *Ten Blocks from the White House: Anatomy of the Washington Riots of 1968* (New York: Praeger, 1968), 44. This book is a synthesis of the Washington Post's coverage of the Washington riots. Gilbert, who was the editor-in-chief along with the staff members of the newspaper examined all the reporters' stories of the riots and produced an hour-by-hour, day-by-day account of what transpired. The book also covers the Poor People's Campaign and provides interviews taken with residents of the riot area five months after the riots.

[4] See U.S. Department of Commerce Bureau of Census. Census of Population: Characteristics of Population, 1950, 1060, and 1970.

[5] Gilbert, *Ten Blocks,* 5.

[6] Ibid. See also "Comment -- The Response of the Washington, D.C. Community and Its Criminal Justice System to the April 1968 Riot," *George Washington Law Review* 37 (May 1969), 864.

[7] "City Girds for Summer; Extra Training for Police, D.C. Guard," *Washington Daily News,* 14 February 1968, sec. B, p. 13.

[8] Drew Pearson and Jack Anderson, "Planning Pays Off in Non-Riot Cities," *Washington Post,* 12 April 1968, sec. B, p. 13.

[9] Martin Weil, "Revolution Needed, Hobson Declares," *Washington Post,* 4 March 1968, sec. B, p. 3.

[10] William Raspberry, "Lessons of the Days of Rage," *Washington Post,* 3 April 1988, sec. A, p. 14.

[11] "Comment," *George Washington Law Review,* 864.

[12] Gilbert, *Ten Blocks,* 13.

[13] Wolden quoted in ibid., 15.

[14] Ibid., 18. See also Leonard Downie, Jr., "A Chronicle of Washington's Burning," *Washington Post Magazine*, 9 April 1978, 7.

[15] Gilbert, *Ten Blocks*, 19.

[16] Ibid., 20-21. See also Miriam Otfenberg, "Test of New Riot Law Seen: Carmichael's Role Assessed," *Washington Evening Star*, 7 April 1968, sec. A, p. 1, and "More Violence and Race War? Effect of Dr. King Tragedy," *U.S. News and World Report* 76 (15 April 1968), 31-32.

[17] Data extracted from Gilbert, *Ten Blocks*, 29. See also "Comment," *George Washington Law Review*, 865.

[18] Elsie Carper, "New Riots Catch Police Short: No Trouble Expected During Day," *Washington Post*, 6 April 1968, sec. A, p. 14.

[19] Gilbert, *Ten Blocks*, 44.

[20] Judge Burka quoted in Donald Hirzel, "Rioters Had No Fear of Arrest, Judge Says," *Washington Evening Star*, 11 June 1968, sec. A, p. 14.

[21] Military District of Washington Message Number 6814, the Commanding General, Military District of Washington to Commanding General United States Continental Army Command, 05165OZ April 68, Subject: MDW Situation Report (SITREP) 01/051200Z April 68, File 103, Record Group 319, Records of the U.S. Army Staff, National Archives, College Park, Maryland (hereafter referred as RG 319, NA).

[22] Minutes of the District of Columbia Council Special Meeting, 8 April 1968, RG 319, NA.

[23] Mayor Walter Washington, Government of the District of Columbia, Executive Office of the Commissioner, Number 68-262, 8 April 1968. Subject: Early Dismissal of Employees on 8 April 1968, RG 319, NA.

[24] Department of the Army, Office of the Chief of Staff, Memorandum for Record, Subject: Interview with Investigators from Senator John L. McClellan's Senate Government Operations Committee, Inquiry on Riots, interview taken at 1000 hours, 24 April 1968, between Messengers Dunne and Morgan, Investigative Staff of Senator McClellan's Government Operations Committee, and General Haines, Vice Chief of Staff and Commanding General Task Force Washington, 4. See also Memorandum to the President of the United States from the Mayor, Director of Public Safety, and the Chief of Police, of the District

of Columbia, Subject: Request for Federal Troops to Restore Order in Washington, D.C. dated 5 April 1968, RG 319 NA.

[25] Memorandum for Record, Subject: Interview with Investigators from Senator John L. McClellan's Senate Government Operations Committee, 4.

[26] It is important to note that National Guard Forces under state control are not bound by the provisions of the Posse Comitatus Act of 1878. The D.C. National Guard, if under the control of the District's mayor, could have operated as "special police," possessing the same authority to enforce laws and arrest and detain law breakers as their civil law enforcement counterparts.

[27] For biographical information on General Ralph Edward Haines, Jr., see the West Point Register of Graduates and Former Cadets (New York: Association of Graduates of the United States Military Academy, 1992), 279.

[28] Department of the Army Message Number 858668, From: Chief of Staff, To: Vice Chief of Staff, 060139Z April 1968, Subject: Designation to Command Task Force, 2, RG 319, NA.

[29] See ibid., 1-7. This entry is a brief synopsis of the letter of instruction issued to General Haines as he assumed command of Task Force Washington in 1968. This is one of the few command situations where the commander does not have the opportunity to impart his vision on the organization, as described in Department of the Army, Field Manual 22-103: Leadership and Command at Senior Levels (Washington: Government Printing Office, 1987), 41.

[30] Ibid.

[31] Task Force Washington After Action Report, 4-16 April 1968, 8, RG 319, NA.

[32] Ibid., 9.

[33] Captain Rhode quoted in Gilbert, *Ten Blocks*, 89.

[34] This note is a synopsis of a report rendered by Washington Post reporter Robert C. Maynard. The story was written by Morton Mintz, "Troops Deploy Through City," *Washington Post*, 7 April 1968, sec. A, p. 1. Missions assigned to the District of Columbia National Guard were oriented toward providing static security of certain critical installations

and protecting firemen. Installations assigned to the D.C. Guard were its own facilities, which included ammunition and ration storage at Camp Simms. Both of these facilities had been thought likely targets during a civil disturbance because of the weapons and ammunition stored there.

[35] Task Force Washington After Action Report, 30.

[36] United States Continental Army Command (USCONARC), Emergency Operations Center Journals, 4-6 April 1968. Information is also found in the USCONARC After Action Report -- Civil Disturbances, April 1968, copy located in the Center of Military History, Washington.

[37] Gilbert, *Ten Blocks*, 90.

[38] Message Number 2709, Commander-in-Chief, Strike Command (CINCSTRIKE), to Commander-in-Chief, Army Strike Command (CINCARSTRIKE), and Commander-in-Chief, Air Force Strike Command (CINCAFSTRIKE), 060230Z April 68, Subject: Garden Plot, RG 319, NA.

[39] Message Number 55378, Commanding General, USCONARC to Commanding General, Third Army, 060128Z April 68, Subject: Movement of Troops, RG 319, NA.

[40] Jean R. Moenk, "USCONARC -- Participation in the Suppression of Civil Disturbances, April 1968," (Fort Monroe, Virginia: USCONARC, October 1968), 52, copy located in File, USCONARC-2, Center of Military History, Washington.

[41] Task Force Washington After Action Report, 24.

[42] Ibid., 24.

[43] Gilbert, *Ten Blocks*, 44.

[44] "Crew rest" refers to the number of hours of rest required by air crews for the safe operation of military aircraft.

[45] Task Force Washington After Action Report, 25. All strength figures, during the troop buildup and phase down, of Task Force Washington are extracted from the Task Force Washington After Action Report. See also Department of the Army After Action Report, 4-17 April Civil Disturbances, 13 August 1968 and Jean R. Moenk, "USCONARC -- Participation in the Suppression of Civil Disturbances."

[46] Task Force Washington After Action Report, 24.

[47] Ibid., 35.

[48] Area responsibility refers to static security of fixed facilities.

[49] Task Force Washington After Action Report, 32.

[50] Ben A. Franklin, "Washington Turmoil Subsides; Hundreds Homeless, Eight Dead," *New York Times*, 8 April 1968, sec. A, p. 1.

[51] Haines relinquished command to assume duties as the acting Army Chief of Staff.

[52] Dates and times of phase down and redeployment of Task Force Washington units extracted from Task Force Washington After Action Report, 34-36.

[53] "So Far, Well Done," *Washington Post*, 8 April 1968, sec. A, p. 16.

[54] Barry Kalb, "Williams Considers Handling Businessmen's Suit on Rioters," *Washington Star*, 12 May 1968, sec. B, p. 4.

[55] Elsie Carper, "Byrd Wants Troops to Stay; Police-Aid Pacts Suggested," *Washington Post*, 9 April 1968, sec. A, p. 5.

[56] Chicago, Baltimore, and Washington, D.C., data extracted from the Department of the Army After Action Report, 12, 15-16. Detroit data extracted from the National Advisory Commission on Civil Disturbances Report, 60-61, and 66. The data in Table 5 represents the ammunition expenditure by federalized troops--Regular Army and National Guardsmen under federal control--only. The Illinois National Guard conducted riot control operations for almost 48 hours before they were federalized. During this 48-hour period the Guard expended 395 rounds of small arms ammunition and 63 tear gas grenades. For data on the Illinois National Guard see Moenk, "USCONARC -- Participation", 52. Questions may arise concerning the implication that there is a correlation between the amount of ammunition expended by the military and the level of violence experienced within an urban center. An examination of urban violence reveals the opposite. Army civil disturbance doctrine writers, from the inception of War Plan White during World War I through the publication of the 1985 edition of FM19-15, were careful to point out that the Army must not appear to as an invading alien force while quelling civil unrest. The Army's mission is to restore order, not to suppress the local populace. In the nation's capital in 1968, the Army focused on restraint. While in Detroit the National Guard violently executed the governor's directive to restore order and stop looters

and arsonist at all cost. As discussed in Chapter II, the unrestrained actions of the Michigan National Guard triggered an equally violent response from local Detroit citizens.

[57] Robin Higham, ed., *Bayonets in the Streets: The Use of Troops in Civil Disturbances* (Lawrence, Kan.: University Press of Kansas, 1969), 8.

[58] William Cavanaugh, quoted in "Comment," *George Washington Law Review*, 870.

[59] The number of troops deployed to quell the 1967 Detroit riot varies with the source consulted. "An American Tragedy, 1967 -- Detroit," *Newsweek* 70 (7 August 1967), 20, contends that Task Force Detroit's troop strength was 4,700. Paul J. Scheips and Karl E. Cocke, "Army and Operational Intelligence in Civil Disturbances Since 1957," (Washington: GPO, 1971), 65, concluded that a little over 6,000 troops were deployed.

[60] Telephone interview, 18 May 1993, Brigadier General (Retired) John Burk with the author. General Burk served as the commander of the 3d Brigade, 28th Infantry Division Pennsylvania National Guard. He also served as the G-3 (Operations Officer) of the 29th Infantry Division and as the assistant division commander of the 28th Infantry Division.

[61] Comment, *George Washington Law Review*, 869.

[62] Carper, "Byrd Wants Troops to Stay," *Washington Post*, 9 April 1968, sec. A, p. 5.

[63] President Lyndon B. Johnson quoted in "Army, Guard Win Praise," *Army Times*, 28 (24 April 1968), 4.

[64] Sarah McClendon, "Army Says Planning, Training Saved City," *Washington Examiner*, 19 April 1968, sec. A, p. 1.

[65] This entry is a summation of "A New Look at New Weapons to Cope With Riots," *U.S. News & World Report*, 64 (1 January 1968), 6-7.

[66] See Task Force Washington After Action Report, 37, for the lessons learned during the Washington riot.

[67] Lines of authority and command relationships refer to the level of control that one command exercised over a subordinate command. Command relationships in 1968 consisted of assigned, attached, operational control, and operational command.

[68] Task Force Washington After Action Report, 39.

[69] Ibid., 39-40.

[70] Oliver Thomas, "Guard Found Duty Rough, Residents Friendly," *Washington Evening Star*, 21 April 1968, sec. B, p. 43.

[71] Ibid.

[72] SEADOC, the Senior Officer Civil Defense Orientation Course was taught at the Army's Military Police School at Fort Gordon, Georgia. SEADOC provided a medium for review of broad civil disturbance policies and procedures, problems and resources by civil officials from priority metropolitan areas and military officials involved in civil disturbance planning and operations. It prepared unit personnel for command, supervision, and planning duties in connection with the commitment of civil police, the Army National Guard and the Regular Army to civil disturbance operations.

[73] "City Girds for Summer: Extra Training for Police, D.C. Guard," *Washington Daily News*, 14 February 1968, p. 5.

[74] District of Columbia, National Guard, Task Force Goblet Glass After Action Report, 5-16 April 1968, 14 May 1968, located in File 103, RG 319, NA.

[75] McClendon, "Army Says Planning, Training Saved City," sec. A, p. 1.

[76] "Troops No Stranger to D.C.: Many Had Briefings Months Ago," *Washington Daily News*, 12 April 1968, p. 43.

[77] Not surprisingly, violation of the Posse Comitatus Act was not an issue during the Washington riots. Possible violations of the Act generally result from a lack of knowledge by the governor, mayor, or local police departments of the missions, roles and responsibilities that federal troops can undertake. Such was not the case in the Federal District of Columbia, where no state governor existed. Mayor Washington, had only held the newly created position since 1967. With respect to requesting and employing troops, the mayor consulted with General Haines, and the assistant attorney general--Warren Christopher. Moreover, several members of the District of Columbia National Guard and the Washington Metropolitan Police Department had undergone training in the SEADOC Course at Fort Gordon, Georgia. Furthermore, the Washington, D.C. contingency plan (Operation Cabin Guard) defined the roles of all military forces assigned to the city, as did the letter of

instruction provide very specific guidance on roles and missions for General Haines. Finally, see McClendon, "Army Says Planning, Training Saved City," sec. A, p. 1, Pearson and Anderson, "Planning Pays Off in Non-Riot Cities," sec B. p. 13, "Troops No Stranger to D.C.: Many Had Briefings Months Age," p. 43, for coverage of the interaction between Regular Army troops, National Guardsmen, and local police as they prepared for the Poor Peoples Campaign scheduled for 22 April. The role of federal troops in Washington, D.C., though not without a blemish, was as close to a "textbook" civil disturbance operation as has been seen during the history of the role.

[78] Thomas, "Guard Found Duty Rough," sec. B, p. 43.

[79] *Field Manual 25-100: Training the Force* (Washington: Headquarters Department of the Army, 15 November 1988), 3-1.

[80] David E. McGiffert, Department of the Army, Office of the Under Secretary of the Army, Memorandum for the Chief of Staff, U.S. Army, dated 17 April 1968, located in RG 319, NA.

[81] Information on Haines, is in the West Point Register of Graduates and Former Cadets, 279. Of interest is that General Haines was against Regular Army troops participating in riot control operations. Haines may have played an active role during his final assignment as the Commanding General, USCONARC in returning the civil disturbance mission to the National Guard. Also of interest is the fact that there is not a single reference by Haines' on his role as the Task Force Washington Commander within his oral history. Transcripts of Haines' interview is located at the U.S. Army War College in Carlisle, Pennsylvania.

[82] Samuel P. Huntington, *The Soldier and the State: The Theory and Politics of Civil-Military Relations* (Cambridge: Belknap Press of Harvard University Press, 1957), 261.

Chapter 4

[1] Allen D. Grimshaw, *Racial Violence in the United States* (Chicago: Aldine Publishing Company, 1969), 334.

[2] Continental Army Command/Army Strike Command, Annual Historical Summary, FY 1970 (Fort Monroe, Va.: Headquarters USCONARC, 28 February 1972), 133, located at the Center of Military History, Washington.

[3] Ibid., 157.

[4] See Memorandum from William J. McCaffrey, Director for Civil Disturbance Planning and Operations, for the Under Secretary of the Army, 30 September 1969, Subject: Federal Response to the Civil Disturbance Threat, RG 319, NA. See also Memorandum from Directorate for Civil Disturbance Plans and Operations, 19 September 1969, Subject: Quick Reaction Response to Civil Disturbances and Table 1--Priority Cities Department of the Army Civil Disturbance Plan, 3 February 1968, Annex I, Appendix L, for priority cities, located in Record Group 319, Records of the U.S. Army Staff, National Archives, College Park, Maryland, (hereafter RG 319 NA).

[5] See Memorandum, Office of Chief of Staff, 2 October 1969, Subject: Federal Response to the Civil Disturbance Threat, RG 319, NA.

[6] Continental Army Command/Army Strike Command Annual Historical Summary, FY 1970, 142.

[7] See Memorandum from the State of Ohio Adjutant General's Department, S. T. Del Corso, Major General, The Adjutant General, for the Chief, National Guard Bureau, 8 June 1970, Subject: After Action Report, Kent State University, 2-8 May 1970, signed by Brigadier General Robert Canterbury Assistant Adjutant General for the Ohio National Guard, 7, located at the National Guard Bureau Historical Branch, the Pentagon, Washington, D.C.

[8] See Joe Eszterhas and Michael D. Roberts, *Thirteen Seconds: Confrontation at Kent State* (New York: Dodd, Mead & Company, 1970), Peter Davies, *The Truth About Kent State: A Challenge to the American Conscience* (New York: Farrar Straus Giroux, 1973), William A. Gordon, *The Fourth of May: Killings and Coverups at Kent State* (Buffalo, N. Y.:

Prometheus Books, 1990), Ottavio M. Casale and Louis Paskoff, eds., *The Kent Affair: Documents and Interpretations* (Boston: Houghton Mifflin, 1971), Joseph Kelner and James Munves, *The Kent State Coverup* (New York: Harper & Row, Publishers, 1980), R.W. Whitney, *Events of Our Time: The Kent State Massacre* (Charlottesville, N. Y.: SamHar Press, 1975), and James A. Michener, *Kent State: What Happened and Why* (New York: Random House, 1971).

⁹ "The Guard vs. Disorder," *The National Guardsman* 24 (June 1970), 3.

¹⁰ See "A *Newsweek* Poll: Mr. Nixon Holds Up," *Newsweek* 75 (25 May 1970), 30.

¹¹ "Diverse Opinions on Kent State," Cleveland *Plain Dealer*, 7 May 1970, 10A.

¹² Statement by Major General James F. Cantwell, President, National Guard Association of the United States, 11 May 1970, located at National Guard Bureau Historical Services, the Pentagon.

¹³ Ibid.

¹⁴ Statement of Major General Winston P. Wilson, Chief, National Guard Bureau at Senate Armed Services Committee during Strength Authorization Hearing, 7 May 1970, 2, located at National Guard Bureau Historical Services, the Pentagon.

¹⁵ Ibid.

¹⁶ "The Guard vs. Disorder," *The National Guardsman* 24 (June 1970), 3.

¹⁷ Ibid. According to Brigadier General Robert Canterbury, Guard casualties totaled 43. Of those injured Canterbury noted that: (1) non-commissioned officer had a heart attack; (2) non-commissioned officers were treated at a hospital for injuries sustained from objects thrown by students; (1) soldier who swallowed glass from a broken windshield was treated at the hospital; (1) Guardsman was hospitalized with an un-identified nervous disorder; (10) soldiers injured by rioters were treated at the battalion medical section and returned to duty; and (3) Ohio Guardsmen sustained injuries serious enough to require extended hospitalization. See After Action Report, Kent State University, 2-8 May 1970, 7.

[18] Richard G. Ellers and Richard C. Widman, "Kent Rioters Driven Back onto Campus," Cleveland *Plain Dealer*, 4 May 1970, 1a and 6a.

[19] Ibid.

[20] Governor Rhodes quoted in Casale and Paskoff, *The Kent State Affair*, 142.

[21] Major General Del Corso quoted in Whitney, *Events of Our Time*, 15.

[22] Brigadier General Robert Canterbury quoted in Michael C. Roberts, "Half of Troops Due to Leave Kent," (Cleveland) *Plain Dealer*, 6 May 1970, 6a.

[23] See the Report of the President's Commission on Campus Unrest, (Washington, D.C.: Government Printing Office, 1970), 283. Although the Commission on Campus Unrest recommended that this practice be eliminated, there are numerous documented instances of armed weapons carried by California National Guardsmen during the 1992 Los Angeles riot.

[24] Paragraph 1-1b of the 1972 edition of *Field Manual 19-15* clearly expressed the purpose and scope of the manual. It stated that the guidance was "intended primarily for use by the U.S. Active and Reserve Component Forces, and should not be applied to State or municipal police operations without certain adaptations or modifications." The aforementioned statement captured the crux of the National Guard versus federal force debate. The Guard under a state governors control can fully engage in state or municipal police operations, as the Posse Comitatus Act does not apply. Moreover, the Garden Plot Contingency Plan for civil disturbances, the Army's standard rules of engagement, and the rules for arming a weapon do not apply to a state controlled National Guard force. Whereas the Regular Army could hope that the Ohio National Guard would exhibit restraint and adhere to the tenets and principles outlined in *FM 19-15*, there was no regulatory requirement that mandated this action.

[25] Roberts, "Half of Troops Due to Leave Kent," Cleveland *Plain Dealer*, 6 May 1970, 6a.

[26] Canterbury quoted in The Report of the President's Commission on Campus Unrest, 270.

[27] See La Rochefoucauld, "Maxims" in Arthur M. Eastman, ed., *The Norton Reader: An Anthology of Expository Prose*, 4th Edition (New York: W.W. Norton and Company, Inc., 1977), 901.

[28] See photographs 50, 51, and 52 in Davies, *The Truth About Kent State*, 110-112.

[29] Military Police units are also an exception, as the M1911A1 (.45 caliber) pistol is basic assigned weapon of military police.

[30] Gordon, *The Fourth of May*, 38.

[31] Ibid., 140.

[32] See Davies, *The Truth About Kent State*, photo 52, 112. This same picture is magnified and is shown on the cover of Davies' book.

[33] There is only one exception to this rule. If an empty clip is inserted into the weapon, the slide stop will lock to the rear automatically upon manually cocking the weapon. It is not very likely that this occurred on 4 May 1970.

[34] See Davies, *The Truth About Kent State*, photo 52, 112.

[35] Ibid., photo 58, 119.

[36] Ibid., photo 59, 120. According to *The New York Times*, the Federal Bureau of Investigation opened an investigation on 7 May 1970. The Bureau confiscated thirteen M1 rifles from the Guard, but did not take any .45 caliber pistols. See John Kifner, "Role of Guns Undefined; Campus Remains Quiet," *The New York Times*, 7 May 1970, 19 col. 1 and 2.

[37] President Richard M. Nixon quoted in "Nixon Sees Tragic Reminder at Kent," (Cleveland) *Plain Dealer*, 5 May 1970, 12a.

[38] Chief Donald Swartzmiller quoted in Richard G. Ellers and Richard C. Widman, "Kent Rioters Driven Back onto Campus," (Cleveland) *Plain Dealer*, 4 May 1970, 1a and 6a.

[39] Major Arthur E. Wallach quoted in ibid., 1a and 6a.

[40] Brian Fisher quoted in "Troops Lost All Their Cool," Joe Eszterhas, (Cleveland)_*Plain Dealer*, 5 May 1970, 1a and 6a. For detailed coverage of events from 1-4 May 1970 and profiles of the four students killed, as well as previews on the initial investigations see Eszterhas and Roberts, *Thirteen Seconds*.

[41] William Hickey, "Kent State University Story One-sided in TV Report," (Cleveland) *Plain Dealer*, 7 May 1970, E6.

[42] Ibid.

[43] John F. Kutcher is quoted in W.D. McGlasson, "From Watts to Kent State: The Guard's Time of Testing," *The National Guardsman* 45 (May 1991), 18.

[44] Major General Francis Greenlief quoted in ibid.

[45] Major General James F. Cantwell quoted in ibid., 20.

[46] <u>Report of President's Commission on Campus Unrest</u>, 290.

[47] See the State of Ohio Adjutant General's Department, <u>Annual Report Fiscal Year 1970</u>, located at the National Guard Bureau Historical Branch, Pentagon, Washington.

[48] See After Action Report, Kent State University, 2-8 May 1970, 7.

[49] <u>Report of President's Commission on Campus Unrest</u>, 289.

[50] Memorandum from Major General Charles M. Gettys, acting Director for Civil Disturbance Plans and Operations, For the Assistant Secretary of the Army, not dated, Subject: Civil Disturbance Training for the Army National Guard, RG 319, NA.

[51] "Army's Rules Tightly Restrict Deadly Force in Riot Situations," *The New York Times*, 6 May 1970, 19, col. 1 and 2. In this article, the chief spokesman for the Department for Public Affairs highlighted the Rules of Engagement for a federalized force as well as the provisions of *Field Manual 19-15*. The spokesman, on the one hand, disavowed any federal ties to the Ohio Guard at Kent State, while, on the other hand created the false notion that federal rules of engagement and the doctrinal tenets of *FM 19-15* were applicable to the state controlled force.

[52] "Who Guards Against the Guard?" *Newsweek* 75 (18 May 1970), 33F.

[53] See Appendix D.

[54] Albert Brien, "The Case for Uniform Regulation of the National Guard," *Boston University Law Review* 50 (Special Issue 1970) 170.

[55] Kenneth Pye, *The Use of Troops in the United States*, (Durham, N.C.: Duke University Center for International Studies, 1982), 14.

[56] Ibid.

[57] James J. Kilpatrick, "Looking Behind the Triggers in Ohio," *The National Guardsman* 24 (June 1970), 15.

[58] Continental Army Command/Army Strike Command, <u>Annual Historical Summary, FY 1971</u> (Fort Monroe, Va.: Headquarters USCONARC, 27 December 1972), 69, located at the Center of Military History, Washington.

[59] Ibid., 76.

[60] During the same year the Army responded to 349 requests for support from the U.S. Secret Service. Continental Army Command/Army Strike Command, <u>Annual Historical Summary, FY 1972</u> (Fort Monroe, Va.: Headquarters USCONARC, 27 November 1973), 296, located at the Center of Military History, Washington.

[61] Ibid., 224.

[62] U.S. Army Forces Command, <u>Annual Report of Major Activities, FY 1977</u> (Fort McPherson, Ga.: Headquarters FORSCOM, 1 October 1978), 630. located at the Center of Military History, Washington.

[63] See James R. Gardner, "The Civil Disturbance Mission of the Department of the Army, 1963-1973," (Ph.D. dissertation, Princeton University, 1977), 271.

[64] Edward S. Farrow, *Farrow's Military Encyclopedia: A Dictionary of Knowledge* (New York: Edward S. Farrow, 1885), 566.

[65] Department of the Army, Directorate of Military Support, Memorandum for the Vice Chief of Staff and the Under Secretary of the Army, 3 March 1973, Subject: Indian Disturbance, Wounded Knee, South Dakota, quoted in Gardner, "The Civil Disturbance Mission," 273.

[66] The ruling was made in Bismarck, North Dakota, by the Southwestern Division of the U.S. District Court. The court decision is quoted in Gardner, 306.

[67] See U.S. House of Representatives, Committee on the Judiciary, U.S. House of Representatives, 97th Congress, 1st session, H.R. 3519, 3 June 1981.

[68] FORSCOM, <u>Annual Report of Major Activities</u>, 630.

[69] See the <u>National Guard Bureau Annual Reports 1969-1991</u> (Washington: Government Printing Office, 1968-1991), located at the National Guard Bureau, the Pentagon.

[70] See Table 9.

[71] David MacIntyre, <u>Narvik</u> (New York: W.W. Norton and Company, Inc., 1960), 1.

[72] Bruce Porter and Marvin Dunn, *The Miami Riot of 1980* (Lexington, Mass.: D.C. Heath and Company, 1984), 93-94.

[73] Ibid., the 750 represented the number of Guardsmen actually dispersed for riot duty. It does not include Guardsmen that constituted the quick reaction force (reserve) or those manning command posts or serving as liaisons with the police or fire departments.

[74] Memorandum from Military Affairs Office of the Adjutant General, to Chief, National Guard Bureau, 12 March 1981, Subject: After Action Report Dade County Civil Disturbance 12-17 May 1980, located at the National Guard Bureau, the Pentagon.

[75] See Mike Clary, "Governor Sends Guard Into Riot Areas," *Miami Herald*, 14 May 1980, 3B, col 2 and 3.

[76] Lesley Valdes, "In 'Black Grove,' Residents Look After their Own- -and Troops, Too," *Miami News*, 20 May 1980, 7a, col 1.

[77] <u>The National Advisory Commission on Civil Disorders</u> (New York: Bantam Books, 1968), charts that follow page 609.

[78] See Grinshaw, *Racial Violence*, 334.

[79] Dunn and Porter, *Miami Riot*, 96.

[80] See "Rage in Miami: A Warning," *U.S. News & World Report* 88 (2 June 1980): 28.

Chapter 5

[1] "Premier Annoyed by Ban on Visit to Disneyland," *The New York Times*, 20 September 1959, p. 40, col. 3. This quote is Mayor Poulson's welcome to Premier Nikita Khrushchev upon his arrival at the Los Angeles Airport in September 1959.

[2] "Sifting Through the Ruins," *Historic Preservation* 44 (September/October 1992), 48. For estimated monetary cost of the riots see "Costly Riots," *Los Angeles Times*, 2 May 1992, A16, and Thomas

S. Mulligan, "L.A. Riots Called Costliest in U.S. History," *Los Angeles Times*, 5 May 1992, B6. For the death toll, see "Counting Up the Human Cost," *Newsweek* 119 (18 May 1992), 47.

[3] Joe Califano, Summary Report on Watts for President, 16 June 1967, 1, located in the Joseph Califano Papers, container 58, at the Lyndon B. Johnson Library and Museum, University of Texas, Austin, Texas. (hereafter L.B.J. Library)

[4] See ibid. See also Anthony Oberschall, "The Los Angeles Riot of August 1965," in David Boesel and Peter H. Rossi, eds., *Cities Under Siege: An Anatomy of Ghetto Riots, 1964-68* (New York: Basic Books, 1971), 86-87. According to Oberschall, in the November 1964 election, California voters repealed the Rumsford Fair Housing Act in a constitutional referendum by a 2:1 margin. Votes to repeal the act were particularly high in Southern California and even higher in the predominately white areas that surrounded the Negro neighborhoods in Los Angeles County. White areas were in favor of the repeal in the 80 to 90 percent range, whereas Negro precincts voted against the measure by almost 90 percent. According to Oberschall, the vote was widely interpreted as a hardening of white public opinion with respect to the issue of integrated housing.

[5] Ramsey Clark, Report of the President's Task Force on the Los Angeles Riots, 11-15 August 1965, 17 September 1965, quotes found on page 17, located in the Ramsey Clark Papers, container 47, L.B.J. Library.

[6] Ibid.

[7] Ibid., 6.

[8] Ibid., 8.

[9] See Daryl Gates, *The Chief: My Life in the LAPD* (New York: Bantam Books, 1992), 108.

[10] Ramsey Clark Report, 20, LBJ Library.

[11] "Race and Rage: The Growing Split Between Black and White," *U.S. News and World Report* 112 (11 May 1992), 22.

[12] See Report by the Special Advisor to the Board of Police Commissioners on the Civil Disorder in Los Angeles, *The City in Crisis* (Los Angeles: Office of the Special Advisor to the Board of Police Commissioners of Los Angeles, 1992,) 33. This report is commonly

known as the "Webster Report" after its special advisor, Judge William H. Webster, and is hereafter cited as the <u>Webster Report</u>.

[13] Ibid., 32.

[14] Crime fighting versus crime prevention refers to a proactive rather than reactive police force. Crime fighting is taking aggressive action against crime and criminals--going on the offense against criminals. Crime prevention generally adheres to passive measures. See <u>Webster Report</u>, 32.

[15] For a synopsis of the "two struggles" in Los Angeles Police Department, see ibid., 31-34.

[16] Former Los Angeles Police Commission President and former Assistant LAPD Chief of Police Jesse Brewer, personal interview with author, 31 May 1995 in Los Angeles.

[17] Deputy Chief of Police Bernard Parks, personal interview with author, 30 May 1995 at Parker Center in Los Angeles.

[18] See <u>Webster Report</u>, 33. The report is careful to point out that Gates' focus was not simply an attempt to retreat from the community based policing policies of his predecessors. Gates faced considerable budgetary constraints, and much like his mentor, Bill Parker, Gates had to do more with less.

[19] Ibid., 38.

[20] Gates, *The Chief*, 37.

[21] Ibid., 38.

[22] Personal interview with Deputy Chief Bernard Parks. The LAPD was called in after a gas company serviceman reported that he had been assaulted by Eula Love while attempting to disconnect her gas line because her account was $69 in arrears. The serviceman reported that if she had paid $22 he would not have disconnected her line. After striking the attendant in the forearm with a shovel, Love purchased a money order in the amount of $22.

[24] The Foothill Division is also the division of assignment of the four officers accused of beating Rodney King in 1991.

[25] See Report of the Independent Commission of the Los Angeles Police Department, 9 July 1991 (henceforth the Christopher Commission Report).

[26] David Ellis, "L.A. Lawless: The Violence Sparked by the King Verdict Reveals Racial Division that have Plagued the City for Years," *Time* 139 (11 May 1992), 28.

[27] Webster Report, 34.

[28] Scott Minerbrook, "A Different Reality for Us," *U.S. News & World Report* 119 (11 May 1992), 36.

[29] Former Los Angeles Mayor Tom Bradley, personal interview with author, 31 May 1995 in Los Angeles.

[30] Former Los Angeles Police Department Chief of Police, Daryl Gates, telephonic interview with author, 31 May 1995.

[31] "One Year Later: The Fires of L.A. Rage On," *Elle* 8 (May 1993), 82.

[32] "Bush: President Pledges Enough Force to Quell Violence," *Los Angeles Times*, 2 May 1992, A22.

[33] Robert Conot, "When Watts' Lessons Are Forgotten," *Los Angeles Times*, 3 May 1992, M1.

[34] Webster Report, 49.

[35] "Counting Up the Human Cost," 47.

[36] Personal interview with Mayor Tom Bradley.

[37] Daniel M. Wientraub, "National Guard Official Cites Series of Delays," Los Angeles Times, 5 May 1992, A4.

[38] General Daniel Brennan quoted in ibid.

[39] Lieutenant General Marvin Covault, telephonic interview with author, 25 September 1996.

[40] Major General Daniel J. Hernandez, telephonic interview with author, 1 October 1996.

[41] James D. Delk, "Military Assistance in Los Angeles," Military Review 72 (September 1992), 13.

[42] Telephonic interview with Chief Daryl Gates.

[43] See Oberschall, "The Los Angeles Riot of August 1965," in Boesel and Rossi, eds., *Cities Under Siege*, 95. Within this passage the authors noted how the partial show of force in 1965 appeared to incite the crowd rather than calm them.

[44] For a troop list of the 40th Infantry Division, see immediate message from the Secretary of the Army to the Governor of the State of California, 2 May 1992, Subject: Calling of California National Guard

into Federal Service (Garden Plot), located at the Center of Military History, Washington, D.C.

[45] General Harrison is quoted in Daniel M. Wientraub, ""Report on L.A. Riots Blasts National Guard," *Los Angeles Times* (Washington, D.C., edition), 3 December 1992, A1.

[46] Ibid.

[47] Governor Wilson is quoted in David Freed and Ted Rohrlich, "Crisis Shows LAPD is Ill-Prepared for Riots, " *Los Angeles Times*, 1 May 1992, A7.

[48] General Brennnan is quoted in Wientraub, " Series of Delays," A4.

[49] Robert Reinhold, "Surprised, Police React Slowly as Violence Spreads," *Los Angeles Times*, 1 May 1992, A1.

[50] See "Questions posed by National Guard Bureau," April 1992, 3, located at the National Guard Bureau, Washington, D.C.

[51] Ibid., 6.

[52] Sergeant Robert Wood and Specialist Denise Blohm, "First in Brigade: 670th Mobilized for the 1992 Los Angeles Riot," *Pride and Power* 1 (10 May 1992), 1.

[53] Colonel John J. Ryneska, Situation Report (SITREP) Number 2, 1-2 May 1992, located at the Center of Military History, Washington, D.C.

[54] Army Public Affairs, Marlin Fitzwater Briefing, 1 May 1992, 2, located at the Center of Military History, Washington, D.C.

[55] "Questions posed by National Guard Bureau," 6.

[56] Ibid., 5.

[57] Draft Talking Paper for Commander, Joint Task Force Los Angeles, 1. Located at the Center of Military History, Washington. D.C.

[58] Telephonic interview with Major General Daniel J. Hernandez.

[59] Under the original contingency plans, units had habitual relations with designated cities. For example, in 1968 the 82d Airborne Division of Fort Bragg, North Carolina, and the 5th Infantry Division of Fort Carson, Colorado, where assigned under Garden Plot to the nation's capital--as were all the units within a one-hundred-mile radius of the

city. However, in 1992 the primary consideration for assignment was proximity.

[60] Telephonic interview with Lieutenant General Marvin L. Covault. Of note: General Covault was not sure why the role was not given to the Marine Corps.

[61] In 1968 when Garden Plot was first published, President Johnson called on the likes of Ramsey Clark, Cyrus Vance, and Warren Christopher to serve as his representative on the ground. These men served in that critical role during the civil rights protest and in Detroit and Washington. In short, Clark, Vance, and Christopher were experienced and were fully capable of fulfilling the duty.

[62] See Joint Task Force Los Angeles Memorandum, "Biography of Major General Marvin L. Covault, Commanding General, 7th Infantry Division (Light)," 7 May 1992, located at the Center of Military History, Washington, D.C.

[63] Telephonic interview with General Covault.

[64] Robert W. Taylor, Principal Deputy Assistant Secretary of the Army, Public Affairs Update--Joint Task Force Los Angeles, 11, located at the Center of Military History, Washington, D.C.

[65] Telephonic interview with General Covault, 25 September 1996.

[66] Draft Talking Paper Joint Task Force Los Angeles, 2.

[67] Memorandum for the Director of Military Support, U.S. Army ODCSOPS, Washington, D.C., 11 July 1992, Subject: CINCFOR AAR on Operation Garden Plot, JTF-Los Angeles, II-25. Located at Sixth Army Headquarters, Presidio, California.

[68] Ibid., II-27.

[69] Greg Seigle, "Police Praise Guard's L. A. Performance," Army Times, 11 May 1992, 1.

[70] G2, 40th Infantry Division Situation Summary, 3-4 May 1992, 3, located at the Center of Military History, Washington, D.C. Of note, Rivas' death occurred on the eve of the twenty-second anniversary of the 1970 Kent State shootings.

[71] Ibid.

[72] Major General James D. Delk, telephonic interview with author, 1 October 1996. General Delk was the Commander of Troops for the California National Guard during the Los Angeles riot.

[73] Major General Marvin Hopgood, telephonic interview with author, 25 September 1996. General Hopgood was the Marine Forces Commander during the Los Angeles riot in 1992.

[74] Telephonic interview with General Covault. According to General Covault, the "Beirut Syndrome" describes the Marine Corps intent to never again experience the loss and helplessness that U.S. Marines experienced in Beirut, Lebanon, during the early 1980's.

[75] Ryneska, Situation Report (SITREP), Number 6, 5-6 May 1992, 2.

[76] Ibid.

[77] Ibid.

[78] Ibid.

[79] Telephonic interview with General Delk, 1 October 1996. "Restoration" of law and order refers to the assistance by a military force in reestablishing civil control, discipline, and law and order. "Maintenance" of law and order implies that civil control, discipline, and law and order have already been attained. During this latter function the military's presence is to ensure that a quelled riot does not reignite.

[80] Telephonic interview with former LAPD Chief Daryl Gates on 31 May 1995.

[81] For specific rules of engagement and arming orders see Appendix C and D.

[82] Telephonic interview with General Delk, 1 October 1996. Both General Hernandez and General Delk pointed out during their telephonic interviews with the author that California Guardsmen fired only twenty- two rounds out of the more than 300,000 that they possessed.

Chapter 6

[1] See George Santayana, The Life of Reason, Volume 1, 1905, at www.quotationspage.com/quotes/George_Santayana/.

[2] Major General (Retired) James Delk stated that local political and police officials were disappointed with the responsiveness once federal forces. He argued that in retrospect, Mayor Bradley had wished that he had not requested such assistance. The general concluded that given similar circumstances, the political leadership of Los Angeles would not seek federal assistance.

[3] Memorandum for Directorate of Military Support, U.S. Army Office of the Deputy Chief of Staff, Operations, Washington, 11 July 1992, Subject: CINCFOR After Action Report (AAR) on Operation Garden Plot, JTF-Los Angeles, II-26, located at Forces Command Headquarters, Fort McPherson, Georgia.

[4] Ibid., II-27.

[5] Ibid.

[6] Kenneth Pye, The Use of Troops in Civil Disturbances in the United States (Durham, N.C.: Duke University Center for International Studies, 1982), 14.

[7] Department of the Army Message Number 858668, from the Chief of Staff to Vice Chief of Staff, 6 April 1968, Subject: Designation to Commander of Task Force Washington, 1-7, located in Record Group 319, National Archives, College Park, Maryland.File 103, (henceforth, RG319, NA). This entry is a brief synopsis of the letter of instruction issued to General Ralph G. Haines as he assumed command of Task Force Washington. Of note, this is one of the few command situations where the commander is not afforded the opportunity to impart his vision on the organization.

[8] The special orders from 1968 and 1992 are listed at Appendix A. Questions and answers distributed to soldiers during the 1992 riots are listed at Appendix B.

[9] Charles P. Stone, "Lessons of Detroit, summer 1967," in Robin Higham, ed., Bayonets in the Streets: The Use of Troops in Civil

<u>Disturbances</u> (Lawrence, Kansas:  University Press of Kansas: 1969), 191.

[10] AAR, II-3.

[11]<u>Field Manual 90-10: Military Operations in Urbanized Terrain</u> (Washington, D.C.: Headquarters, Department of the Army, 15 August 1979), G-8. During an interview with the author, Major General (Retired) James D. Delk (commander of troops for the California Army National Guard during the Los Angeles riot) asserted that over 200 rounds were fired by Marines during this incident. See also James D. Delk, <u>Fire and Furies: The L.A. Riots</u> (Palm Springs, Calif.: EPC Publications, 1994), 222.

[12] Information provided by Brigadier General (Retired) Douglas Kinnard during telephonic interview with author on 23 May 1996.

[13] Garden Plot Appendix 2 (Quick Reaction Force) to Annex C (Operations) to Commander-in-Chief Forces Command (CINCFOR) Civil Disturbance Plan (Garden Plot), C-2-1. Located at Fort McPherson, Georgia.

[14] Ibid., 7. The Garden Plot contingency plan states that the unit will be fully capable of quelling a riot per its arrival in a riot situation. This is highly unlikely given the fact that the DRB does not train on riot-related skills.

[15] <u>FM 100-19, FMFM 7-10: Domestic Support Operations</u> (Washington, D.C.: Headquarters, Department of the Army and U.S. Marine Corps, 1993), 9-0.

[16] Ibid., C-12-1.

[17] AAR, II-5.

[18] George Marshall, quoted in <u>FM 25-100</u>, 3-1.

[19] See discussion of Bonus March 1932 and Detroit 1943 riots in Chapter II this study.

[20] See Table 9: Annual Training Requirement for Civil Disturbance Operation, Chapter V this study. See also Continental Army Command, Appendix XV, Training in Civil Disturbance Operations, 22 October 1968, RG319, NA.

[21] William Hazlitt, "Characteristics," in Arthur M. Eastman, ed., The Norton Reader: An Anthology of Expository Prose, 4th Edition (New York: W.W. Norton and Company, Inc., 1977), 898.

[22] Office of the Special Consultant to the Secretary of the Army, Bicentennial of the United States Constitution: A Resource Guide, Supplement IV: 1991 The Adoption of the Bill of Rights (Washington, D.C.: Office of the Special Consultant to the Secretary of the Army, 1991), 93.

[23] Major General Daniel Hernandez telephonic interview with author on 1 October 1996. General Hernandez was the commander of the 40th Infantry Division, California Army National Guard and the Army Forces Commander during the 1992 Los Angeles riot.

[24] Jody J. Elwell, "Riot Read," Soldiers 48 (November 1993), 50.

[25] Maria L. LoVasco, "Dedicated Rioters Ensured Louisiana Guard Soldiers Undergoing Civil Disturbance Training Got . . . No Time Out," Soldiers 50 (March 1995), 22.

[26] Stone, "Lessons of Detroit, summer 1967," 191.

[27] See John O. Edwards, www.NewsMax.com, Friday, Nov. 21, 2003, "Gen. Franks Doubts Constitution Will Survive WMD Attack." General Franks is also quoted in www.propagandamatrix.com/211103martial-law.html.

[28] Henry David Thoreau quoted in: https://en.wikiquote.org/wiki/Civil_Disobedience_(Thoreau).

[29] Field Manual 19-15: Civil Disturbances and Disasters. (Washington, D.C.: Government Printing Office, 1967), 19-20.

[30] The Prophet Muhammed quoted in: www.rumisgarden.co.uk/.../prophet-muhammed-four-things-support-the-world

Chapter 7

[1] Charles Dickens, A Tale of Two Cities (London, England: James Nisbet & CO., Limited, 1902), 1.

[2] Alan Dawley, Struggles for Justice: Social Responsibility and the Liberal State (Cambridge, 1991), 416.

[3] Bible King James, Matthew 5:14.

[4] Kerner Report, 117

[5] https:www.mappingpolicevoilence.org/

[6] Ibid.

[7] Ibid.

[8] Ibid

[9] Ibid

[10]The Holy Bible, English Standard Version Text Edition: 2016. Copyright 2001 by Crossway Bibles, a publishing ministry of Good News Publishers

[11]https:www.mappingpoliceviolence.org/

[12] Report of the National Advisory Commission on Civil Disturbances (New York: Bantam Books, 1968), 483. Hereafter referred to as the Kerner Report.

[13] Ibid., vii.

[14] Andrew Hacker, *Two Nations*, (New York: Macmillan, 1992), 218.

[15]George M. Fredrickson, "A Man But Not a Brother: Abraham Lincoln and Racial Equality," Journal of Southern History, 41 (February 1975), 39-58.

[16] Michael Omi and Howard Winut, "Racism Is Prevalent Today," in Bruno Leone, ed., *Racism Opposing Viewpoints: The Isms: Modern Doctrines and Movements* (St. Paul, Minn.: Greenhaven Press, 1986), 138.

[17] Ibid., 139.

[18]John Hope Franklin, *The Color Line: Legacy for the Twenty-First Century* (Columbia, Mo.: University of Missouri Press, 1993), 72.

[19] Hacker, *Two Nations*, 219.

[20] Ibid., 98. See also National Urban League, Inc., State of Black America, 1994 (New York: The National Urban League, Inc., 1994), 214.

[21] Hacker, *Two Nations*, 100. See also National Urban League, State of Black America, 218.

[22] Hacker, *Two Nations*, 103. See also National Urban League, State of Black America, 223.

[23] Harvard Sitkoff, *The Struggle for Black Equality: 1954-1992* (New York: Hill and Wang, 1993), 227.

[24] Barbara Ritchie, *The Riot Report: A Shortened Version of the Report of the National Commission on Civil Disorders* (New York: The Viking Press, 1969), 7.

[25] Kerner Report, xv.

## Epilogue

[1] George Santayana, *The Life of Reason: Reason in Common Sense.* (New York: Scribner's, 1905), 284..

[2] Thaddeus Hoffmeister, (2010). "An Insurrection Act for the Twenty-first Century." *Stetson Law Review*, 39: 898.


[3] 45 Quotes of our Beloved Prophet Muhammad About the Discipline of Life

# *APPENDIX A*

## SPECIAL ORDERS GIVEN TO SOLDIERS ENGAGED IN CIVIL

## DISTURBANCE OPERATIONS[1]

1.  Carry out your assigned duties in a military manner and present a neat military appearance at all times. Be sure that everything you do reflects credit upon your country, the military service, your unit, and yourself.

2.  Have regard for the human rights of all persons. Be as courteous toward civilians as possible under the circumstances. Do not mistreat anyone or withhold medical attention from anyone needing it. Do not damage property unnecessarily.

3.  Use only the minimum amount of force required to accomplish your mission and, if necessary, to defend yourself. When under the control of an officer, you will load or fire your weapon only on his orders. When not under the control of an officer, you will load or fire your weapon only when required to protect your own life or the lives of others, to protect specified property designated as vital to public health or safety, or to prevent the escape of persons endangering life or vital facilities; you are not authorized to use firearms to prevent offenses which are not likely to cause death or serious bodily harm, not endanger public health or safety.

4.  When firing is necessary, shoot to wound, not to kill.

5.  When possible, let civilian police arrest lawbreakers. But when assistance is necessary or in the absence of the civil police, you have the duty and the authority to take lawbreakers into custody. Take such persons to the police or designated military authorities as soon as possible. Cooperate fully with the police by safeguarding evidence and completing records as instructed.

6.  Allow properly identified news reporters freedom of movement, so long as they do not interfere with the mission of your unit.

7.  Do not talk about this operation or pass on information or rumors about it to unauthorized person; refer all civilians who ask for information about what you are doing to your commanding officer.

8.  Become familiar with these special orders, and carry this card on your person at all times when engaged in civil disturbance operations.

---

[1] Special orders remain unchanged from 1967. See Department of Defense, Graphic Training Aid 21-2-7: October 1967, Special Orders For All Military Personnel Engaged In Civil Disturbance Operations, located in File 103, Record Group 319, National Archives, College Park, Maryland, (RG 319, NA). For 1992 special orders refer to Tab A (Special Orders) to Appendix 12 (Rules of Engagement) to Annex C (Concept of Operations) to CINCFOR Civil Disturbance Plan (Garden Plot), C-12-A-1, 21 November 1992, located at Forces Command (FORSCOM), Fort McPherson, Georgia.

# *APPENDIX B*

# QUESTIONS AND ANSWERS 1992 RIOTS[1]

Joint Information Bureau's Question and Answer Handout for JTF LA Forces Q: What unit are you with?

A: Answer forthrightly.

Q: How do you feel about being out here? A: Answer forthrightly.

Q: Does the possibility of using deadly force against fellow citizens bother you?

A: We are trained to use the minimum force necessary to perform our mission. We, however, do not want to even doe that.

Q: Have you seen any looting/violence/arson activity?

A: Answer forthrightly.

Q: Do you have live ammunition in your weapon?

A: Answer truthfully.

Q: How long do you expect to be out here?

A: I really couldn't speculate. That will be determined by civilian and military authorities.

Q: Have you ever been involved in an operation like this before?

A: Answer truthfully.

Q: How do you feel about the verdict in the Rodney King trial?

A: It would be inappropriate for me to comment on that matter.

Q: Did you think the verdict from the trial would have resulted in violence to such an extent?

A: I really couldn't speculate.

Q:  Can you pursue and arrest individuals engaged in illegal activity?

A:  We are here to support civil law enforcement authority. We will only use the minimum force necessary. We are authorized to assist, but do not discuss rules of engagement.

---

[1]  See Immediate Message from the Secretary of Defense, 2 May 1992, Subject: Public Affairs Guidance Update Joint Task Force Los Angeles, located at the Center of Military of Military History Washington, D.C. See also Department of Defense, 7 May 1992, Subject: Role and Mission Statement of Joint Task Force Los Angeles, Questions and Answers, Biographies of Task Force Commanding General and the Division Commander of the California National Guard; and Office of the Assistant Secretary of Defense, Public Affairs, 7 May 1992, Subject Questions and Answers for California Unrest, both located at the Center of Military History. See also Nora Zamicho "Marching Orders Include Script for Answering Queries," Los Angeles Times, 4 May 1992, 4.

# *APPENDIX C*

## ARMING ORDERS[1]

| Arming Order | Rifle | Bayonet Scabbard | Bayonet | Pistol * | Baton * | Ammo | Chamber |
|---|---|---|---|---|---|---|---|
| 1 | Sling | on belt | Scabbard | holstered | belt | in pouch | empty |
| 2 | Port | on belt | Scabbard | holstered | belt | in pouch | empty |
| 3 | Sling ** | on belt ** | Fixed | holstered | hand | in pouch | empty |
| 4 | Port | on belt | Fixed | holstered | hand | in pouch | empty |
| 5 | Port | on belt | Fixed | holstered | hand | in weapon | empty |
| 6 | Port | on belt | Fixed | in hand | belt | in weapon | loaded |

\* Denotes weapons that were not included in the Arming Orders during the 1968 post-Martin Luther King assassination riots.

\*\* Denotes changes on the 1992 Arming Orders. On the 1968 Arming Orders at level three the rifle was at port arms and the scabbard was on the bayonet.

NOTE: Each of the above options represents an escalation in the level of force. They are not, however, a mandatory sequence requiring a commander to initially select the first option, or to proceed from one to another in any particular order. So long as the option selected is appropriate, given the threat, the minimum necessary force principle is not violated.

---

[1] For 1968 Arming Orders see Task Force Washington After Action Report (AAR), 4- 16 April 1968, Appendix B (Letter of Instructions), B-4, File 103, RG 319, NA. For 1992 Arming Orders see Appendix 12 (Rules of Engagement) to Annex C (Concept of Operations) to CINCFOR Civil Disturbance Plan (Garden Plot), C-12-7. See also The International and Operational Law Department, Operational Law Handbook, (Charlottesville, Virginia: The Judge Advocate General's School, 1995), 21-8, and Bruce Irwin, "Security of the Force: A Commanders Call," Infantry, 83 (January - February 1993), 42.

# *APPENDIX D*

## RULES OF ENGAGEMENT[1]

1.  Every serviceman has the right under law to use reasonable and necessary force to defend himself against violent and dangerous personal attack. The limitations described below are not intended to infringe this right, but to prevent the indiscriminate use of force.

2.  Force will never be used unless necessary, and then only the minimum force necessary will be used.

    (a) Use non-deadly force to:

        (1) Control the disturbance.

        (2) Prevent crimes.

        (3) Apprehend or detain persons who have committed crimes.

    (b) Use deadly force only when:

        (1) Lesser means of force exhausted or unavailable; and

        (2) Risk of death or serious bodily harm to innocent persons is not significantly increased by the use; and

        (3) Purpose of use:

            (a) Self-defense to avoid death or serious bodily harm.

            (b) Prevention of crime involving death or serious bodily harm.

            (c) Prevention of destruction of public utilities which have been determined vital by the task force commander.

            (d) Detention or prevention of escape of persons who present a clear threat or loss of life.

            (e) When possible, the use of deadly force should be preceded by a clear warning that such force is contemplated or imminent.

            (f) Warning shots will not be used.

            (g) When firing, shots will be aimed to wound, if possible, rather than kill.

            (h) Weapons will not be fired on automatic.

(i)    When possible, let civilian police arrest lawbreakers.

(j)    Allow properly identified news reporters freedom of movement, so long as they do not interfere with your mission.

(k)    Do not talk about this operation or pass on information or rumors about it to unauthorized persons; refer them to your commander.

(l)    Joint task force commander withholds authority for use of riot control agents and sniper teams.

---

[1]  This entry depicts the Rules of Engagement (ROE) for military personnel committed to the 1992 Los Angeles riot. See International and Operational Law Division, Operational Law Handbook (Charlottesville, Virginia: The Judge Advocate General's School, 1995), 21-7.

# *REFERENCES*

## Primary Sources

<u>U.S. National Archives, Washington, D.C.:</u>

Record Group 165: Records of the War Department General and Special Staffs, War Plans Division General Correspondence, 1920-1942:

War Department. Memorandum for the Deputy Chief of Staff from Brigadier General George V. Strong, 21 April 1939, Subject: Emergency Plan White, Washington Provisional Brigade.

Record Group 338: Records of U.S. Army Commands, 1942-1945:

Headquarters 387th Engineer Combat Battalion. Memorandum for the Commanding General, Third United States Army, 16 August 1946, Subject: Negro Manpower.

The Officers of the 92d Infantry Division, United States Army of America. Memorandum for the Commander in Chief of the United States Armed Forces, 18 November 1943, Subject: Grievances of Black Officers.

Record Group 407: Records of the Adjutant General:

Memorandum for the Commanding General, District of Washington, Washington, D.C., 8 June 1923, Subject: Emergency Plans--White.

War Department. Emergency Plan White, Basic, 1940.

## U.S. National Archives II, College Park, Maryland:

Record Group 319: Records of the Army Staff:

Background Papers for the Role of Federal Forces in Civil Disturbances, 1945-1971: Department of the Army, After Action Report, 4-17 April Civil Disturbances. Washington, D.C.: Office of the Deputy Chief of Staff for Military Operations, 1968.

Department of Defense. Graphic Training Aid 21-2-7: Dated October 1967, Special Orders for All Military Personnel Engaged in Civil Disturbance Operations.

Department of the Army, David E. McGiffert, Office of the Under Secretary of the Army. Memorandum for the Chief of Staff, U.S. Army, 17 April 1968.

Department of the Army. Memorandum for Record, Office of the Chief of Staff, 18 April 1968, Subject: General Haines, Vice Chief of Staff and Commanding General Task Force Washington Interview with Investigators from Senator John L. McClellan's Senate Government Operations Committee, Inquiry on Riots.

Department of the Army. Memorandum Number 000.5, Office of the Chief of Staff, for the Department of the Army Staff, August 1967, Subject: Army Preparedness in Civil Disturbance Matters.

Department of the Army. Memorandum Number 67-316, Office of the Chief of Staff, 4 August 1967, Subject: Army Preparedness in Civil Disturbance Matters.

Department of the Army. Message Number 826762, Deputy Chief of Staff, Operations to Commanding General United States Continental Army Command, 7 August 1968, Subject: Use of Military Personnel, Equipment, and Facilities During Civil Disturbances and Disorders.

Department of the Army. Message Number 858668, Chief of Staff to Vice Chief of Staff, 6 April 1968, Subject: Designation to Command Task Force Washington.

District of Columbia, National Guard. "Task Force Goblet Glass, After Action Report 5-16 April 68," 14 May 1968.

Memorandum, "Using D.C. National Guardsmen as Special Police In Surrounding Suburban Areas," no author or date.

Memorandum from the Mayor, Director of Public Safety, and the Chief of Police, of the District of Columbia, to the President of the United

States 5 April 1968. Subject: Request for Federal Troops to Restore Order in Washington, D.C.

Message Number 2709. Commander-in-Chief, Strike Command (CINCSTRIKE), to Commander-in-Chief, Army Strike Command (CINCARSTRIKE), and Commander-in-Chief, Air Force Strike Command (CINCAFSTRIKE), 6 April 1968, Subject: Garden Plot.

Message Number 55378. CG, USCONARC to CG, Third Army, 6 April 1968, Subject: Movement of Troops.

Military District of Washington Message Number 6814. Commanding General, Military District of Washington to Commanding General United States Continental Army Command, 5 April 68, Subject: MDW Situation Report (SITREP) 1-5 April 1968.

Minutes of the District of Columbia Council Special Meeting, 8 April 1968. Washington, Walter. Government of the District of Columbia, Executive Office of the Commissioner, Number 68-262, 8 April 1968. Subject: Early Dismissal of Employees on 8 April 1968.

Record Group 389: Records of the Provost Marshal General:

Office of the Adjutant General, Alabama State Military Department. Report of Riot Duty in Mobile, Alabama, 25 May - 5 June 1943.

Office of the Commanding General, Army Service Forces. Memorandum for the Army Staff, Commanding General All Service Commands, Commanding General All Defense Commands, the Navy, the Federal Bureau of Investigation, and the Inspector General, 10 July 1945, Subject: Domestic Racial Estimate.

War Department, Military Intelligence Division. Summary of Information, 7 April 1943, Subject: March on Washington Movement, Chicago, Illinois.

Record Group 407: Records of the Adjutant General:

Bureau of Public Relations, War Department. Press Release, 2 May 1946, Subject: Army Adopts Policy on Postwar Utilization of Negro Manpower.

A. J. Burke. Letter to President Franklin Delano Roosevelt, 9 April 1942, Subject: Military Police Beating a Black Soldier in a Fort Worth, Texas, Restaurant.

Brigadier General I. H. Edwards, Assistant Chief of Staff, U. S. Army. Letter in Reply to Inquiry by Judge Hastie, 12 August 1942, Subject: The Suggested Use of Negro Troops in Amphibious, Parachute, and Commando Units.

W. J. Faulkner, President Interdenominational Ministers Alliance. Petition for the Honorable Henry L. Stimson, Secretary of War, 3 April 1942, Subject: Brutalizing and Terrorizing of Negro Men, Women, and Children by a Riot Squad of White Civilian and Military Police in Nashville, Tennessee.

Lieutenant Colonel Palham D. Glassford, Instructor-Observer Group, Office of the Provost Marshal General. Memorandum to the Provost Marshal General, 15 April 1942, Subject: Report on Race Discrimination and Race Problems in IV Corps Area.

Military District of Washington Emergency Plan White, 10 June 1947.

Office of the Commanding General, Headquarters Eighth Service Command. Memorandum to the Commanding General, Army Service Forces, Washington, D.C., 26 June 1943, Subject: Report of Race Riot at Beaumont, Texas.

Office of the Provost Marshal General, War Department. Memorandum to the Director, Operations and Training Division, Secret and Confidential Section, Room 2B939, The Pentagon, 16 October 1943, Subject: Use of Troops in Domestic Disorders.

____. Memorandum to the Commanding Generals, First, Second, Third, Fourth, Fifth, Sixth, Seventh, Eighth, and Ninth Service Commands; Military District of Washington, 25 October 1943, Subject: Plans for Action in Domestic Disturbances.

War Department, Military Intelligence Division. Memorandum for the Assistant Chief of Staff, G-1, 15 April 1942, Subject: Assignment of Colored Troop Units to Theaters of Operation and Overseas Stations.

_____. Memorandum for the Assistant Chief of Staff, OPD, 8 May 1942, Subject: Negro Civilians & Military Personnel Alexandria, Louisiana, and Vicinity.

_____. Memorandum to the Assistant Chief of Staff, G-3, 17 June 1942, Subject: The Negro Problem in the Army.

Major General Edward F. Witsell, The Adjutant General of the United States Army. Personal Letter to Mr. William T. Lawrence, General Delivery, Los Angeles, California, 6 December 1946. Subject: Integration of the Armed Forces.

**Lyndon Baines Johnson Presidential Library, Austin, Texas:**

Personal Papers of Assistant Attorney General Warren Christopher, 1 August 1967, Subject: Racial Disturbances 1967.

Personal Papers of Cyrus Vance, not dated, Subject: Gift of Personal Statement by Cyrus Vance.

Personal Papers of Joe Califano, 16 June 1967, Subject: Problems of the Ghetto: Negro in Watts, Mexican-American in Los Angeles.

_____. Summary Report on Watts for President of the United States, 16 June 1967,

_____. Subject: Riot Control Demonstration, 503rd Military Police Battalion, 82d Airborne Division, 27 September 1967.

_____. Civil Disturbances 1967, Memorandum to State Governors, not dated, Subject: Procedures for Requesting Federal Troops.

_____. not dated, Subject: Riot Toll in Cities 1964-1967.

Personal Papers of Lyndon Baines Johnson, President 1963-1969. Office Files of Harry McPherson, Speech: Talking Points to the Commission on Civil Disorders, 29 July 1967.

_____. Memorandum from Joseph Califano to President Johnson, 28 February 1968.

_____. Memorandum from David Ginsburg for Henry B. Taliaferro, Jr., 11 March 1968, Subject: Inaccuracy of Some Press Comments or Reports.

_____. Memorandum from Joe Califano for Harry McPherson, 4 April 1968, Subject: Kerner Commission Report.

_____. Memorandum from Roger Wilkins for Harry McPherson, 4 April 1968, Subject: The Kerner Commission Report.

Personal Papers of U.S. Attorney General Ramsey Clark, 29 September 1967, Subject: Speech in Detroit, Michigan, to the State Bar.

Presidential Task Forces, Riots and Riot Control 1968, not dated, Subject: Civil Disturbance Orientation Course.

Report of the President's Task Force on the Los Angeles Riots, 11-15 August 1965, 17 September 1965.

### Center for Military History, Washington, D.C.:

California Air National Guard After Action Report. Operation Sudden Shield, 1-7 May 1992, 8 May 1992.

California National Guard After Action Report. California Civil Disturbance After Action Review: Los Angeles Civil Disturbance, 1-14 May 1992.

Commander in Chief Forces Command. After Action Review of Operation Garden Plot, Joint Task Force Los Angeles, 12 July 1992.

Department of Defense, 7 May 1992, Subject: Role and Mission Statement of Joint Task Force Los Angeles, Questions and Answers, Biographies of Task Force Commanding General and the Division Commander of the California National Guard.

Immediate Message from the Secretary of Defense, 2 May 1992, Subject: Public Affairs Guidance Update Joint Task Force Los Angeles.

Office of the Assistant Chief of Staff, G2, 40th Infantry Division. Intelligence Summary 2150 hours, 29 April-0400 hours 4 May 1992.

Office of the Assistant Secretary of Defense, Public Affairs, 7 May 1992, Subject Questions and Answers for California Unrest.

Office of the Secretary of the Army, 8 May 1992, Subject: Remarks of President George Bush at Police/Military Staging Area in Los Angeles, California.

Secretary of the Army, 2 May 1992, Immediate Message, Subject: Calling the California National Guard into Federal Service.

Task Force Washington, After Action Report, 4-16 April 1968., United States Continental Army Command (USCONARC), Emergency Operations Center Journals, 4-6 April 1968.

United States Army Forces Command (FORSCOM) Annual Historical Summary, fiscal years, 1974-1992.

United States Continental Army Command (USCONARC)/United States Army Strike Command (USARSTRIKE) Annual Historical Summary, fiscal years 1968-1973.

## National Guard Bureau, Historical Services, The Pentagon Washington, D.C.:

Letter from Major General James F. Cantwell, President of the National Guard Association of the United States, to the Honorable Melvin R. Laird, Secretary of Defense, The Pentagon, 19 May 1970.

Memorandum from the State of Florida Department of Military Affairs, Office of the Adjutant General, St. Augustine, Florida, for Chief, National Guard Bureau, ATTN: NGB-MS, Washington, D.C., 12 March 1981, Subject: After Action Report, Dade County Civil Disturbance, 17-26 May 1980.

Memorandum from the State of Ohio Adjutant General's Department, Columbus Ohio, for the Chief, National Guard Bureau, ATTN: NGNGBS, Washington, D.C., 8 June 1970, Subject: After Action Report, Kent State University, 2-8 May 1970.

Statement by Major General James F. Cantwell, President of the National Guard Association of the United States, 11 May 1970, Subject: Kent State.

Statement of Chief, National Guard Bureau at Senate Armed Services Committee during Strength Authorization Hearings, 7 May 1970.

**Combined Arms Research Library, Fort Leavenworth, Kansas:**

Air War College Air University Maxwell Air Force Base, Alabama, Report number 3901, Lieutenant Colonel John G. Doty, Jr., "A Blue Print for Crisis: A Case Study of the Air National Guard's Utilization in Detroit," April 1970.

Department of the Army, Office of the Adjutant General, 28 September 1967, Subject: Operations Report--Lessons Learned, Report 5-67--"Civil Disorders--TF Detroit."

Lieutenant General John L. Throckmorton, Headquarters XVIII Airborne Corps and Fort Bragg, North Carolina, 13 November 1967, Subject: After Action Report Task Force Washington, 19-23 October 1967.

Memorandum from Major General Charles P. Stone, Deputy Commander Task Force Detroit, for Chief of Staff, U.S. Army, 4 August 1967, Subject: Report of the Deputy Commander Task Force Detroit--Operations and Observations.

Memorandum from Robert S. McNamara, Secretary of Defense, for the Secretary of the Army, Secretary of the Air Force, and Secretary of the Navy, 24 July 1967, Subject: Implementation of Executive Order 11364, "Providing Federal Assistance in the State of Michigan."

U.S. Army War College, Carlisle Barracks, Pennsylvania, Case Study by Colonel Joe Baker, Jr., Policy Decisions for Civil Disturbance Operations, 10 March 1969.

## Police Departments:

After Action Report of the Las Vegas Police Department based on 30 April- 25 May 1992 Civil Unrest in Las Vegas, Nevada.

Los Angeles Police Department After Action Report for the April/May 1992 Riots.

Los Angeles Police Department Six Month Status Report in Implementing the Christopher Commission Recommendations, 14 January 1992.

Report of the Independent Commission of the Los Angeles Police Department. Warren Christopher Commission Report, 9 July 1991.

## Personal Interviews:

Block, Sherman. (Sheriff of Los Angeles County). Personal interview with author, 2 June 1995.

Bradley, Tom. (Former Los Angeles Police Department Lieutenant and Mayor of Los Angeles, California, from 1972 to 1992). Personal interview with author, 31 May 1995.

Brewer, Jesse. (Former Los Angeles Police Department Deputy Chief of Police and President of the Los Angeles Police Department Police Commission). Personal interview with author, 31 May 1995.

Burk, John. (Colonel, Army National Guard and Brigade Commander of National Guard forces in Baltimore, 1968; retired Brigadier General, 1975). Telephone interview with author, 18 May 1993.

Covault, Marvin, (Lieutenant General (retired) and Former Commander of Joint Task Force Los Angeles and the 7th Infantry Division (Light), 1992). Telephone interview with author on 25 September 1996.

Delk, James D. (Major General (retired) and Former Commander of Troops for the California National Guard during the 1992 Los Angeles riot). Telephone interview with author on 1 October 1996.

Dinse, Rick. (Former Police Captain, later a Commander with the Los Angeles Police Department). Personal interview with author, 30 May 1995.

Duke, William. (Sergeant with the Los Angeles Police Department's 77th Division Crash (Gang) Unit). Personal interview and tour through the entire riot area with author on 31 May 1995.

Epperson, Shirley. (Director of Urban Programs, Washington, D.C., Urban League). Personal interview with author on 12 May 1995.

Gates, Daryl. (Former Chief of Police for the City of Los Angeles). Telephone interview with author, 2 June 1995.

Grimes, Milton. (Rodney King's attorney during the second--Civil Rights-- trial against the four Los Angeles Police Officers charged with beating his client). Personal interview with author, 1 June 1995.

Hernandez, Daniel J. (Major General (retired) and Former Army Forces Commander for Joint Task Force Los Angeles and Commander of the California National Guard). Telephone interview with author on 1 October 1996.

Hewitt, John. (Assistant Sheriff Orange County, California, Sheriff's Department). Personal interview with author on 1 June 1995.

Hopgood, Marvin (Major General (retired) United States Marine Corps and Marine Forces Commander during the 1992 Los Angeles riot). Telephone interview with author on 25 September 1996.

Kinnard, Douglas, (Brigadier General, Retired, and former operations officer for United States Army Continental Command (USCONARC), 1968. Telephone interview with author on 23 May 1996.

Kuykendyll, Daniel. (U.S. Congressman from Memphis, Tennessee, at the time Martin Luther King, Jr. was assassinated). Personal interview with author on 6 September 1994.

Newburn-Williams, Mary. (Former director of the Los Angeles Urban League). Personal interview with author on 27 May 1995.

Parks, Bernard. (Former Deputy Los Angeles Chief of Police and later Assistant Chief of Police for the city of Los Angeles). Personal interview with author, 30 May 1995.

Robinson, Hugh, (Major General, Retired, and Former Military Aide to President Lyndon B. Johnson, 1965-1969). Telephone interview with author on 18 May 1996.

Schofield, Gary. (Lieutenant with the Las Vegas Metropolitan Police Department and Commander of the department's Special Weapons and Tactics Unit). Personal interview with author on 8 June 1995.

Sheehan, Kathleen. (Former Executive Officer for Chief of Police Darryl Gates, later a Police Lieutenant tasked with implementing the department's leadership training program). Personal interview with author, 30 May 1995.

Whitman, Joe. (Operations Officer, III Corps Office of the G-3, Major, U.S. Army, 1968). Personal interview with author, 18 June 1993.

Williams, Willie. (Chief of Police for the City of Los Angeles). Personal interview with author, 30 May 1995.

Williamson, Daniel C. (A. L. Brown High School junior, 1968; Lieutenant Colonel, U.S. Army 1993). Telephone interview with author, 12 February 1993.


**Newspapers and Magazines:**

America. "CNN Does It Again," 186 (1 May 1993), 16-17.

Army Times. Gene Famiglietti. "D.C. Riot Troops Praised," 28 (24 April 1968), 1.

_____. "Army, Guard Win Praise," 28 (8 May 1968), 4.

Coast Weekly. "Where's Justice?: D-Day in L.A.: The Day Fort Ord Invaded Los Angeles," 7 May 1992.

Detroit Free Press. "Police and Guard Move in as Mobs Run Rampant," 24 July 1967, 1a.

_____. John A. Hamilton. "The Meaning of Detroit's Riot," 24 July 1967, 4a.

_____.William Serrin. "National Guard Is Told: Shoot to Kill If Fired On; 8,000 Troops on Patrol with 5,000 Law Officers," 25 July 1967, 5a.

_____.Gene Goltz. "Men and Machines: A Battle Against Madness," 25 July 1967, 7a.

_____."Troops Fight Pitched Battle With Snipers," 25 July 1967, 8a.

_____."Violence of 1943 Recalled," 25 July 1967, 3b.

_____."Grim U.S. Troops Cool Riot Ardor," 26 July 1967, 4a.

_____."Dr. King Supports Use of GI's in Riot," 26 July 1967, 5b.

_____.George Walker. "Nerves Frayed: Fatigue Adds to Tension on Troops, Police," 27 July 1967, 8a.

_____."Guard Reviewing Training for Riots," 28 July 1967, 8a.

_____."How to Control Riots," 29 July 1967, 8a.

_____.Don Oberdorfer. "LBJ Orders New Riot Training for National Guard," 30 July 1967, 15a.

_____."Riots Shock GI's," 2 August 1967, 6a.

_____."Call for Guard in Rioting Was Too Late, General Says," 5 August 1967, 3a.

_____."Girl's Death Explained: Guard Defends Riot Shooting," 8 August 1967, 3a.

Maclean's. "Streets of Hate," 105 (11 May 1992), 20-28.

Miami Herald: Gene Miller. "Cops Meted Out 'Street Justice,' State Charges," 17 May 1980, 1b.

_____."Cops Freed in McDuffie Case: Rage at Verdict Erupts Into Violence," 18 May 1980, 1a.

_____.William R. Amlong. "Angry Blacks, Police Clash; 4 Die in Night of Violence," 18 May 1980, 1a.

_____.Barry Bearak, "How Police Recaptured Justice Building," 18 May 1980, 33a.

_____.Stephen Doig. "Scores Injured by Angry Crowds: Victims Overflow Jackson Hospital," 18 May 1980, 1b.

_____.Mike Clary. "Governor Sends Guard Into Riot Areas," 19 May 1980, 3b.

_____.Carl Hiaasen and Joan Fleischman. "Guard-Duty Cops Vandalized Cars in Shopping Plaza," 20 May 1980, 1a.

_____."2,500 More Guards Sent to Miami," 20 May 1980, 17a.

_____."Nothing Changed From 68 Riots," 20 May 1980, 22b.

_____.Andy Rosenblatt. "Guard Shows Dade a New Face," 21 May 1980, 1c.

_____.Edna Buchanan. "Savagery Blamed on Gang of Crazies," 22 May 1980, 1a.

_____. "Schools Open, But Most Guardsmen on Standby," 22 May 1980, 21a.

_____. "Ghetto Voices: Violence Is Way to Get Action," 23 May 1980, 21a.

_____.Fredric Tasker and Fitz McAden. "Healing Miami: What Has to Be Done," 25 May 1980, 1a.

_____.William R. Amlong. "Homemade 'Justice' Miami's Frustration Exposed, Not Answered, by Eruption of Rage," 25 May 1980, 26a.

_____.Joan Fleishchman. "Dade Lifts Emergency Restrictions," 27 May 1980, 1a.

Miami News. Jack Knarr. "Deadly Tide of Violence Recedes After Worst Riot in Dade History," 19 May 1980, 1a.

_____.Terry Williams. "Jones, LaFleur, Adams, McDuffie: Time Bombs That Finally Exploded," 19 May 1980, 1a.

_____.Milt Sosin. "Scores of Blazes Unfought Because of Rioting Dangers," 19 May 1980, 5a.

_____.Howard Kleinberg. "Violence, Inequities Festered for Years," 19 May 1980, 16a.

_____. Marilyn A. Moore. "Some Troops Just Left Duty in Key West," 20 May 1980, 7a.

_____.Lesley Valdes. "Not Letting Guard Down: In 'Black Grove,' Residents Look After Their Own--and Troops, too," 20 May 1980, 7a.

National Guard. "A City in Pain," 34 (July 1980), 8-11.

_____.W.D. McGlasson, "From Watts to Kent State: The Guard's Time of Testing," 45 (May 1991), 16-21.

The National Guard Magazine. "The California Guard Secures Los Angeles," 46 (July 1992), 16-19.

The National Guardsman. "Riot Duty," 21 (September 1967), 2-3.

_____."Operation Sundown," 21 (September 1967), 6-7.

_____. "Lessons Learned in Detroit," 21 (September 1967), 12-13.

_____. "The Guard versus Disorder," 24 (June 1970), 2-7.

_____. "Bomb Blasts Memorial," 24 (June 1970), 8-12.

_____. James J. Kilpatrick. "Looking Behind the Triggers in Ohio," 24 (June 1970), 15.

_____."The Guard on the Campus: A Commentary on the Report of the President's Commission on Campus Unrest," 24 (November 1970), 31-33.

The New York Times. Ben A. Franklin. "Army Troops in Capital as Negroes Riot: Guard Sent Into Chicago, Detroit, Boston; Johnson Asks a Joint Session of Congress," 6 April 1968, sec. A, p.1.

_____."Washington Turmoil Subsides; Hundreds Homeless, Eight Dead," 8 April 1968, sec. A, p. 1.

_____.Nathaniel Sheppard, Jr. "Miami's Blacks Have "Nothing to Lose," 23 May 1980, sec. B, p. 4.

Newsweek. "An American Tragedy, 1967--Detroit," 70 (7 August 1967), 18-26.

_____."The U.S. Epidemic of Negro Riots," 70 (7 August 1967), 32.

_____.Edward Kosner. "Seven Days in April: A Momentous Week Brings Hope for Peace--Then National Tragedy," 71 (15 April 1968), 26-38.

_____.Edward Kosner. "It May Be a Tolling for Me," 71 (22 April 1968), 23- 33.

_____. "Who Guards Against the Guard?" 75 (18 May 1970), 33f.

_____."A Newsweek Poll: Mr. Nixon Holds Up," 75 (25 May 1970), 30-35.

_____."The Siege of L.A.," 119 (11 May 1992), 30-34.

_____."A Night of Hell at Ground Zero," 119 (11 May 1992), 35.

_____. "Blacks and Police: Up Against the Wall," 119 (11 May 1992), 52.

_____."A Powerful Reminder of the Rage of the Dispossessed," 119 (11 May 1992), 54-55.

_____. "Looking Past the Verdict," 121 (26 April 1993), 20-29.

_____."Larger Than Life: Rodney King's Case Resonated Because It Strengthened a Widespread Perception of Unequal Justice for Blacks. Can One Trial Even the Score?" 121 (26 April 1993), 30-31.

(Cleveland, Ohio) Plain Dealer. Richard G. Ellers and Richard C. Widman. "Kent Rioters Driven Back Onto Campus," 4 May 1970, 1a and 6a.

_____.Joe Esztherhas. "Troops Lost All Their Cool," 5 May 1970, 1a and 6a.

_____.John P. Hayes. "Victory Bell Called Crowd," 5 May 1970, 10a, 11a, and 12a.

_____."Nixon Sees Tragic Reminder at Kent," 5 May 1970, 12a.

_____. "Divers Opinions on Kent State," 7 May 1970, 10a.

_____. William Hickey. "KSU Story One-sided in TV Report," 7 May 1970, 6e.

_____. David L. Hopcraft. "State to Cut Use of Troops," 8 May 1970, 1a.

Sunburst: 40th Infantry Division, California National Guard. "Federalized Division Soldiers Quell Riots," 6 (7 May 1992).

_____."President Hails Guard, Others for Efforts During Devastating Los Angeles Riots." 6 (10 May 1992).

Time. "An Hour of Need," 91 (12 April 1968), 17-21.

_____."Rampage and Restraint," 91 (19 April 1968), 13-19.

_____."A Jarring Verdict, An Angry Spasm," 139 (11 May 1992) 10-11.

_____."Fire this Time," 139 (11 May 1992), 18-25.

_____. "L.A. Lawless," 139 (11 May 1992), 26-29.

_____. "Anatomy of an Acquittal," 139 (11 May 1992), 30-32.

_____. "We Have to Start Talking to Each Other," 139 (11 May 1992), 37.

_____. "Video Warriors in Los Angeles," 139 (11 May 1992), 68.

_____. "Rodney King Redux," 141 ( 8 March 1993), 17.

U.S. News & World Report. "A New Look at New Weapons to Cope With Riots," 64 (1 January 1968), 6-7.

_____."More Violence and Race War? Effects of Dr. King Tragedy," 64 (15 April 1968), 31-34.

_____. "Aftermath of Riots--What Next?" 64 (22 April 1968), 27-30.

_____. "Insurrection: Outlook in U.S.: Interview with an Authority on Riots," 64 (29 April 1968), 38-41.

_____. "Race and Rage: The Growing Split Between Black and White," 112 (11 May , 1992), 20-26.

_____. "Cops in the Crossfire," 112 (11 May 1992), 27-35.

_____. "Different Realities," 112 (11 May 1992), 36.

Washington Daily News. "City Girds for Summer: Extra Training for Police, D.C. Guard", 14 February 1968, p. 5.

_____. "Troops No Stranger to D.C.: Many Had Briefings Months Ago," 12 April 1968, p. 43.

Washington Evening Star. Adams, Michael. McGrory, Mary. Otfenberg, Miriam. "Test of New Riot Law Seen; Carmichael's Role Assessed," 7 April 1968, sec. A, p. 1.

_____."King Death: A Turning Point?" 7 April, 1968, sec. A, p. 14.

_____."Voice of the City . . . School Plan in the Aftermath," 13 April 1968, sec. A, p. 20.

_____.Thomas, Oliver. "Guard Found Duty Rough, Residents Friendly," 21 April 1968, sec. B, p. 1.

_____. Kalb, Barry. "Williams Considers Handling Businessmen's Suit on Rioters," 12 May 1968, sec. B, p. 4.

_____. Hirzel, Donald. "Rioters Had No Fear of Arrest, Judge Says," 11 June 1968, sec. A, p. 14.

Washington Examiner. McClendon, Sarah. "Army Says Planning, Training Saved City," 19 April 1968, sec. A, p. 1.

Washington Post. Weil, Martin. "Revolution Needed, Hobson Declares," 4 March 1968, sec. B, p. 3.

_____.Mintz, Morton. "Troops Deploy Through City," 6 April 1968, sec. A, p. 1.

_____. Carper, Elsie. "New Riots Catch Police Short: No Trouble Expected During Day," 6 April 1968, sec. A, p. 14.

_____. "So Far, Well Done," 8 April 1968, sec. A, p. 16.

_____. "Byrd Wants Troops to Stay; Police-Aid Pacts Suggested," 9 April 1968, sec. A, p. 5.

_____. Clopton, Willard and Carl W. Sims. "D.C. Turns to Mammoth Relief Effort as Violence Abates," 9 April 1968, sec. A, p. 11.

_____.Pearson, Drew, and Jack Anderson. "Planning Pays Off in Non-Riot Cities," 12 April 1968, sec. B, p. 13.

_____. Raspberry, William. "Lessons of the Days of Rage," 3 April 1988, sec. A, p. 14.

_____.Gaines-Carter, Patrice. "The Fires of April 20 Years Later: For Riot Victims' Kin, the Pain Endures," 5 April 1988, sec. A, p. 1.

_____."The Fires of April: 20 Years Later," 7 April 1988, sec. A, p. 14.

Washington Post Magazine. Downie, Leonard. "A Chronicle o f Washington's Burning," 9 April 1978, 7-44.

## Additional Newspapers Consulted or Reviewed:

Atlanta Daily World.

Atlanta University Center Digest. Californian, Sacramento, California.

Central Missouri State University Mule Skinner. Commercial Appeal, Memphis, Tennessee.

Gannett News Service, Arlington, Virginia. Houston Chronicle.

Houston Post. Kansas City Star.

Los Angeles Daily News.

Maroon Tiger, Morehouse College, Atlanta, Georgia. Memphis World.

Meter, Tennessee State University Newspaper. Nashville Tennessean.

Navy Times. Oklahoma Eagle.

Orange County Register, Orange County California. Press Telegram, Long Beach, California.

San Francisco Examiner. San Jose Mercury News. St. Louis Post Dispatch.

<u>Stars and Stripes</u>, European Edition. <u>Tacoma Morning New Tribune</u>.

<u>Tri-State Defender</u>, Memphis, Tennessee. <u>Tulsa Daily World</u>.

<u>Union Tribune</u>, San Diego, California. <u>U.S.A. Today</u>.

<u>Washington Times</u>.

## Government Documents

<u>U.S. Army Center for Military History, Washington, D.C.</u>:

Military Support of Law Enforcement During Civil Disturbances: A Report Concerning the California National Guards Part in Suppressing the Los Angeles Riot--August 1965.

Trip Report. Civil Disturbance Seminar (22-24 July 1992) in Washington, D.C., Sponsored by the International Association of Chiefs of Police.

<u>U.S. Army Combined Arms Command, Fort Leavenworth, Kansas: Center for Army Lessons Learned,</u> :

Operations Other Than War (OOTH), Vol. III, <u>Civil Disturbance</u>, Number 93- 7, November 1993.

<u>U.S. Army Military History Institute, Carlisle Barracks, Pennsylvania</u>:

Flynn, Ronald B. "The National Guard Drug Interdiction Mission: A Circumvention of Posse Comitatus?" U.S. Army War College Military Studies Program Paper, 2 April 1990.

Rice, Paul Jackson, "New Laws and Insights Encircle the Posse Comitatus Act." U.S. Army War College Military Studies Program Paper, 26 May 1983.

Van Horn, Jonathan S. "Civil Disturbance Management: What Commanders Must Know." U.S. Army War College Monograph, 26 February 1973.

## Other Government Sources:

Department of the Army. <u>Army Regulation 500-50: Emergency Employment of Army Resources</u>. Washington, D.C.: Government Printing Office, 1956.

Department of the Army. <u>Field Manual 19-15: Civil Disturbances and Disasters</u>. Washington, D.C.: Government Printing Office, July 1945.

Revised April 1952, September 1958, December 1964, March 1968, March 1972, October 1975, and November 1985.

Department of the Army. <u>Field Manual 22-103: Leadership and Command at Senior Levels</u>. Washington, D.C.: Government Printing Office, 1987.

Department of the Army. <u>Field Manual 25-100: Training</u> the Force. Washington, D.C.: Government Printing Office, 1988.

Department of the Army. <u>Field Manual 90-10: Military Operation in Urban Terrain.</u> (Washington, D.C.: Government Printing Office, 1979.

Department of the Army. <u>Military Aid to the Civil Power</u>. Fort Leavenworth, Kansas: General Service Schools Press, 1925.

Headquarters, National Guard Bureau. <u>National Guard Bureau Annual Review</u>, Washington, D.C.: Government Printing Office, 1968-1992.

Report by the Special Advisor to the Board of Police Commissioners on the Civil Disorder in Los Angeles. <u>The City in Crisis</u>. Los Angeles: Office of the Special Advisor to the Board of Police Commissioners City of Los Angeles, 1992.

U.S. Army Inspector-General's Office. <u>The Brownsville Affray: Report of the Inspector-General</u>. Washington, D.C.: Government Printing Office, 1908.

U.S. Congress. House Committee on Armed Services. <u>Report of the Special Subcommittee to Inquire into the Capability of the National Guard to Cope with Civil Disturbances</u>. 90th Congress, 1st session. Washington, D.C.: Government Printing Office, 1967.

U.S. Congress. House Committee on the District of Columbia. <u>Civil Disturbances in Washington: Hearings</u>. 90th Congress, 2d session. Washington, D.C.: Government Printing Office, 1968.

U.S. Department of Commerce, Bureau of Census. <u>Census of Population: Characteristics of Population</u>. Washington: Department of Commerce, 1950, 1960, 1970, 1980, and 1990.

U.S. Department of Justice. Federal Bureau of Investigation. <u>Prevention and Control of Mobs and Riots</u>. Washington, D.C.: Government Printing Office, 1967.

U.S. National Advisory Commission on Civil Disorders. <u>One Year Later: An Assessment of the Nation's Response to the Crisis Described by the National Commission on Civil Disorders</u>. Washington, D.C.: Urban Coalition, 1968.

U.S. National Advisory Commission on Civil Disorders. <u>Report</u>. Washington, D.C.: Government Printing Office, 1968.

_____.<u>Supplemental Studies</u>. Washington, D.C.: Government Printing Office, July 1968.

U.S. National Commission on the Causes and Prevention of Violence. <u>Final Report: To Establish Justice, To Insure Domestic Tranquility</u>. Washington, D.C.: Government Printing Office, 1969.

U.S. President's Commission on Campus Unrest. <u>Report</u>. Washington, D.C.: Government Printing Office, 1970.

**Secondary Sources Books:**

Ambrose, Stephen E. <u>Upton and the Army</u>. Baton Rouge: Louisiana State University Press, 1964.

_____,and James A. Barber. The Military and American Society: Essays and Readings. New York: Free Press, 1972.

Babcock, Louis L. Manual for the Use of Troops: In Aid to the Civil Authority. New York: George H. Doran Company, 1918.

Belknap, Michael R., ed. Civil Rights, The White House, and The Justice Department, 1945-1968. New York: Garland Publishing, Inc., 1991.

Bellows, Harry A. A Treatise on Riot Duty for the National Guard. Washington: Government Printing Office, 1920.

Binkin, Martin, and Mark J. Eitelberg. Blacks in the Military. Washington, D.C.: The Brookings Institution, 1982.

Boehme, Lillian R. Carte Blanche for Chaos. New Rochelle, New York: Arlington House, 1970.

Boesel, David, and Peter H. Rossi. Cities Under Siege: An Anatomy of the Ghetto Riots, 1964-1968. New York: Basic Books, 1971.

Boskin, Joseph. Urban Racial Violence in the Twentieth Century. Beverly Hills: Glencoe Press, 1976.

Boyer, Paul S., Clifford E. Clark, Jr., Joseph F. Kett, Neal Salisbury, Harvard Sitkoff, and Nancy Woloch. The Enduring Vision: A History of the American People, vol. 2, second edition, Lexington, Massachusetts: D.C. Heath and Company, 1993.

Capeci, Dominic J., and Martha Wilkerson. Layered Violence: The Detroit Rioters of 1943. Jackson, Mississippi: University Press of Mississippi, 1991.

Chikota, Richard A., and Michael C. Moran. Riot in the Cities: An Analytical Symposium on the Causes and Effects. Rutherford, New Jersey: Fairleigh Dickinson University Press, 1968.

Christian, Garna L. Black Soldiers in Jim Crow Texas, 1899-1917. College Station, Texas: Texas A&M University Press, 1995.

Coakley, Robert W. The Role of Federal Military Forces in Domestic Disorders, 1789-1878. Washington: Center of Military History/ Government Printing Office, 1988.

Cohen, Norman S. Civil Strife in America: A Historical Approach to the Study of Riots in America. Hinsdale, Illinois: Dryden Press, 1972.

Connery, Robert H. Urban Riots: Violence and Social Change. New York: Academy of Political Science, 1968.

Cooper, Jerry M. The Army and Civil Disorder: Federal Military Intervention in Labor Disputes, 1877-1900. Westport, Connecticut: Greenwood Press, 1980.

Deane-Drummond, Anthony. Riot Control. New York: Crane Russak & Company, 1975.

Elliff, John T. Crime, Dissent and The Attorney General: The Justice Department in the 1960's. Beverly Hills, California: Sage Publications, 1971.

Farrow, Edward S. Military Encyclopedia: A Dictionary of Military Knowledge. New York: Edward S. Farrow, 1885.

_____. Riots and Riot Duty. New York: Edward S. Farrow, 1919.

Fine, Sidney. Violence in the Model City: The Cavanagh Administration, Race Relations, and the Detroit Riot of 1967. Ann Arbor, Michigan: The University of Michigan Press, 1989.

Fogelson, Robert M. Violence as Protest: A Study of Riots and Ghettos. Garden City, New York: Doubleday and Company, 1971.

Franklin, John Hope. The Color Line: Legacy for the Twenty-first Century. Columbia, Missouri: University of Missouri Press, 1993.

Gates, Daryl F. Chief: My Life in the LAPD. New York: Bantam Books, 1992. Gilbert, Ben W. Ten Blocks from the White House: Anatomy of the Washington Riots of 1968. New York: Praeger, 1968.

Gordon, Leonard. A City in Racial Crisis: The Case of Detroit Pre- and Post- the 1967 Riot. New York: Wlliam C. Brown Publishers, 1971.

Grant, Joanne. Black Protest: History, Documents, and Analyses 1619 to the Present. New York: Fawcett Premier, 1968.

Grier, William H., and Price M. Cobbs. Black Rage. New York: Harper Collins, 1992.

Grimshaw, Allen D, ed. Racial Violence in the United States. Chicago: Aldine Publishing Company, 1969.

Hacker, Andrew. Two Nations. New York: MacMillan, 1992.

Harris, Fred R. and Roger W. Wilkins. Quiet Riots: Race and Poverty in the U.S.: The Kerner Report Twenty Years Later. New York: Pantheon Books, 1988.

Harris, Leonard. Philosophy Born of Struggle: Anthology of Afro-American Philosophy from 1917. Dubuque, Iowa: Kendall Hunt, 1983.

Haynes, Robert V. A Night of Violence: The Houston Riot of 1917. Baton Rouge: Louisiana State University Press, 1976.

Higham, Robin, ed. Bayonets in the Streets: The Use of Troops in Civil Disturbances. Lawrence, Kansas: University Press of Kansas, 1969.

Hope, Richard O. Racial Strife in the U.S. Military: Toward the Elimination of Discrimination. New York: Praeger, 1979.

Huntington, Samuel P. The Soldier and the State. Cambridge: Belknap Press of Harvard University Press, 1957.

Institute for Alternative Journalism. Inside the L.A. Riots: What Really Happened and Why it Will Happen Again. Los Angeles: Institute for Alternative Journalism, 1992.

Jacobs, Paul. Prelude to Riot: A View of Urban America from the Bottom. New York: Random House, Inc., 1966.

Janowitz, Morris. Social Control of Escalated Riots. Chicago: University of Chicago, Center for Policy Study, 1968.

Jensen, Joan M. Army Surveillance in America, 1775-1980. New Haven: Yale University Press, 1991.

255

Johnson, Lyndon Baines. The Vantage Point: Perspectives of the Presidency, 1963-1969. New York: Holt, Rinehart and Winston, 1971.

Lane, Ann J. The Brownsville Affair: National Crisis and Black Reaction. New York: Kennikat Press, 1971.

Lee, Alfred M. and Norman D. Humphrey. Race Riot: Detroit, 1943. New York: Octagon Books, Inc., 1968.

Lee, Ulyssess Grant. U.S. Army in World War II Special Studies: The Employment of Negro Troops. Washington, D.C.: Office of the Chief of Military History/Government Printing Office, 1966.

Leone, Bruno. Racism Opposing Viewpoints: The Isms: Modern Doctrines and Movements. St. Paul, Minnesota: Greenhaven Press, 1976.

Lieberson, Stanley. A Piece of the Pie: Blacks and White Immigrants Since 1880. Los Angeles: University of California Press, 1980.

Locke, Hubert G. The Detroit Riot of 1967. Detroit: Wayne State University Press, 1969.

Lohman, Joseph D. The Police and Minority Groups. Chicago: Chicago Park District, 1947.

Los Angeles Times Staff. Understanding the Riots: Los Angeles Before and After the Rodney King Case. Los Angeles: The Los Angeles Times, 1992.

Mahon, John K. History of the Militia and the National Guard. New York: Macmillan Publishing Company, 1983.

Martin, James Kirby, Randy Roberts, Steven Mintz, Linda O. McMurry, and James H. Jones. America and its People. Glenview, Ilinois.: Scott, Foreman and Company, 1989.

Masotti, Louis H. and Don R. Bowen, eds. Riots and Rebellion: Civil Violence in the Urban Community. Beverly Hills: Sage Publications, Inc., 1968.

Methvin, Eugene H. The Riot Makers: The Technology of Social Demolition. New Rochelle, New York: Arlington House, 1970.

Millett, Allan R. and Peter Maslowski. For the Common Defense: A Military History of the United States of America. New York: Free Press, 1984.

Moss, Robert. The War for the Cities. New York: Coward, McCann and Geoghegan, 1972.

Nalty, Bernard C. Strength For the Fight: A History of Black Americans in the Military. New York: Free Press, 1986.

_____.and Morris MacGregor, eds. Blacks In the Military: Essential Documents. Wilmington, Delaware: Scholarly Resources Inc., 1981.

National Urban League. The State of Black America 1994. New York: National Urban League, Inc., 1994.

Newton, Michael and J.A. Newton. Racial and Religious Violence in America: A Chronology. New York: Garland Press, 1995.

Office of the Special Consultant to the Secretary of the Army. Bicentennial of the United States Constitution: A Resource Guide, Supplement IV: 1991 The Adoption of the Bill of Rights. Washington, D.C.: Office of the Special Consultant to the Secretary of the Army for the Bicentennial of the United States Constitution, 1991.

O'Neill, William L. Coming Apart: An Informal History of America in the 1960's. New York: Quadrangle, 1971.

Ordway, Albert. Drill Regulations for Street Riot Duty. Washington, D.C.: James J. Chapman, 1891.

Perry, Mark. Four Stars. Boston: Houghton Mifflin Company, 1989.

Rye, Kenneth A. The Use of Troops in Civil Disturbances in the United States. Durham, North Carolina: Duke University Center for International Studies, 1982.

Ryan, Garry D., and Timothy K. Nenninger, eds. Soldiers and Civilians: The U.S. Army and the American People. Washington, D.C.: National Archives and Records Administration, 1987.

Sandburg, Carl. The Chicago Race Riots July, 1919. New York: Harcourt, Brace and Howe, 1919.

Sauter, Van Gordon and Burleigh Hines. Nightmare in Detroit: A Rebellion and Its Victims. Chicago: Henry Regnery Co., 1968.

Sefton, James. United States Army and Reconstruction, 1865-1877. Baton Rouge: Louisiana State University Press, 1967.

Shogan, Robert and Tom Craig. The Detroit Race Riot: A Study in Violence. New York: Chilton Books, 1964.

Sitkoff, Harvard. The Struggle for Black Equality. New York: Hill and Wang, 1993.

Sorley, Lewis. Thunderbolt: General Creighton Abrams and the Army of His Times. New York: Simon and Schuster, 1992.

Steele, Philip. Riots: Past and Present. New York: New Discovery, 1993.

Tuttle, William M. Race Riot: Chicago in the Red Summer of 1919. New York: Atheneum, 1977.

Vernon, Robert L. L.A. Justice: Lessons from the Firestorm. Colorado Springs, Colorado: Focus on the Family Publishing, 1993.

Waddington, David P. Contemporary Issues in Public Disorder: A Comparative and Historical Approach. New York: Routledge Publishing, 1992.

Wall, Brenda. The Rodney King Rebellion: A Psychopolitical Analysis of Racial Despair and Hope. Chicago: African American Images, 1992.

Waskow, Arthur I. From Race Riot to Sit-In. New York: Doubleday, 1966.
Weaver, John D. The Brownsville Raid. New York: W.W. Norton, 1970.

Weinstein, Allen, and Frank Otto Gatell. Freedom and Crisis: An American History, third edition. New York: Random House, 1981.

West, Cornel. Race Matters. Boston: Beacon Press, 1994.

West Point Register of Graduates and Former Cadets. New York: Association of Graduates of the United States Military Academy, 1992.

Wilson, Amos. Understanding Black Adolescent Male Violence. New York: African World Info Systems, 1992.

Wood, Sterling A. Riot Control by The National Guard. Harrisburg, Pennsylvania: The Military Service Publishing Company, 1940.

Wright, Nathan, Jr. Black Power and Urban Unrest. New York: Hawthorn Books, 1967.

Yarmolinsky, Adam. The Military Establishment. New York: Harper & Row, 1971.

**Articles and Book Chapters**

Beaumont, Roger A. "The Embryonic Revolution: Perspectives on the 1967 Riots." In Robin Higham, ed. Bayonets in the Streets: The Use of Troops in Civil Disturbances. Lawrence, Kansas: University Press of Kansas, 1969, 205-22.

_____."Must the Guard Be a Police Force?" Army 70 (September 1970), 35-37.

Blumenson, Martin. "The Army as Cop." Army 26 (May 1976), 50-56.

_____ ."On the Function of the Military in Civil Disorders." In Roger Little, ed. Handbook of Military Institutions. Beverly Hills, California: Sage Publications, 1971, 493-528.

Brien, Albert. "The Case for Uniform Regulation of the National Guard." Boston University Law Review 50 (Special Issue, 1970), 169-77.

Cockerham, William, and Lawrence E. Cohen. "Attitudes of U.S. Army Paratroopers Toward Participation in the Quelling of Civil Disturbances." Journal of Political and Military Sociology 7 (Fall 1979), 257-69.

"Comment--The Response of the Washington, D.C. Community and Its Criminal Justice System to the April 1968 Riot." George Washington Law Review 37 (May 1969), 863-1013.

Cooper, Jerry M. "Federal Military Intervention in Domestic Disorders." In Richard H. Kohn, ed. The United States Military Under the Constitution of the United States, 1789-1989. New York: New York University Press, 1991, 120-50.

Elle Magazine. "One Year Later: The Fires of L.A. Rage On," 8 (May 93), 82 and 88.

Fogelson, Robert. "Violence as a Protest." In Roger Lane and John J. Turner, Jr. eds. Riot, Rout, and Tumult: Readings in American Social and Political Violence. New York: University Press of America, 1978, 327-48.

Friedman, David and Joel Kotkin. "The Los Angeles Riots: Causes, Myths, and Solutions." Commentary 2 (February 1993), 1-30.

Furman, H.W.C. "Restrictions upon the Use of the Army Imposed by the Posse Comitatus Act." Military Law Review 7 (January 1960), 85-129.

Gans, Herbert J. "The Ghetto Rebellions and Urban Class Conflicts", in Robert H. Connery, ed. Urban Riots: Violence and Social Change. New York: Vintage Books, 1968, 42-51.

Hacker, Barton C. "The United States Army as a National Police Force: The Federal Policing of Labor Disputes, 1877-1898." Military Affairs 33 (April 1969), 255-64.

Hill, Herbert. "Racial Discrimination in the Nation's Apprenticeship Training Programs." Phylon 23 (Fall 1962), 215-24.

Laurie, Clayton D. "Civil Disorder and the Military in Rock Springs, Wyoming; The Arm's Role in the 1885 Chinese Massacre." Montana: The Magazine of Western History 40 (Summer 1990), 44-59.

_____."The U.S. Army and the Omaha Race Riot of 1919." Nebraska History 72 (Fall 1991), 135-43.

Lieberson, Stanley and Arnold Silverman. "The Precipitants and Underlying Conditions of Race Riots." American Sociological Review 30 (December 1965), 887-98.

Marshall, Thurgood. "The Gestapo in Detroit." In Joseph Boskin, ed. Urban Racial Violence in the Twentieth Century. Beverly Hills: Glencoe Press, 1969, 41-5.

Mattic, Hans W. "The Form and Content of Recent Riots." Midway (Summer 1968), 3-32.

McNamara, Robert J. "The Ethics of Violent Dissent." In Robert H. Connery, ed.Urban Riots: Violence and Social Change. New York: Academy of Political Science, 1968, 140-45.

Meeks, Clarence I. "Illegal Law Enforcement: Aiding Civil Authorities in Violation of the Posse Comitatus Act." Military Law Review 70 (1975): 70- 136.

The Public Opinion Quarterly. Joe R. Feagin and Paul B. Sheatsley, "Ghetto Resident Appraisals of a Riot," 32 (Fall 1968), 352-362.

____.Benjamin D. Singer. "Mass Media and Communication Processes in the Detroit Riot of 1967," 34 (Summer 1970), 236-245.

Rustin, Bayard. "A Way Out of the Exploding Ghetto." New York Times Magazine (13 August 1967), 16-17, 54, 59-60, 62, 64-65.

Scheips, Paul J. "The Army and Civil Disturbances: Oxford and Detroit." In Garry D.Ryan and Timothy K. Nenninger, eds., Soldiers and Civilians: The U.S. Army and the American People. Washington, D.C.: National Archives and Record Administration, 1987, 179-94.

Schubert, Frank N. and Michael Robinson. "David Fagen: An Afro-American Rebel in the Philippines, 1899-1901." Pacific Historical Review 44 (February 1975), 68-83.

Sitkoff, Harvard. "Racial Militancy and Interracial Violence in the Second World War." In Roger Lane and John J. Turner, Jr., eds. Riot, Rout, and Tumult: Readings in American Social and Political Violence. New York: University Press of America, 1978, 305-26.

Stone, Charles P. "Lessons of Detroit, Summer 1967." In Robin Highham, ed. Bayonets in the Streets: The Use of Troops in Civil Disturbances. Lawrence, Kansas: University Press of Kansas, 1969, 185-203.

White, Walter. "What the Negro Thinks of the Army." Annals of the American Academy of Political and Social Science, 223 (September 1942), 67-71.

Zickel, Lewis L. "The Soldier and Civil Disorder." Military Review, 57 (May 1977), 63-72.

## Unpublished Sources

Center for Military History, Washington, D.C.:

Coakley, Robert W. "Operation Arkansas" (OCMH Monograph 158M). Washington, D.C.: Office of the Chief of Military History, 1967.

_____, Paul J. Scheips, and Vincent H. Demma. "Use of Troops in Civil Disturbances Since World War II" (OCMH Study 75), revised edition. Washington, D.C.: Office of the Chief of Military History, 1971.

Moenk, Jean R. "USCONARC--Participation in the Suppression of Civil Disturbances, April 1968." Fort Monroe, Virginia: Historical Branch, U.S. Continental Command, October 1968, File, USCONARC-2.

Scheips, Paul J. "The Role of the Army in the Oxford, Mississippi, Incident, 1962-1963" (OCMH Monograph 73-M). Washington, D.C.: Office of the Chief of Military History, 1965.

_____,and Karl E. Cocke. "Army Operational and Intelligence Activities in Civil Disturbances Since 1957." Washington, D.C.: Office of the Chief of Military History, 1968.

_____,and John N. Albright. "Use of Troops in Civil Disturbances, 1963- 1968" (OCMH Annex 6). Washington, D.C.: Office of the Chief of Military History, 1968.

_____,and M. Warner Stark. "Use of Troops in Civil Disturbances Since World War II, Supplement II (1967)." Washington, D.C.: Office of the Chief of Military History, 1968.

_____."Use of Troops in Civil Disturbances Since World War II, Supplement I (September 1965-October 1966)" (OCMH Study 74). Washington: Office of the Chief of Military History, 1973.

## Theses and Dissertations:

Fabiano, Gerald James. "The Analysis and Interpretation of the Use of Presidential Authority to Order United States Armed Forces into Military Action to Quell Domestic Disturbances." Ph.D. dissertation, New York University, 1962.

Gardner, James R. "The Civil Disturbance Mission of the Department of the Army, 1963-1973." Ph.D. dissertation, Princeton University, 1977.

Gill, Loren L. "The Tulsa Race Riot." M.A. Thesis, University of Tulsa, 1946.

Price, Barrye L. "The Use of Federal Troops in Quelling Unrest in Washington, D.C., in April 1968." M.A. Thesis, Texas A&M University, 1994.

Reichley, Martin Sherwood. "Federal Military Intervention in Civil Disturbances." Ph.D. dissertation, Georgetown University, 1939.

Sedlack, Richard Guy. "Riots as Disasters: An Exploratory Case Study of Selected Aspects of the Civil Disturbance in Washington, D.C., April 1968." Ph.D. dissertation, University of Maryland, 1973.

## Internet Resources

Addicott, Jeffrey. *Drafting the Military: The Posse Comitatus Act and the Hunt for the D.C. Sniper.* **Jurist** October 17, 2002. **Available online at:** http://jurist.law.pitt.edu/forum/forumnew62.php

Baker, Bonnie. *The Origins of the Posse Comitatus.* **Aerospace Power Chronicles** November 1, 1999. **Available online at:** http://www.airpower.maxwell.af.mil/airchronicles/cc/baker1.html

Center for Defense Information. **Posse Comitatus: Caution Is Necessary**, by David Isenberg. August 6, 2002. **Available online at:** http://www.cdi.org/terrorism/pcomitatus.cfm

Center for Strategic and International Studies. **Posse Comitatus - Has the Posse Comitatus Act Outlived Its Usefulness?**. by Craig T. Trebilcock. **Available online at:** http://www.csis.org/burke/hd/reports/trebilcock.pdf

Edwards, John O. www.NewsMax.com, Friday, Nov. 21, 2003, "Gen. Franks Doubts Constitution Will Survive WMD Attack." General Franks is also quoted in www.propagandamatrix.com/211103martiallaw.html.

Grove, Gregory D. **The U.S. Military and Civil Infrastructure Protection: Restrictions and Direction under the Posse Comitatus Act**. Stanford, CA, Center for International Security and Cooperation, Stanford University, October 1999. **Available online at:** http://www.ciaonet.org/wps/grg02/GrovePosse Comitatus99.pdf

Military Law and Legal Links: Posse Comitatus & Aiding Civilians. **Air War College Gateway to Internet Resources**. **Available online at:** http://www.au.af.mil/au/awc/awcgate/awc-law.htm #posse Provides access to sections applicable to the subject of Posse Comitatus in Tiles 10, 18 and 42 of the United States Code.

*The Posse Comitatus Act: A Principal in Need of Renewal.* **Washington University Law Quarterly** 75: Summer 1997. **Available online at:** http://law.wustl.edu/WULQ/75-2/752-10.html

Trebilcock, Craig T. *The Myth of Posse Comitatus.* **Journal of Homeland Security** October 2000. **Available online at:** http://www.homelandsecurity.org/journal/articles/ Trebilcock.htm

United States. Dept. of Defense. **Military Assistance for Civil Disturbances (MACDIS)**. Washington, February 4, 1994. **Available online at:** http://www.dtic.mil/whs/directives/corres/pdf/d3 02512_020494/d302512p.pdf DOD Directive 3025.12.

United States. Dept. of Defense. **Military Assistance to Civil Authorities**. Washington, February 18, 1997. **Available online at:** http://www.dtic.mil/whs/directives/corres/pdf/d3 02515_021897/d302515p.pdf DOD Directive 3025.15.

United States Northern Command. **The Posse Comitatus Act (Newsroom Fact Sheets).**
**Available online at:** http://www.northcom.mil/index.cfm?fuseaction=news.factsheets&factsheet=5

Bolgiano, David G. *Military Support of Domestic Law Enforcement Operations.* **FBI Law Enforcement Bulletin** 70:16-24 December 2001.
Also available online at: http://search.epnet.com/direct.asp?an=5791719&db=aph

*Consequences of Violating the Posse Comitatus Act.* **Army Lawyer** No.272:61-68 July 1995.
Also available online at: http://search.epnet.com/direct.asp?an=9510250862&db=f5h

Cragin, Charles L. *A Ready, Capable Total Force.* **National Guard** 53:10-11 March 1999.

D'Agostion, Joseph A. *Bush Will Review Law of Domestic Use of Military.* **Human Events** 58:6 July 29, 2002.
Also available online at: http://search.epnet.com/direct.asp?an=7069875&db=aph

Kayyem, Juliette N. *War on Terrorism Will Compel Revisions to Posse Comitatus.* **National Defense** 87:41-42 December 2002.
Also available online at: http://www.nationaldefensemagazine.org/article.cfm?Id=1000

King, Martin Luther, Jr.   quoted in https://www.brainyquote.com/quotes/martin_luther_king_jr_110202.

Kiser, George C. *Military Policing of the United States.* **Humanist** 57:32-33 May-June 1997.
Also available online at: http://search.epnet.com/direct.asp?an=290793&db=f5h

Lujan, Thomas R. *The Legal Consequences of Domestic Employment of the Army.* **Parameters** 27:82-97 Autumn 1997.
Also available online at: http://carlisle-www.army.mil/usawc/parameters/97autumn/lujan.htm

https:www.mappingpolicevoilence.org/

Meeks, Clarence I, III. *Illegal Law Enforcement: Aiding Civil Authorities in Violation of the Posse Comitatus Act.* **Military Law Review** 70:83-136 Fall 1975.

*Military Resists Domestic Role.* **Government Executive** 33:28 November 2001.
Also available online at: http://search.epnet.com/direct.asp?an=5504484&db=mth

*Misusing the Military.* **Air Force Times** 63:5 August 5, 2002.

Navas, William A., Jr. *Posse Comitatus: The Army of the 21st Century and the Law of Unintended Consequences.* **National Guard** 53:34 January 1999.

Muhammed, Prophet. www.rumisgarden.co.uk/.../prophet-muhammed-four-things-support-the-world.

Quillen, Chris. *Posse Comitatus and Nuclear Terrorism.* **Parameters** 32:60-74 Spring 2002.

Also available online at: http://carlisle-www.army.mil/usawc/parameters/02spring/quillen.htm

Rice, Paul J. *New Laws and Insights Encircle the Posse Comitatus Act.* **Military Law Review** 104:109-138 Spring 1984.

Rossi, C. T. *Modifying Posse Comitatus Puts Americans in Danger.* **Insight on the News** 18:45 September 2, 2002.
Also available online at: http://search.epnet.com/direct.asp?an=7307991&db=f5h

Thompson, Mark and Dickerson, John F. *Soldier on the Beat.* **Time** 158:60+ December 3, 2001.
Also available online at: http://search.epnet.com/direct.asp?an=5566398&db=aph

Thoreau, Henry David quoted in: https://en.wikiquote.org/wiki/Civil_Disobedience_(Thoreau).

Major General Barrye L. Price, Ph.D., Retired U.S. Army is a 1985 Distinguished Military Graduate of the University of Houston's College of Business Administration. He earned a Master of Arts Degree in History in 1994 from Texas A&M University and in 1997 he became the first African-American to obtain a doctorate from the Department of History in the 140-year history of Texas A&M University. He also earned a Master of Science Degree in National Security Strategy from the National Defense University in 2004.

Major General Price's previous assignments include: Commander of the 5th Replacement Company, Fort Polk, La.; Regimental Adjutant for the 11th Armored Cavalry Regiment in both Doha, Kuwait, and Fulda, Germany; Assistant Professor of Military History at the United States Military Academy, West Point, N.Y.; G1, 13th Corps Support Command, Fort Hood, Texas; White House Fellow and Special Assistant to the Director, U.S. Office of Personnel Management, Washington, D.C.; Battalion Commander, 4th Personnel Services Battalion, Fort Carson, Colo.; Executive Officer and Military Assistant to the Deputy Assistant Secretary of the Army for Manpower and Reserve Affairs (Human Resources) Pentagon, Washington, D.C.; Commander, Eastern Sector, United States Military Entrance Processing Command; Director, J1, United Forces-Iraq; the Deputy Commanding General of the United States Army Cadet Command at Fort Knox, KY, the Director of Human Resources Policy Directorate, Army G1 Pentagon, Washington, D.C. and his final active duty assignment was as Deputy Chief of Staff, G-1 Army Forces Command in Fort Bragg, North Carolina.

Major General Price served on the President and First Lady's Task Force on "Raising Responsible and Resourceful Teenagers" in 2000; served on President Clinton's "Mississippi Delta Task Force" which sought to revitalize the 207-county, seven-state region that comprises the Mississippi River flood plain from 1999 through 2000, served on the Board of the National PTA, currently serves on the National Gun Violence Collaborative and the National Suicide Action Alliance. He is the author of the 2001 volume: *Against All Enemies Foreign and Domestic: A Study of Urban Unrest and Federal Intervention Within the United States*; and the 2016 volume: *Life on the Other Side of You.*

Major General Price received many personal honors during his Army career. Those included the Army Distinguished Service Medal, the Defense Superior Service Medal, three Legions of Merit, and the Bronze Star Medal. He is also entitled to wear the Army Staff Badge and the Airborne and Air Assault Badges.

Made in the USA
Columbia, SC
11 November 2020